THE UPRISING OF 1857

THE UPRISING OF 1857

Before and Beyond

Edited by

KAUSHIK ROY

MANOHAR
2010

First published 2010

ISBN 978-81-7304-891-3

Published by
Ajay Kumar Jain for
Manohar Publishers & Distributors
4753/23 Ansari Road, Daryaganj
New Delhi 110 002

Typeset at
Digigrafics
New Delhi 110 049

Printed at
Salasar Imaging Systems
Delhi 110 035

In honour of Prof. Rajat Kanta Roy
who introduced '1857' to me during my
undergraduate days

Contents

Preface

The year 2007 witnessed the celebration of 150th anniversary of the 1857 Uprising. Publishers especially in India commissioned flashy books as the market was considered favourable for selling quasi-academic products on 1857. At about the same time, within the academicians, two trends emerged. A large section of India historians (who were previously Marxists) argued that 1857 was an all India uprising. They argued that massive popular rebellions occurred at Bengal, Bombay, Punjab and even in south India. On the contrary, British historians not only considered 1857 as a military mutiny but also shifted the focus to the study of literature (novels, poems, plays) associated with 1857. This collection of ten essays shows that the 1857 Uprising was neither merely a military mutiny (though the military played a very vital role) nor an all India anti-colonial uprising. Further, an attempt is made in two essays of this volume to integrate 1857 as part of pan-Asian history. I am hopeful that the collection will encourage further research in new directions in the near future. Lastly, I thank the contributors and the publisher for making the volume possible.

KAUSHIK ROY

Acknowledgements

I am grateful to all the contributors for their patience, which made this volume possible. Special thanks are due to my ex-students Pratyay Nath and Priyadarshini Sen. Pratyay provided many crucial sources which are utilized in this volume and Priyadarshini and Suhrita helped to improve my English.

Kolkata,
January 2010

KAUSHIK ROY

Abbreviations

BL	British Library
BNI	Bengal Native Infantry
CSSH	*Comparative Studies in Society and History*
EIC	East India Company
FD	Foreign Department
GoI	Government of India
IESHR	*Indian Economic and Social History Review*
IJHS	*Indian Journal of History of Science*
IOR	India Office Records
JICH	*Journal of Imperial and Commonwealth History*
JMH	*Journal of Military History*
JOS	*Journal of the Ordnance Society*
JSAHR	*Journal of the Society for Army Historical Research*
JSS	*Journal of Strategic Studies*
JUSII	*Journal of the United Service Institution of India*
JWH	*Journal of World History*
MAS	*Modern Asian Studies*
MD	Military Department
PIF	Punjab Irregular Force later renamed as the Punjab Frontier Force
WBSA	West Bengal State Archives

Glossary

adda	a group of Bengalis gossiping together.
anna	16 *anna* was equivalent to one rupee.
babu	Bengali gentleman.
badshah	also called *Padshah* meaning the Mughal Emperor.
Banjaras	itinerant grain merchants.
batta	special allowance given to troops for service in outlying areas.
begum	wife of a Muslim ruler.
bhisti	water carrier.
budmash	goon, criminal.
chapa khana	printing press.
chaplis	sandals made of grass.
chowk	central region of the town square or the market.
crore	one crore is equivalent to 100 lakh. One crore means 10 million.
deen	religion for the Muslims.
dharamsala	cheap guest house.
dharma	code of conduct for the Hindus meaning righteous conduct broadly in accordance with the Hindu religion. It is both individual and collective.
dharma yuddha	just war conducted by the Hindus.
fatwa	proclamation issued by the *maulvi.*
ferangi	literally meaning Franks. This term refers to the Christians, meaning British.
fitna	internal struggle within the Islamic domain.
gazi	Islamic religious warrior.
haveli	palace or traditional big residential house.
jagirdar	person who was granted *jagir* (a piece of land) by the ruling authority for maintaining troops out of the revenue extracted from the *jagir.*

jati	literal meaning sub-caste, but also meant sub-nationalism or nationalism of a particular religious community in a particular region.
jirgas	tribal assembly.
Khalsa	Sikh theocracy.
kothi	house.
lashkar	war band of the North-West Frontier tribes.
mahajan	Hindu moneylender.
mofussil	district area.
mohalla	locality within a city.
mullah	somewhat equivalent to *ulema*. The term refers to Islamic clergy or teacher of Koran.
nabob	British adventurer who made a windfall in India. After returning to Britain such a person displayed his wealth by building a huge mansion, etc. He was caricatured as the equivalent to the *nawab* famous for ostentatious display of wealth.
nautch girl	dancing girl.
nawab	independent Mughal subadar.
nawabi	domain of the *nawab*.
Nizam	independent Mughal Governor of Deccan who later established the Hyderabad *nawabi*.
Pandies	derogatory term used by the British officers of mid-nineteenth-century India for the rebellious high-caste soldiers of the Bengal Army. Literally, the term was derived from Mangal Pandey.
pargana	subdivision of a district.
Peshwa	Prime Minister of the Maratha Confederacy.
pugris	turbans or headgear.
Raj	rule or realm, here refers to British rule in India.
sabha	Meeting.
sahid	martyr, one who gave life while fighting for Islam.
sangar	fortification constructed at mountaintops made of stones and rocks.
sarai	rest house.
sardar	chieftain.
seth	Hindu businessman.

talukdar	semi-autonomous landed magnate of Awadh who also maintained armed retainers.
taluka	administrative subdivision, i.e. district.
topi	hat.
topkhana	artillery establishment.
trace Italienne	also known as *alla moderna*. It means star-shaped fortress designed to resist gunpowder artillery. This new architectural design first emerged in Italy in the early modern era and then spread to north-west Europe.
zamburaks	also known as *shutarnals*. They were the camel swivel guns.

Introduction

The Great Uprising of 1857 started on 10 May at the Meerut Cantonment and continued until April 1859. While writing a history of the 1857 Uprising, a scholar faces the problem of having at his disposal mostly one-sided evidence. Besides official documents, there are private papers, memoirs, biographies and even fiction on 1857 that were mostly generated by the British.[1] As James Belich has stated in another context, Victorian records are imbued with the conviction that the British were inherently superior to their opponents.[2]

This edited volume is divided into two parts. The first section has eight essays (based on original documents) which throw light on the social, cultural, literary, technological, and military aspects of 1857. The two essays in the second section attempts to contextualize the 1857 Uprising in a global context. Instead of merely summarizing these essays, I will locate them within the wider historiographical matrix.

The collection in this edited volume shows that research on 1857 has moved a long way from the traditional debates regarding the nature of the rebellion. Whether 1857 was a forward looking national uprising or a reactionary feudal upsurge, shaped the debates within the academic circuit during the 1950s and the 1960s. In the 1980s, the debate was about whether 1857 represented a popular agrarian uprising or a rebellion of the magnates and their retainers suffering from relative economic deprivation. One of the principal strength of this volume is that the contributors do not fall within any particular school. While Satyaki Kanjilal somewhat in line with the post-modernist thinking goes for literary criticism, Uttara Chakraborty's analysis of a Scottish soldier's memoir is empirical. Iqbal Husain's essay is an exercise in urban/architectural history. Anasua Dutta's piece attempts to reconstruct the mindset of anxiety and fear among the Bengali *babus* within the confined space of a city— Calcutta— mainly from oral history and vernacular sources. Swarupa Gupta studies the texts generated by the Bengali intelligentsia during late nineteenth century to show how the memory of 1857 shaped the Bengali discourse on *jati* and *samaj*.

Most studies of 1857 focus on north and central India. In contrast, this compilation has two essays on Bengal and one on the Indus frontier. Again, to some extent both Husain and Dutta's pieces are representative of urban history and Gupta's essay falls within the paradigm of social history. Whereas Raymond Callahan contributes traditional military history with a view from the top, T.R. Moreman's piece brings the 'frontier' within the mainstream of Indian history of the nineteenth century. R. Balasubramaniam and R. Brown's joint essay shows the necessity of having metallurgists dabbling in history in trying to understand the technological history of nineteenth-century India. Two essays, by Kaushik Roy and Madhavi Thampi respectively in Section II, attempt to locate 1857 within the global history paradigm by comparing and contrasting the Sepoy Mutiny with the Taiping Rebellion, the Crimean War, and the American Civil War.

One of the principal pillars of British power in India was the land forces which comprise of the British Army, the EIC's private white army with indigenous forces allied to it. In 1837, India produced a land revenue of 12 million sterling while Britain with a much smaller population generated 40 million sterling. About half the Government of India's income went to support its armies. In case of emergencies, in order to sustain military operations, the government also resorted to loans.[3] During the 1857 Uprising, the British government raised a loan from the merchants of Peshawar.[4]

The evolution of the armies under the direct control of the EIC from the late eighteenth century to the onset of the 1857 Uprising constitutes the subject of Callahan's essay. The British Army, like the British-Indian Sepoy Army, was a long service force. In the 1840s, the British Army required 11,000–12,000 men to replace annual wastage. In 1855, the male population of Britain was 13,575,000 and the size of the army was 136,932. In 1860, the male population in the United Kingdom was 14,553,000 and the army numbered 219,631 men. In other words, the proportion of men under arms varied between 1.2 to 1.6 per cent between these two dates. Military service was not popular in Britain. The use of dishonest and disreputable methods of recruitment ensured enlistment from the lowest strata of the population. Most of the recruits joined because they lacked any employment or because of family quarrels, and so on. Service in the British Army was characterized by drunkenness and desertions. Despite the army's preference for agricultural labourers, most of the recruits were from the unskilled and unemployed urban proletariat. For disciplining the personnel, the army depended on corporal punishment. The British Army always suffered from recruitment problems and during emergencies was unable to expand quickly.[5] Especially during emergencies, indigenous colonial armies became vital for Britain.

The lynchpin of the British-Indian Army or the Sepoy Army was the sahib–sepoy relationship. The relationship between the Indian soldiery and their white officers remains an enigma. It is time to reject the liberal Victorian picture of honest and brave, childlike Indian soldiers led by courageous British officers. The sahib–sepoy relationship was something like a *mai-bap* relationship. Jeffrey Greenhut asserts that the British officers believed that they functioned as country squires and the sepoys and sowars as their retainers. In contrast, the sepoys and the sowars considered that serving with loyalty was part of their caste *dharma*. And the Indian soldiers considered their British officers as patrons. Hence, Indian private soldiers, unlike their European counterparts, gave obedience to the man wearing the uniform, not to the uniform itself. In other words, a strong personal bond developed between sahibs and sepoys. Besides, in order to acquire obedience, the British officers had to develop linguistic skills and in return had to acquire the trust of the men under their command.[6]

1857 was in many ways a large-scale insurgency. Insurgency is an armed political movement aiming at a particular objective. And insurgency need not be revolutionary in its political design. Thomas A. Marks says that neither ethnicity, nor national identity or ideology is the key to the mobilization of insurgents. Societal causes are a necessary but not sufficient factor. While the leaders might be swayed by ideology, the followers are guided by more mundane causes. The leaders sustain an insurgency by mobilizing those who consider themselves alienated from the system, the grievance guerrillas. Occasionally, the leaders draw on the power of religion for greater socialization of the followers. To sum up, rather than any specific grievances of the populace, a breakdown of the negotiated relationship between the rulers and the ruled results in insurgency.[7]

The sahib–sepoy relationship became dysfunctional for both organizational and economic reasons. Like Haraprasad Chattopadhyay, Callahan in his essay in this volume agrees that the increasing disdain of overbearing British officers for the sepoys contributed to the breakdown of the loyalty bond. Again, both agree that the 1857 Mutiny was not inevitable. If the British officers had been more caring towards the sepoys and the sowars, and if the military bureaucracy had paid due attention to religious and cultural sensibilities, the Mutiny could have been averted. The 'penny-pinching' policy of the government, admit Chattopadhyaya and Callahan, caused increasing financial burden to the Indian soldiery and alienated them from the Raj.[8] In addition, the decline of the Indian officers' status due to the induction of arrogant young British junior officers, further completed the breakdown.[9] James W. Hoover asserts that in 1857, opposition to the government's land tenure policy was expressed in religious and political terms. Religious and political symbols were utilized for rallying the discontented peasantry against the Raj.[10]

Most of the sepoys of the Bengal Army hailed from Awadh and Bihar. Lucknow, Gorakhpur, Rohilkhand, Allahabad, Banaras, Jaunpur, Arrah, and Agra were the most heavily recruited districts. The Brahmins who joined the Bengal Army's infantry were from the agricultural and not the priestly class.[11] The Bais and Chauhan clans of the Rajputs and Bhumihar Brahmins especially from Banaras region filled the ranks of the Bengal Army. Most of the sepoys came from families of small farmers, joining up to tide over economic decline.[12] Even in 1837, the immediate families of the Bengal Army's soldiers numbered about 50,000 to 60,000 individuals. They took advantage of being Company's servants to petition the Awadh durbar through the Resident for settling land disputes in their favour.[13] When Awadh was annexed by the EIC, the soldiers' families lost this privilege and turned against the Raj. In addition, pay and pension of the sepoy and sowar were not increasing with time and their career prospects were becoming gloomier. When the EIC annexed Awadh, about 70,000 soldiers of the Awadh *Nawabi* army was discharged, and many soldiers now joined the rebels during the

1857 Uprising.[14] Most of the *talukdars*, being petty rajas, maintained mud forts and cannons. In 1856, the British counted 623 forts in Awadh of which 351 were formidable.[15] About 60,000 ex-soldiers of the Awadh *Nawabi* army, the retainers of the zamindars and the *talukdars* who had about 250 forts under them fought against the British.[16] The peasants joined the *talukdars* during the 1857 Mutiny, writes Thomas R. Metcalf, due to the loyalty they felt for the deposed *nawab* and partly also because they were overawed by the military might of the rebellious *talukdars*.[17]

Military rebellion by the colonial soldiery was nothing new in British India. The Madras Army was rocked by large-scale disturbances in 1806 in what is known as the Vellore Mutiny. At least one-fourth of the Madras Army (total number of Indian personnel was 48,000) was directly and indirectly affected. Hoover asserts that it is wrong to assume that the Indian soldiers were simpletons led astray by machinations of the malicious indigenous elite. At least, the Indian officers were politically conscious. Hoover claims that during the Vellore crisis the sepoys opposed certain policies of the EIC, not the Company itself. Rather than instigation by Tipu Sultan's descendants, the sepoys and the sowars had grievances connected with the military service which had linkages with culture of the local society in south India. In the mentality of the Madras soldiers, religious values and cultural values were fused with each other. One of the grievances of the Indian soldiers was that due to inflation, the real value of their wages was declining. Moreover, the new generation of British officers no more cared for the cultural and religious sensibilities of the men under them. The new regulations introduced in November 1805 prevented the Hindu sepoys from applying *vibhuti* (caste marks) on their foreheads. Further, the new shape of turbans was disliked by both the Hindu sepoys and Muslim sowars. They thought that the new turban introduced by the Madras Army high command looked like a European *topi*. The local communities considered that the Madras soldiers were becoming Europeans or Christians and refused to have any social and cultural interaction with them. The process of dialogue that lead to negotiations and compromise between the employers (i.e. British officers) and the employed (Indian soldiers) broke down in the Madras Army. The policy of Europeanizing and bureaucratizing the Madras Army resulted in the disintegration of traditional dialogic transactions between the sahibs and the sepoys. Hence, the only way left for the disgruntled sepoys and sowars to protest was to display violence and this occurred on 10 July 1806.[18] In a way, the Madras soldiers of 1806 were grievance insurrectionists.

It is erroneous to believe that only the Indian soldiery was prone to rebel. In fact, the white soldiers and the white officers rebelled several times in British India with disastrous results for the Raj. Just after suppression of the 1857 Mutiny, British India was rocked by the White Mutiny of 1859–60. The EIC's private white army, unlike the British Army, comprised of a large proportion of artisans and clerks whereas the British Army's recruits were mostly poor labourers who had joined out of desperation. The Queen's Army discouraged clerks from joining its ranks. The Queen's Army was suspicious of literates in its ranks but a large proportion of literates had joined the Bengal European regiments. In fact, the EIC's white contingent comprised of a large number of surveyors, draughtsmen, chemists, and druggists. They enlisted with the objective of bettering themselves. After 1857, the British authorities decided to transfer India from the EIC to the Crown and abolish the Company's private white army. The existing personnel of the EIC's private white army were either to be absorbed into the British Army or else discharged. The transfer of personnel angered many because it threatened the security and promotion of the white personnel of the EIC's white army.[19]

Despite numerical inferiority, the British emerged supreme in 1859 partly due to superior technology at their disposal. It is necessary to assess the important role played by technology in general, and military technology in particular, in the course of British expansion in South Asia without falling into the trap of technological determinism. The issue of technological backwardness of pre-colonial India is a problematic one. Jean Deloche writes that even in the late eighteenth century, the Indian military engineers, unlike the Europeans, continued to build high curtain walls and towers because they thought that the thickness of their masonry was strong enough to resist cannon balls. This meant that the siege artillery used by the indigenous powers was weak by European standards. Most of the guns used by the south Indian powers till the end of the eighteenth century were cast bronze cannons and wrought iron cannons composed of iron bars hooped together by iron rings. Some of the cannon pieces were massive, one weighing about 55 tons. Towards the end of the seventeenth century, the Mughals started using wrought iron shots instead of stone cannon balls for the siege guns.[20] During the Second Anglo–Sikh War, at Ramnagar (2 December 1848), the Sikhs had only 9-pounders whereas the EIC deployed 18-pounders.[21] It is to be noted that the role of artillery in west European battles was increasing from late eighteenth century. Battle doctrine of the time emphasized that artillery should start battles and the cannons were to be massed in the battlefield for firepower effect. Jean de Gribeauval (1715–89) introduced standardized artillery in the army of the *ancien regime:* 4, 6, 8 and 12-pounder cannons, and 6-inch howitzers. Standardization aided in rapid, regular and predictable fire. This was further accelerated by the introduction of pre-packaged rounds. French artillery also underwent the introduction of stronger and larger wheels, shorter barrels, and lighter weight cannons. Accuracy was improved by better sights, the issue of gunnery tables and inclination markers.[22]

Balasubramaniam and Brown forcefully claim that at least in the first half of the nineteenth century, there was no serious technological gap between the EIC and the indigenous powers especially as regards military hardware. The views of these two scholars are similar to that of Pradeep Barua who asserts that the pre-colonial powers failed against the onslaught of the EIC because, despite modernizing their military machines, the indigenous rulers failed to upgrade state infrastructures, which happened to be feudal and centrifugal.[23] In other words not technological but managerial failures, especially in the field of statecraft, resulted in the collapse of India's *ancien regime* against the Company.

The Mughals were great builders. Zahir-ud-din Babur introduced in India the 'paradise gardens' constructed by the Timurids in Central Asia. Like his ancestor Timur (CE 1336-1405), he preferred residence in gardens. Timur's residential gardens in Samarkand were large enclosures with running water, pools, fruit trees, etc. At Dholpur located on the Chambal River, Babur built the Lotus Garden. The Lotus Garden represents the symbiosis of Timurid garden ideals with Indian architectural heritage. Babur's successors constructed hundreds of gardens in north India.[24] Mughal royal women too indulged in garden building. Ebba Koch writes that Shah Jahan's ever blooming palace gardens had a definite political significance. They were intended as an image of his reign and empire, as garden paradises of the ideal king whose good government, so it claimed, had brought about a golden age of unending spring.[25]

The British did not care much about the architectural heritage of Delhi but took care about buildings related to security concerns. The city wall of Delhi was rebuilt and fortified by the British military authorities in 1816. And ironically, this piece of fortification was used well by the rebels. The built-up areas of Delhi comprised Paharganj, Kishanganj, and Sabzimandi in the west. And the cantonment was on the north Ridge.[26] After the collapse of rebel resistance in Delhi on 15 September 1857, the British troops got drunk and engaged in widespread looting. The British officers lost control over their men and the indisciplined British soldiers often fought with each other for the spoils. Shops and houses were broken and ransacked indiscriminately.[27] And about 27,000 persons were executed by the victorious British in Delhi.[28] Only in January 1858, the Hindus were allowed to return to the city and the Muslims came back at the end of that year. Delhi's population fell below the pre-Mutiny level. The population of the city and the suburbs was 160,270 in 1846 but in 1863 it numbered only 141,709.[29]

Iqbal Husain shows that the architectural landscape of Mughal Delhi was not only altered but also destroyed by the British in the immediate aftermath of 1857. The alteration of urban landscape of Delhi was partly due to the security concerns of an anxious colonial regime and partly the product of retaliation on the part of the victors towards the defeated power. About 80 per cent of the Red Fort had been destroyed when the British recaptured Delhi.[30] The mosques were destroyed and some were used for accommodating the army and the police. In the immediate post-Mutiny era, the city functioned mostly as a cantonment and the army controlled one-third of the city.[31]

Colonialism in the paradigm of cultural studies school, was also partly a cultural project. Satyaki Kanjilal's essay analyses the nature of British Mutiny novels. The ideological roots of such writings were the product of both immediate and long-term causes. The immediate factor behind the production of such novels was the Mutiny itself. However, the continued appeal for such novels among the British was the product of the long-term forces within which British imperialism was operating. Besides the pragmatic demands of the empire, racial anthropology and social Darwinism also shaped the attitudes and methodologies of the British writers.[32]

Douglas M. Peers writes that much of what was written about India during the colonial period was written by military officers posted in India. And their accounts emphasize exotic location, dramatic stories of bravery, heroism, and tragedy. Such romanticized accounts overlook British brutalities and justify the empire.[33] To give an example, G.A. Henty (1832–1902) wrote more than a hundred books dealing with the adventures of the British gentlemen in various parts of the empire. Nine of these were set in India. *In Times of Peril* (1881) was jingoistic while the tone of *Rujub the Juggler* (1895) was more moderate.[34] Henty emphasized justice, fairness, and avoidance of inflicting torture on the 'natives' as characteristics of his British heroes. True courage, wrote Henty, comprised of magnanimity and gentleness.[35] Somewhat similar attitudes, asserts Uttara Chakraborty in her essay, are present in William Forbes Mitchell's memoir. Mitchell, the Scot soldier, in his autobiography displays empathy with the rebels and Uttara Chakraborty rightly claims that the standard view of the British 'othering' all the Indians need to be revised.

Analysing nineteenth-century British fiction, Gautam Chakravarty writes that self-serving and self-congratulatory high talk about civilizing the savages justified British violence over the 'natives'. 1857 became a site of heroic adventures for British writers. Most of the Mutiny novels targeted a juvenile readership and the emphasis was on character building, military exploits, state security, and espionage. Chakravarty claims that the characteristic features of the Mutiny novels were already laid out in the fictions generated during the first half of the nineteenth century. For example, John Kaye's Punjab War novel, *Peregrine Pultuney* (1844), focuses on militarism and the reformist missions of the British. In British literature, Indian polities are represented as 'oriental kingdoms' which were despotic, profligate, picturesque, and simultaneously anarchic, impoverished, and horrific.[36]

The boundaries between fact and fiction became blurred in the writings of the gentleman-officer-scholar. Such British writings which Peers categorizes as 'Orientalist', established the structures of dominance over the colonized. These writings were products of assumptions of innate British superiority as well as of apprehensions of the survivability of British rule in the alien landscape. The 'Orientalist' literature, continues Peers, is characterized by binary oppositions like masculine/feminine, progress/stagnation, reason/superstition, in order to heighten distinctions.[37] Rationality becomes the preserve of the British.[38] The works of the British officers portray India as an exotic landscape with endless curiosities which fascinated readers back in Britain.[39]

Bruce Watson claims that the ideology of the British during the 1850s was characterized by heady evangelicalism and xenophobic nationalism.[40] The 1850s witnessed an extraordinary upsurge of Christian militarism which spread the notion of soldiers as heroes and the missionaries as exporting Christian values to the uncivilized regions of the world. Henry Havelock emerged as a heroic Christian soldier. A more secular strain of militarism, writes Peter Burroughs, emerged after 1870 due to the rivalry among the European powers. This new militarism emphasized physical and moral fitness and Anglo–Saxon virtues.[41]

In a somewhat similar tune, Ralph Crane and Radhika Mohanram assert that 1860s witnessed the emergence of the modern militaristic hero in British fiction. This reflected the shift in bourgeois preoccupations. The powerful Evangelicals, with their emphasis on a daily spiritual life and the establishment of the Christian missionary movement that had the objective of Christianizing India, constructed the masculinity of the Christian soldier. It is to be noted that Henry Havelock, the 62-year old general who relieved Lucknow, was a practising Baptist. The shift from a monastic to a militaristic ethos, claim Crane and Mohanram (in contrast to Burroughs), was the product of the Mutiny. In the new cult of masculinity, the emphasis was less on spiritual autonomy and intellectual maturity than on sports, games, male bonding, i.e. qualities considered necessary in the production of ideal soldier for the empire. And in British political history also, as a corollary, greater importance was given to the British Empire and especially to India.[42]

British adventure fiction emphasized alien lands. From the seventeenth century onwards, a linkage developed between the adventurer and the soldier who journeyed overseas in search of fortune. The structure of the adventure is linked with perilous journeys and crucial struggles. Adventure is linked with a romantic plot which concentrates on the marvellous and the fantastic. The dislocation that the hero underwent through his journeys, write Crane and Mohanram, generated in him enduring courage, bravery, and lack of doubt. The adventure story helped to shore up the ideology that enabled the British to perceive themselves as a racially superior people.[43]

Like Peers, Indrani Sen writes that in colonial fiction connected with the Mutiny, the historical figures are constructions or ideologically loaded projections of reality instead of reflections of reality. Hence, these texts reveal more about the colonial perceptions than about the colonized, and also show the shifts in colonial attitudes and ideologies. The majority of the Mutiny novels were romances of love and adventure which marked a polarization between Indians/mutineers and the British, thus feeding into myths pertaining to race, culture, sexuality, power, and gender. Racial and cultural stereotypes like Asiatic cruelty, treachery, and lechery towards white women, and British courage, manliness and chivalry abound in the fictional literature. By producing and circulating imperial knowledge about the colonies, the function of this genre of literature was to establish military and moral superiority over the 'natives'. The images of Indian women in the Mutiny novels were shaped by race, class, and gender perceptions of the colonizers. Most of the prostitutes and *begums* were portrayed as licentious, sexually voracious and as examples of 'native' female cruelty.[44] In reality, asserts Lata Singh, the prostitutes of the British documents were actually *tawaifs* who had joined the uprising out of political conviction.[45]

Aishwarya Lakshmi writes that Mutiny novels portray India as a feminine land, subservient to the masculine West, but there are variations within the Mutiny novels. Philip Meadow Taylor's *Seeta,* published in 1872, depicts an inter-racial marriage which is central to the plot. Such marriages though common in the early nineteenth century became anathema for the British in India during the second half of the nineteenth century.[46] Taylor in *Seeta,* claims Sen, portrays the image of the *virangana* (warrior woman of India) as far as the Rani of Jhansi was concerned. Taylor presents the Rani as a victim of British injustice and treachery. This was because, unlike many other British writers, Taylor had a benevolent paternalistic admiration for Indian culture. The late nineteenth-century novel titled *The Rane* by Colonel J.N.H. Maclean, portrays the Rani as a cruel unscrupulous lady using her sexuality among the British males for getting back her kingdom. Sen concludes by saying that the Rani is portrayed within the trope of androgyny. Alluring female sexuality is fused with masculine physical prowess and martial skills.[47]

Charles Edward Pearce was a newspaper editor and a prolific author of popular biographies. He published three mutiny novels, *Love Besieged: A Romance of the Defence of Lucknow* (1909), *Red Revenge: A Romance of Cawnpore* (1911) and *A Star of the East: A Romance of Delhi* (1912). This proved the enduring appeal of the imperial adventure romance as a genre in the early decades of twentieth-century Britain. The 'Indian Mutiny' continued to exert a tremendous hold on the British imagination even sixty years after 1857. The event, write Crane and Mohanram, defined British imperial identity. G.O. Trevelyan, author of *The Competition Wallah* (1864), wrote that 1857 reminded the British that they were an imperial race who dominated the land by dint of white valour and foresight. The Mutiny was a significant factor in the process of rewriting of imperial history by the imperialists and in re-imagining Britain as a colonial power. Reports of the murder and rape of British women and the slaughter of children obscured the part played by the British in instigating the rebellion and shifted the focus on the 'demonic tendencies' and 'treacherous nature' of the 'natives'. The vengeance wreaked on the mutineers was met with approval even among the intellectuals in Britain. Along with Flora Annie Steel, no less a figure than Charles Dickens wanted to avenge the loss of British lives.[48]

The shift in the imagining of British masculinity also led to a reconfiguration of white feminity and an idealization of white womanhood. Within gender relations, white women functioned as the 'other' that gave men their identity. Crane and Mohanram assert that from the time of the Mutiny, the home and the woman had to be protected from the dangerous species of outside space and white women became a metaphor for the space inhabited by white people. The British home in India became a place of refuge and also an endangered space. In *Love Besieged*, Jean Atherton is the white virginal heroine who gives the besieged, especially Jack Hawke, a cause to fight for and in Dr. Lennard's case a cause to die for.[49]

In recent times, many Indian historians have claimed that although the rebellion actually occurred in north India, various peripheral regions also simmered with the possibilities of uprising. In other words, though the feeling of common people in Bengal and Punjab did not cross the threshold from antipathy to active rebellion, complex anti-colonial undercurrents engulfed the whole of the subcontinent.[50]

The traditional view is that Bengal remained untouched by sentiments of rebellion against the colonial order. However, the loyalty of the Bengali middle class was not straightforward. Benoy Ghose asserts that the loyalty of the Bengali intelligentsia towards the British was conditional. The educated Bengali middle class supported the British during the 1857 Uprising because the Company Raj supported their class interests. The high-caste Bengal Army soldiers who had rebelled stood for social conservatism. Again, indirectly the Bengali intelligentsia, by remaining loyal to the British liberals, also opposed the conservatives within the British ruling class.[51] Gopal Haldar concurs by saying that under the leadership of Iswar Chandra Vidyasagar (1820–91), the educated Bengali middle class gained a victory in the passing of the Widow Remarriage Act in 1856. Such social reforms were anathema to the high-caste soldiery of the Bengal Army. The foundation of three universities at Calcutta, Bombay, and Madras was another victory for the indigenous intelligentsia. The Bengali intelligentsia were patriotic but could not establish a joint front with the 'reactionary' sepoys.[52] For Ghose and Haldar, the rebels represented a feudal reaction. Hence, the liberal bourgeois intelligentsia could not join them in an anti-colonial struggle.[53]

Sekhar Bandopadhyay writes that the expression of loyalty was, for the Bengali middle class more a product of the head than the heart.[54] Swarupa Gupta asserts that it is too simplistic to categorize the Bengali middle class of that time as loyalists. While there were no armed rebellions in Bengal, 1857 forced the Bengalis to rethink the concept of nation, people, and land. The event shaped the Bengali search for identity and encouraged development of the *samaj* through self-help. The late 1850s witnessed the glimmerings of the idea of *Bharat*/Hindustan. Many Bengali literati belonging to the middle class emphasized in their writings the unity of Hindus and Muslims. Some Bengali writers used the idea of Aryan greatness of India and Hindu-Muslim unity in order to reconfigure their ideas about nationhood.[55] Gupta develops this line of argument in her essay and turns the limelight from English texts generated by the colonizers to vernacular texts (both historical and fictional) written by the Bengali intelligentsia in the aftermath of 1857 Uprising. It is interesting that though the British officers assumed that the Bengalis being non-Aryan were not martial, the Bengali Hindu literati of the late colonial period considered themselves descendants of the great Aryan race. What we need is further studies of the texts generated by the Muslim intelligentsia of Bengal of that period to see how they perceived the 1857 Uprising, their role in it, and their interaction with the Hindus of Bengal.

Basudeb Chattopadhyay asserts that in February 1857 the British administration was anxious about the attitude of the 19th Native Infantry Regiment and the Irregular Corps stationed in Baharampur. Baharampur was close to Murshidabad, the residence of the Nawabs of Bengal. A parallel could be drawn with British fear about Tipu's relations in Vellore instigating Madras sepoys in 1806. History seemed to be repeating itself. Rumours played a very important role in heightening British anxiety in Calcutta, shows Anasua Dutta, during the stormy days of 1857. Basudeb Chattopadhyay adds that rumours were afloat that some of the discharged Pandies did not return to their 'native' villages in west Bihar or in Uttar Pradesh but were hovering around Barrackpur, Barasat, Chinsura, and even Calcutta. Calcutta was perceived by the European community as better guarded, hence a 'mini' migration occurred of European settlers from the *mofussil* to Calcutta. Within Calcutta, the EIC administration was also afraid that Wajid Ali Shah, the deposed Nawab of Awadh and his followers might join hands with the rebellious Indian soldiers.[56] On 15 June 1857, the ex-Nawab of Awadh was arrested.[57] The British high command panicked. Sabyasachi Bhattacharya writes that during the panic in Calcutta on 13 June 1857, Governor-General Canning moved a bill in the legislature of Calcutta to ensure absolute and summary control over the press and within a day the bill was rushed through to the statute book as Act XV of 1857. This law was applicable both to the English and vernacular press, and gagged the indigenous intelligentsia in Calcutta and Bombay. Some newspapers in Calcutta stopped publications in protest.[58]

Before trying to place the 1857 Uprising on a global plane, it is necessary to analyse the concept of world/global history. Some scholars differentiate between the global and world history. Bruce Mazlish writes that interactions between peoples participating in large-scale historical processes comprise one of the chief concerns of world history. Trans-civilizational encounters, interaction among peoples of diverse cultures, is another objective of the world history approach. So, world history is concerned with historical phenomena that arise on a world scale. In contrast, writes Mazlish, the history of globalization is the heart and novelty of global history. The synergy and synchronicity of the various factors, their unprecedented interactions in ever-increasing extent and force, despite the fact that all of these factors originated in differentiated pasts, represents globalization. Globalization affects every person of the globe and all the regions in widely differing local contexts. Thus, global history takes up the challenge of studying the factors of globalization in relation to the local realities which take different forms. Globalization, warns Mazlish, is not foreordained. The practitioners of global history accept that globalization's future course is unpredictable and contingency and uncertainty of human affairs shape the process of globalization. Though global history is transnational in its subjects of study, it cannot afford to neglect the study of nations. National history merits re-examination in the light of how the forces of globalization have affected the nation states and vice versa. Nations still exist. So global history is also concerned with the study of the nations as major actors. In contrast, the main focus of world history is not the nations but civilizations.[59]

The agenda of world history is to challenge Eurocentrism or Western-centrism. World history is also transcultural history. The objective is exploration of spaces beyond the nation states. The theories of alternative spaces cut across cultural and national boundaries. The aim is to understand global transformations, entanglements and adaptations. Gradually, the nation should be abandoned as the key unit of historical analysis. Another important aim of world history is to challenge the dominance of one vision of the global past. Studies of world history should never insist on one rigid global structure, as propounded by Immanuel Wallerstein and Geoffrey Parker. In the 1960s, the dependency theorists while tracing the development of underdevelopment on a global scale focused on the core, periphery and semi-periphery in order to explain the global logic of capital accumulation. The introduction of the concept of semi-periphery is an innovation compared to the imperialist historiography's use of core (metropolitan European countries) and the periphery (colonies) while trying to tell the grand narrative of the rise of modernity and state. Nevertheless, the dependency theorists accept the state as the unit of analysis and go for monocausal (economic) explanations. However, world history aims to transcend state centrism by emphasizing on transnational comparisons and processes of interactions.[60] World history should rather throw up plural visions of the past and seeks to include alternative perspective. The principal challenges of the practitioners of world history would be to combine and balance the local with the global. Dominic Sachsenmaier claims that what is required is a synthesis of abstract global theories and detailed local studies, so that world history could be something more than global in scope and local in structures.[61]

The editor of this volume equates global history with world history. The argument against micro history is that the practitioners of this type of history writing suffers from narrow over-specialization while the criticism against the practitioners of macro history/world history is that they suffer from lack of control over the various languages and do not possess proximity to the sources. Nevertheless, world history could provide broad perspectives and comprehensive interpretations at the world stage.[62]

One of the characteristics of global history is the comparative angle. Chris Lorenz points out the importance of comparative history, by saying that history written from the national perspective omits the international perspective. Such analysis creates the illusion that national problems must have 'national' causes. History is, after all, writes Lorenz, a mixture of general (international) and specific (national) ingredients. Comparative history writing is the only way to identify and explain both differences and similarities between national historiographical traditions.[63] Jurgen Kocka writes: 'comparing in history means to discuss two or more historical phenomena systematically with respect to their similarities and differences in order to reach certain intellectual aims'.[64] Historical comparisons also aid in clarifying the profiles of single cases, occasionally just one single case by contrasting it with others. Comparative approaches, international and intercultural comparisons enriches to understanding of transnational historical processes.[65]

However, comparative history has come under the challenge of entangled histories or connected history. Connected history is part of global history. In recent times 'entangled histories' or *histoire croisee* is coming up. Rather than focusing on similarities and differences between two or more cases as is the case in comparative history, entangled histories focus on reciprocal interactions between the two or more units and case studies of historical comparisons. The entangled process of constituting each other is the main agenda of *histoire croisee*. So, from the entangled history point of view, comparative history separates reality into different pieces in order to analyse by comparing the pieces as units of comparison whereas in reality these so-called separate pieces constitute one web of entanglement. Kocka attempts to fuse *histoire compare* and *histoire croisee*. He continues that comparative historians should incorporate elements of entangled histories into the comparative design of their research. The act of comparison presupposes the analytical separation of the cases to be compared but that does not mean ignoring or neglecting the interrelationship between the cases. Rather, such interrelations should become an integral part of the comparative framework by analysing them as factors that have led to similarities and differences, convergence and divergence between the cases one compares.[66]

Mid-nineteent-century China and India provide a good case study of comparative history and connected/entangled history within the world/global history approach. China and India remain the two most populous countries of the world. Both these countries experienced massive anti-state movements in the 1850s. The great Taiping Rebellion (1851–64) in China, writes Madhavi Thampi, offers similarities and contrasts with the 1857

Uprising in India. Arising in a remote corner of south-west China from a crisis caused by a combination of domestic and external factors, the Taiping Rebellion eventually covered all of south and central China, cost an estimated 20 million lives, and took thirteen years to put down. True, the 1857 Uprising did not spread throughout India. But, the regions which revolted were equal in area to France, Austria, and Prussia put together.[67] In the mid-nineteenth century, there were about 170 million people in the subcontinent.[68] Irfan Habib asserts that temporarily, the rebel *sarkar* came to control about one-fourth of the populace of British India.[69] In Awadh alone, about 150,000 men (including 35,000 sepoys) succumbed against the British.[70]

Both the Taiping Rebellion and the 1857 Uprising were large-scale peasant rebellions. As regards 1857, Eric Stokes claims that the peasant rebellion was triggered off not by the intrusion of the *mahajans* as part of British land-revenue policy but due to the differing effect of land revenue on different communities. The other two causes were the decaying Muslim aristocracy (gentry) and the clan organization of the peasant communities.[71] Bearing features of China's long tradition of peasant rebellions, as well as elements of a radically new social programme and ideology influenced by messianic Christianity, the Taiping Rebellion, writes Thampi, stands at the conjunction of pre-modern and modern China. Although it was completely exterminated, it continues to live on powerfully in the oral traditions and folklore as well as the consciousness of Chinese people.

Like the Taiping Rebellion, the 1857 Uprising was also characterized by a strong streak of religiosity. For instance Maulvi Muhammad Baqir, the editor of *Dihli Urdu Akhbar*, wrote in May 1857 that the rebellion was an act of god to punish the *kafirs* for their arrogant plans to wipe out the traditional religions of India.[72] The rebel leaders sought legitimation through authoritative religious prescriptions. The *maulvis' fatwas* and proclamations sometimes provided the template for the political magnate's proclamations.[73] The *mujahideens* and the *ghazis* who were the Wahhabi *maulvis* and militant *naqshbandis* arrived in Delhi and fought with the rebel soldiery against the Delhi Field Force.[74] K.M. Ashraf asserts that the Wahhabis played an important role, especially in Delhi. General Bakht Khan was a Wahhabi and he appointed Sarfaraz Ali as the leader of the *jihadis*. Between 1850 and 1857, the Wahhabis repeatedly instigated the North-West Frontier tribes to raise the banner of rebellion against the British. Under Wahhabi influence, the ruler of Swat and Akhund contacted the Indian soldiery in Punjab to rebel against the Company Raj. In order to fight the *ferangis* in Delhi, Wahhabi volunteers came from Jaipur, Jhansi, Hissar, Bhopal, Nasirabad, Najibabad, and Tonk.[75] Sabyasachi Bhattacharya cautions that the term *jihad* in the context of 1857 Uprising referred to righteous war or *dharmayuddha*. Bhattacharya rightly says that we need to be context-specific and context-sensitive while analysing religious categories.[76]

In the mid-1850s, Britain the global superpower was engaged in military operations in China and India. The Second Opium War (1856–60) was fought by Britain and France against China.[77] The looting of Delhi and Lucknow in September 1857 and March 1858 by British soldiers could be compared with the looting of Beijing by the French Army in 1860.[78] The course of British military operation in China was entangled with contemporary events in India. In March 1857, the British government sent reinforcements from Britain and Mauritius to teach the Manchu regime and the Taiping rebels a lesson, but the 1857 Uprising resulted in the diversion of the troops to India. As a result, reinforcements reached China a year later.[79] For the Indians, a feature of particular interest is the connection of Indian soldiers with the Taiping Rebellion. Indian soldiers were used in China in the First Opium War (1840–2) and the Second Opium War. The Indian soldiers deserted the British and joined the Chinese rebels only in 1857. This change of sides by the Indian soldiery, says B.R. Deepak, was spontaneous. Unlike some of the Westerners, the Indian soldiery who sided with the Taiping, claims Deepak, fought not for money but for a cause.[80] Rebels in China and India were also thinking of a joint front against Britain. In late 1859, Chalafenta, a Tartar general of Sinkiang and the *mandarin* Fahfooli acting on the advice of the Russian consul in Sinkiang, were thinking of sending a mission to India to conclude an alliance against Britain.[81] By late 1859, the rebels in India were a spent force. Had such a mission been sent a year earlier, history might have taken an alternate course.

While the Indian Uprising was directed primarily against the alien power, the Chinese rebellion was against a domestic regime. Nevertheless, the Taiping Rebellion also indirectly challenged imperialism. It is essential to note that even the 1857 Uprising was not totally an anti-colonial movement. E.I. Brodkin rightly says that the disappearance of British authority in much of northern India was followed by the re-emergence of traditional rivalries among different Indian communities. The British withdrawal, continues Brodkin, marked the beginning of a gigantic power struggle for succession.[82] The difference in the nature of the Indian and Chinese uprisings, writes Deepak, was partly due to the differing nature of imperialism. While London established direct imperialism in India, it established indirect imperialism in China and ruled that country through the Qing regime. After the Opium War, Britain used the Manchu government as a tool for opening up China for trade and economic exploitation. The Chinese peasantry realized the degeneration of the Manchu government and launched a massive movement to get rid of it.[83] Thampi's essay in this volume shows that the Taipings had a forward looking social agenda. In contrast, the rebels of 1857 were insensitive to the issues of social justice.[84] The British mobilized an international force to crush the Taipings and in addition utilized the Manchu regime to fight the Taiping rebels. Similarly, the British also used the loyal PIF and the units of Madras and Bombay armies to fight the rebels within India.

CONCLUSION

Unlike the Taiping rebels, the rebels of 1857 India had a negative social programme which prevented the educated indigenous middle class in Calcutta, Madras and Bombay from throwing their lot against the Company Raj. Again, British military operations both in China and India which occurred simultaneously were entangled like a double helix. Counter-factual history cannot prove anything except by challenging linear determinism. As Callahan suggests, the mutiny in the Bengal Army was not inevitable. To establish a direct connection between the Vellore Mutiny of 1806 and the 1857 Uprising would be an example of crass linear teleology. Had the 1857 Mutiny occurred a year earlier when Britain was conducting the Persian War, or during the Crimean War, or if a joint front among the three great land powers (Russia, China and India) actually came into existence, then Eurasian history would have taken a different course. In fact, then the British Empire would have collapsed long before the Second World War. Herein, lies the importance of entangled history and counter-factual history. Rather than merely a parlour game, it opens up new vistas to think beyond the existing lines. Hence, the relevance of analysing the 1857 Uprising on a global plane especially taking into account the role of the contingent and unforeseen.

NOTES

1. There are Urdu documents generated by the rebels in particular and some contemporary Indians in general which have been used extensively by S. Mahdi Husain in his biography of Bahadur Shah Zafar titled *Bahadur Shah Zafar and the War of 1857 in Delhi* (1958, rpt. Delhi: Aakar Books, 2006). But a complete cataloguing and translation of these documents is yet to be done. W. Dalrymple in *The Last Mughal: The Fall of a Dynasty, Delhi 1857* (New Delhi: Penguin, Viking, 2006) claims to be the first to use Urdu sources and does not mention Husain's book either in the bibliography or in the endnotes. Note that numerous Urdu documents have been translated and published in the multi-volume *Freedom Struggle in Uttar Pradesh*, ed. S.A.A. Rizvi and M.L. Bhargava.
2. James Belich, 'The Victorian Interpretation of Racial Conflict and the New Zealand Wars: An Approach to the Problem of One-Sided Evidence', *JICH*, vol. 5 (1986–7), pp. 123, 140.
3. Douglas M. Peers, 'War and Public Finance in Early Nineteenth-Century British India: The First Burma War', *International History Review*, vol. 11, no. 4 (1989), pp. 634, 636, 640.
4. Talmiz Khaldun, 'The Great Rebellion', in P.C. Joshi (ed.), *Rebellion 1857: A Symposium* (1957, rpt., Calcutta: K.P. Bagchi, 1986), p. 34.
5. E.M. Spiers, *The Army and Society: 1815–1914* (London: Longman, 1980), pp. 35–6, 40–1, 44, 48, 49, 62–3.
6. Jeffrey Greenhut, 'Sahib and Sepoy: An Inquiry into the Relationship between the British Officers and Native Soldiers of the British Indian Army', *Military Affairs*, vol. XLVIII, no. 1 (1984), pp. 15–18.
7. Thomas A. Marks, 'Ideology of Insurgency: New Ethnic Focus or Cold War Distortions?', *Small Wars & Insurgencies*, vol. 15, no. 1 (2004), pp. 108–12, 122–3, 126.
8. Haraprasad Chattopadhyay, *The Sepoy Mutiny, 1857: A Social Study and Analysis* (Calcutta: Bookland Pvt. Ltd., 1957), pp. 56–60.
9. James W. Hoover, 'The Recruitment of the Bengal Army: Beyond the Myth of the Zemindar's Son', *Indo-British Review*, vol. 21, no. 2 (1996), p. 152.

10. Hoover, 'Recruitment of the Bengal Army', p. 151.
11. Haraprasad Chattopadhyay, 'Sepoy Army: Its Strength and Composition', *Calcutta Review*, vol. 30 (July 1956), p. 32.
12. Hoover, 'Recruitment of the Bengal Army', pp. 144–9.
13. Michael H. Fisher, 'British Expansion in North India: The Role of the Resident in Awadh', *IESHR*, vol. 18, no. 1 (1981), pp. 73–4.
14. Khaldun, 'The Great Rebellion', in Joshi (ed.), *Rebellion 1857*, p. 16.
15. Thomas R. Metcalf, 'From Raja to Landlord: The Oudh Taluqdars, 1850–70', in Metcalf, *Forging the Raj: Essays on British India in the Heyday of Empire* (New Delhi: Oxford University Press, 2005), p. 52.
16. P.C. Joshi, '1857 in our History', in Joshi (ed.), *Rebellion 1857*, p. 137.
17. Thomas R. Metcalf, 'The Influence of the Mutiny of 1857 on Land Policy in India', in Metcalf, *Forging the Raj*, p. 38.
18. James W. Hoover, *Men Without Hats: Dialogue, Discipline and Discontent in the Madras Army, 1806-1807* (New Delhi: Manohar, 2007), pp. 25, 27, 29, 35, 39–41, 44, 47–8, 55, 57.
19. Peter Stanley, ' "Dear Comrades": Barrack Room Culture and the "White Mutiny" of 1859-60', *Indo-British Review*, vol. 21, no. 2 (1996), pp. 165–75.
20. Jean Deloche, *Studies on Fortification in India* (Pondichery: Institut Francais de Pondichery, 2007), pp. 235–6, 240, 242.
21. John Fraser, 'The Letters of Brevet Lieutenant-Colonel Robert Abercomby Yule: Part One', *JSAHR*, vol. 61 (1983), p. 225.
22. Jeremy Black, 'Revolutionary and Napoleonic Warfare', in J. Black (ed.), *European Warfare: 1453-1815* (Houndmills, Basingstoke: Macmillan, 1999), pp. 227–8.
23. Pradeep Barua, 'Military Developments in India: 1750–1850', *JMH*, vol. 58, no. 4 (1994), pp. 599–616.
24. Elizabeth B. Moynihan, 'The Lotus Garden Palace of Zahir al-Din Muhammad Babur', *Muqarnas*, vol. 5 (1988), pp. 135–45.
25. Ebba Koch, 'Mughal Palace Gardens from Babur to Shah Jahan (1526–1648)', *Muqarnas*, vol. 14 (1997), pp. 147, 159.
26. Narayani Gupta, 'Military Security and Urban Development: A Case Study of Delhi, 1857–1912', *MAS*, vol. 5, no. 1 (1971), p. 62.
27. Raffi Gregorian, 'Unfit for Service: British Law and Looting in India in the mid-Nineteenth Century', *South Asia*, vol. 13, no. 1 (1990), pp. 71–2, 75.
28. Joshi, '1857 in our History', in Joshi (ed.), *Rebellion 1857*, p. 163.
29. Gupta, 'Military Security and Urban Development', pp. 62–3.
30. Sekhar Bandopadhyay, 'Eighteen Fifty-Seven and its Many Histories', in *1857: Essays from Economic and Political Weekly* (Hyderabad: Orient Longman in association with the Sameeksha Trust, 2008), p. 11.
31. Gupta, 'Military Security and Urban Development', pp. 63, 65.
32. Gautam Chakravarty, *The Indian Mutiny and the British Imagination* (Cambridge: Cambridge University Press, 2006), pp. 78–9.

33. Douglas Peers, 'South Asia', in Jeremy Black (ed.), *War in the Modern World Since 1815* (London/New York: Routledge, 2003), p. 44.
34. Ralph Crane and Radhika Mohanram, 'Introduction', in R. Crane (ed.), *Love Besieged: A Romance of the Defence of Lucknow*, by Charles E. Pearce (New Delhi: Oxford University Press, 2003), pp. xiii–xiv.
35. Rod Thornton, 'The British Army and the Origins of its Minimum Force Philosophy', *Small Wars & Insurgencies*, vol. 15, no. 1 (2004), p. 90.
36. Chakravarty, *Indian Mutiny and the British Imagination*, pp. 2, 6, 9, 63.
37. Douglas M. Peers, 'Colonial Knowledge and the Military in India, 1780–1860', *JICH*, vol. 33, no. 2 (May 2005), pp. 157–61.
38. Crane and Mohanram, 'Introduction', in Crane (ed.), *Love Besieged*, p. xix.
39. Peers, 'Colonial Knowledge and the Military in India', p. 166.
40. Bruce Watson, *The Great Indian Mutiny: Colin Campbell and the Campaign at Lucknow* (New York, Westport, Connecticut, London: Praeger, 1991), p. 25.
41. Peter Burroughs, 'Imperial Defence and the Victorian Army', *JICH*, vol. 15, no. 1 (1986), pp. 62–3.
42. Crane and Mohanram, 'Introduction', in Crane (ed.), *Love Besieged*, pp. xii–xiii.
43. Ibid., pp. xiv–xvi.
44. Indrani Sen, 'Inscribing the Rani of Jhansi in Colonial "Mutiny" Fiction', in *1857*, pp. 253–4, 262.
45. Lata Singh, '1857: Visibilising the "Other" in History: Courtesans and the Revolt', in *1857*, pp. 329–38.
46. Aishwarya Lakshmi, 'The Mutiny Novel: Creating the Domestic Body of the Empire', in *1857*, pp. 229, 234.
47. Sen, 'Inscribing the Rani of Jhansi', in *1857*, pp. 258–60, 263, 265.
48. Crane and Mohanram, 'Introduction', in Crane (ed.), *Love Besieged*, pp. ix, xi–xii.
49. Ibid., pp. xiii, xviii–xix.
50. Smita Pandey, *Vision of the Rebels during 1857: Aspects of Mobilisation, Organisation and Resistance* (New Delhi: Rupa, 2008); Sitaram Yechury, 'Introduction', in Sitaram Yechury (ed.), *The Great Revolt: A Left Appraisal* (New Delhi: People's Democracy, 2008), pp. xv–xxiv.
51. Benoy Ghose, 'The Bengali Intelligentsia and the Revolt', in Joshi (ed.), *Rebellion 1857*, pp. 103, 112.
52. Gopal Haldar, 'Bengali Literature Before and After 1857', in Joshi (ed.), *Rebellion 1857*, pp. 258–9.
53. Ghose, 'Bengali Intelligentsia', and Haldar, 'Bengali Literature', in Joshi (ed.), *Rebellion 1857*, pp. 116–17, 260.
54. Bandopadhyay, 'Eighteen Fifty-Seven', in *1857*, p. 13.
55. Swarupa Gupta, '1857 and Ideas about Nationhood in Bengal: Nuances and Themes', in *1857*, pp. 279–302.

56. Basudeb Chattopadhyay, 'Panic Sunday in Calcutta: 14 June 1857', in Sabyasachi Bhattacharya (ed.), *Rethinking 1857* (New Delhi: Orient Longman, 2007), pp. 168–70.
57. Chattopadhyay, *The Sepoy Mutiny*, p. 16.
58. Sabyasachi Bhattacharya, 'Rethinking 1857', in S. Bhattacharya (ed.), *Rethinking 1857*, p. xxxii.
59. Bruce Mazlish, 'Comparing Global History to World History', *Journal of Interdisciplinary History*, vol. 28, no. 3 (1998), pp. 385–7, 390, 392–3.
60. Heather Sutherland, 'The Problematic Authority of (World) History', *JWH*, vol. 18, no. 4 (2007), pp. 505–8.
61. Dominic Sachsenmaier, 'World History as Ecumenical History?', *JWH*, vol. 18, no. 4 (2007), pp. 465-89. Sachsenmaier implies a subtle distinction between the concepts of world history and global history.
62. Jurgen Kocka, 'Comparison and Beyond', *History and Theory*, vol. 42, no. 1 (2003), p. 43.
63. Chris Lorenz, 'Comparative Historiography: Problems and Perspectives', *History and Theory*, vol. 38, no. 1 (1999), pp. 28–9.
64. Kocka, 'Comparison and Beyond', p. 39.
65. Ibid., pp. 40, 42.
66. Ibid., pp. 42-4.
67. Joshi, '1857 in our History', in Joshi (ed.), *Rebellion 1857*, p. 176.
68. K.C. Yadav, 'Interpreting 1857: A Case Study', in Bhattacharya (ed.), *Rethinking 1857*, p. 5.
69. Irfan Habib, 'Understanding 1857', in Bhattacharya (ed.), *Rethinking 1857*, p. 60.
70. Joshi, '1857 in our History', in Joshi (ed.), *Rebellion 1857*, p. 195.
71. Eric Stokes, 'Rural Revolt in the Great Rebellion of 1857 in India: A Study of the Saharanpur and Muzaffarnagar Districts', *Historical Journal*, vol. 12, no. 4 (1969), pp. 606–27.
72. William Dalrymple, 'Religious Rhetoric in the Delhi Uprising of 1857', in Bhattacharya (ed.), *Rethinking 1857*, p. 24.
73. Bhattacharya, 'Rethinking 1857', in Bhattacharya (ed.), *Rethinking 1857*, pp. xxiii–xxiv.
74. Dalrymple, 'Religious Rhetoric', in Bhattacharya (ed.), *Rethinking 1857*, p. 26.
75. K.M. Ashraf, 'Muslim Revivalists and the Revolt of 1857', in Joshi (ed.), *Rebellion 1857*, pp. 71, 82, 98.
76. Bhattacharya, 'Rethinking 1857', in Bhattacharya (ed.), *Rethinking 1857*, pp. xix, xxi.
77. Yu Sheng-Wu and Chang Chen-Kun, 'China and India in the mid-19th Century', in Joshi (ed.), *Rebellion 1857*, p. 338.
78. Gregorian, 'Unfit for Service', p. 84.
79. Sheng-Wu and Chen-Kun, 'China and India', in Joshi (ed.), *Rebellion 1857*, pp. 340–2.

80. B.R. Deepak, 'The 1857 Rebellion and Indian Involvement in the Taiping Uprising of China', in Madhavi Thampi (ed.), *India and China in the Colonial World* (New Delhi: Social Science Press, 2005), pp. 140, 146–7.
81. Sheng-Wu and Chen-Kun, 'China and India', in Joshi (ed.), *Rebellion 1857*; pp. 344–5.
82. E.I. Brodkin, 'The Struggle for Succession: Rebels and Loyalists in the Indian Mutiny of 1857', *MAS*, vol. 6, no. 3 (1972), pp. 277–90.
83. Deepak, 'Indian involvement in the Taiping Uprising of China', in Madhavi Thampi (ed.), *India and China*, 139.
84. Bhattacharya, 'Rethinking 1857', in Bhattacharya (ed.), *Rethinking 1857*, p. xxvi.

PART I

1857 UPRISING IN INDIA

CHAPTER 1

From Mornington to the Mutiny: Some Thoughts and Questions about the Company's Army 1805–1857

RAYMOND CALLAHAN

There are two pictures that, taken together, frame this essay. The failed attempt by the EIC's Bengal Army to take Bharatpur in 1805, during the Second Anglo–Maratha War (1803–5) that consolidated the Company's position as the dominant power in the subcontinent, is the first. Committed to a hopeless assault on an inadequate breach in the city's walls, the 15th BNI was shot to pieces, losing nearly half its strength. Its shredded battle flag, destined to be ceremonially cremated, then mysteriously vanished during the army's crestfallen retreat from Bharatpur. Twenty years later, the Company's army returned—a different war, a larger force, and a somewhat better commander. The 15th BNI had become, in one of the Bengal Army's periodic reorganizations, the 31st BNI. Again facing the walls of Bharatpur—this time effectively breached—the regiment asked, through its senior Indian officers, to be part of the assault column. When the attack went in, the 31st BNI carried before it the shredded remnants of the 1805 battle flag, carefully cut up and distributed among the survivors of the failed assault, passed on from fathers to the sons who followed them into the regiment, until the stain on the unit's honour that was the failure in 1805 could be triumphantly expunged, as it was on 17 January 1826. It is a story whose almost cinematic drama underscores the tremendous *esprit de corps* that had made the Company's armies so unstoppable a force.

But, then a second snapshot: the 6th BNI at Allahabad in June 1857. The regiment reacted to the mutinies that had begun on 10 May 1857 at Meerut and then spread to other Bengal Army stations by volunteering to serve against the mutineers who had seized Delhi. At an evening parade on 6 June, the thanks of the Governor-General for the regiment's fidelity was read to troops, who responded with cheers and renewed assertions of loyalty. A few hours later, spooked by rumours that, despite their loyalty, they would be disarmed by British troops, they rose in mutiny, shooting down five of their officers on the same parade ground where they had so recently proclaimed their fidelity.

The EIC never planned to have an empire, much less a large standing army, a navy, a diplomatic service, and a foreign policy, not to mention a very large bureaucracy to fund, feed, move, and control it all. That nonetheless is what it acquired between 1740 and 1805. The trigger mechanisms that set-off this astounding transformation were two, one internal and one external: the political balkanization of India (to which the Company would make its own contribution), and the worldwide Anglo–French struggle. Those sixty years saw war after war in India, climaxing in the manic imperial drive of Richard Colley Wellesley, Lord Mornington (Governor-General from 1798–1805).

The narrative arc of the Company's armies from the end of Wellesley's multiple wars, wars that made the Company 'paramount', until the outbreak of the 'Great Sepoy Mutiny' in 1857 is, from one angle, a story of the decline of its largest component, the Bengal Army, from a very formidable fighting force to a dissent-ridden, only precariously stable organization whose ultimate collapse took the Company with it. To see matters that way, however, is to forget F.W. Maitland's warning to historians that while history is written and interpreted in retrospect, it is lived going forward into an unknowable future. With that in mind, this essay will attempt to look at the Company's armies, not from the point of view of an inevitable 1857, but as a remarkable amalgam of Western and Indian personnel, technology and military customs, perhaps the most remarkable institution created by the British during their long overseas adventure and created by them in an ambiguous partnership with those they had come to rule.[1]

WHAT THE COMPANY'S ARMIES WERE

Born in an *ad hoc* fashion in the middle years of the eighteenth century and forged in an almost non-stop series of wars, the

Company's armies had, by the early nineteenth century, become institutionally mature. They had, moreover, become the backbone of what has been called a 'military fiscal state'—a governmental structure in which sustaining the army became the top priority.[2] This military fiscal state was, however, structured in a very unusual way. Each of the Company's three Indian presidencies had its own army, with its own distinctive customs, traditions, and recruitment patterns. Furthermore, the officers of each army had developed their own set of professional prejudices, of which the most marked was the assumption by the officers of the Bengal Army (the youngest of the presidency armies) that their service and sepoys were much superior to the other two. At no time during the Company's life— nor indeed, for forty years after its demise—was there a unified Indian Army. The Company's military began to grow from 'factory guards' into armies on the Coromandel Coast, and then named as the Madras (or 'Coast') Army, which bore the brunt of the Company's early wars and, indeed, provided the sepoys with whom Clive won Bengal. However, its days as the Company's senior army passed rapidly. The size, wealth, and importance of the Bengal Presidency were reflected quickly in the primacy accorded its army. The commander-in-chief of India was also the commander-in-chief of the Bengal Army and, as a member of the governor-general's council, spent his time at Calcutta or on tour in his own presidency. Only when physically present at the other presidencies did he take precedence over their commanders-in-chief. Far from being effective head of the Company's armies, he was at best *primus inter pares*, having neither the authority, the staff, nor, until the coming of the cable and telegraph, the communication infrastructure to exercise effective command over the Madras and Bombay armies. The comparative isolation of the other two presidencies from Bengal would have important long-term consequences.

From the late eighteenth century, when London began to pay close and continuing attention to India, the three presidency commanders-in-chief were usually from the regular British Army rather than from the Company's service. This meant that Company officers (who could not rise above the rank of colonel until after 1796) could not normally expect to become the professional heads of their services, a situation that was only the most obvious example of a toxic mix of professional jealousy, social snobbery, and avidity for 'jobs for the boys' that would mark the British Army's relationship with the Company's service throughout, and that would survive the Company's demise, affecting British Army attitudes to Indian Army officers until the end of the Raj. The costs of this arrangement were very high. Many commanders-in-chief knew little and understood less about the Company's service and, in particular, about its 'native black troops'. A Madras Commander-in-Chief, Sir John Craddock, precipitated the worst mutiny prior to 1857 at Vellore in 1806 by an ill-advised attempt to make Madras sepoys look more European. A Bengal (and India's) Commander-in-Chief, Sir Edward Paget, turned what was a manageable situation into a bloody shambles in 1824 by treating the presentation of grievances by sepoys of the 47th BNI at Barrackpur as mutiny, which he suppressed savagely, killing some 300 sepoys outright and hanging more in the aftermath. A case can be made that the change in attitude by the Bengal sepoys towards their employers had its origin at Barrackpur on that day. The problems arising from two different types of officers controlling Company troops present one of the most anomalous features of the Company's military structure and were a continuing source of problems.[3]

The Company's own officer corps, like its armies, was not a unitary professional group, but three separate groups that had a paymaster, but little else, in common. All three had come into existence, like the armies they commanded, in an *ad hoc*, improvisatory way as the Company lurched from trading concern to a tax gathering militarized state. The Bombay Army, with its roots in the mid-seventeenth century, had long had to cope with constricted territories and therefore limited resources, financial and demographic. Perhaps, for that reason its officers got accustomed to handling a very broad cross-section of Indian troops—the Bombay Army could not afford to turn anyone away. The variegated composition of its units proved to be a stabilizing force in 1857. In the Company's last years, the Bombay Army threw up one of the most striking and original talents in the history of the Company's military service: John Jacob. He founded a regiment, left his name on the Indian landscape in the city of Jacobabad, and—in his ideas on the recruitment, training and leadership of Indian units—prefigured some of the post-

Mutiny reforms (a mutiny he foresaw and warned against in trenchant pamphlets that were ignored).[4]

The Madras Army was born as the Company was drawn into a complex struggle for dominance in south India, triggered by both the instability accompanying Mughal decline and the local impact of the worldwide Anglo–French struggle. Its rapid growth in the middle years of the eighteenth century, and the fact that southern India was the scene of a series of hard-fought wars with the Sultanate of Mysore, made the Madras Army perhaps the most battle-tested of the Company's armies until the century's end. The final conquest of Mysore and a shift in the focus of military activity to central and then northern India gradually turned the Madras Army into a military backwater after the last of the Maratha Wars (i.e. the Third Anglo–Maratha War of 1817–18), although it served abroad in Ceylon, at Malacca and in Burma and had as well continuing responsibility for providing garrisons for the Company's Burmese holdings. Some units served briefly—and unhappily—in Sind in the 1840s. There is some evidence that the relationship of the Madras officers to their sepoys (who were recruited largely in south India from groups with a tradition of military service and were therefore more homogeneous than the Bombay Army) remained good even as those in Bengal deteriorated, something that would be important in 1857.[5]

The largest by far of the Company's armies, however, and the dominant force throughout the period covered by this essay, was the Bengal Army. Created in the aftermath of the battle of Plassey and the conquest of Bengal (1757), supported by wealth extracted from a very rich province, and fed by a recruitment area that soon included the heartland of the north Indian military manpower market, it rapidly became the most significant of the Company's military services. As the centre of gravity of the Company's concerns moved from south India to the Ganga Valley and the expansionism of Richard Colley Wellesley drove the Company's frontiers north-west, the size and importance of the Bengal Army steadily increased, as did its officers' sense of their own indispensability. On the eve of Wellesley's drive to make Britain paramount in India, the Bengal officers, faced with plans crafted by Lord Cornwallis (Governor-General from 1786–92) and Henry Dundas (Prime Minister William Pitt's manager of Indian affairs) to 'nationalize' the Company's armies, mounted a furious defence of the status and prerogatives of the Company's service, intimidating Cornwallis's successor as Governor-General, Sir John Shore, and checkmating London's plans. Ironically, one of the threats the Bengal officers deployed was the willingness of their sepoys to stand behind them in any clash with the Governor-General—and the few British Army units available to him. The consequent compromise 'reform' of 1796 gave the Company's officer corps the shape it would retain for the next fifty years.[6]

That officer corps was based on one dominant fact: career military service in India was undertaken by those for whom a commission in the regular British Army was out of reach. 'We are not men of Interest' was how the London representatives of the Bengal officers put it in their tense negotiations with the government and the Company in the 1790s. Lacking the connections and patrons—'interest'—of the sort very common among British Army officers of the era (connections that could accelerate a career significantly), they built their service on strict seniority. To make worthwhile the risks of Indian service for the thirty and more years it would take to reach the senior ranks, they simultaneously built an incredible network of payments and perquisites for themselves, taking advantage of the fact that while the Company's weaponry and tactics were European, as was much of its administration, its logistics were not. In these carry-overs from Mughal (or even older) practices, there were abundant opportunities for profit: after all, the officers argued, such emoluments were merely appropriate compensation for long service in India which resulted in most of the officers dying either due to campaigning or climate.[7] None of the peculiarities of Company service meant that military professionalism was lacking—the Company's 'military seminary' at Addiscombe (established in 1809) represented the same impulse to modernize and professionalize as the British Army's Sandhurst. Those peculiarities did mean, however, that there were strong, inbuilt, forces of institutional conservatism in the Company's officer corps—especially in the Bengal Army—that made it slow to react when the changing circumstances began to unsettle the soldiers.

A comprehensive history of sepoy recruitment in the Company's armies has yet to be written, but enough has been done to make possible a reasonably accurate overall picture. The Bombay

Army, as noted, took a very wide range of recruits because in its early, formative years it had no choice, while Madras recruited mostly in southern India. Neither recruited large numbers of men from northern India. That great reservoir of military manpower drained almost exclusively into the Bengal Army. The Company tapped, as soon as it was able, many of the same sources of manpower as had the Mughals and other north Indian rulers before them. Military service in India was, by and large, contractual; as the Company's power steadily grew, it offered the best chance of gainful military employment. Many of the problems that would arise later in the relationship of the sepoy to his employer (sahib) were the product of the shifting balance in the minds of Indian soldiers between the gains realized by service to the Company and the constraints that had to be accepted in the employ of people alien in race, culture, and belief. For a long time the gains outweighed the losses. The Company was winning. Sepoy pay, if not much better than that offered by many Indian rulers, was generally received regularly. The perquisites, allowances, pensions, and shares in frequent hauls of loot were good. A sepoy in the Company's service could usually pass his valuable place along to his son. As the Company settled down after its era of expansion under Wellesley, it was in control of some of the richest recruiting tracts in India—the client *Nawabi* of Awadh and its own north-western provinces stretching from Awadh to Delhi. This guaranteed a steady flow of military manpower and allowed the Bengal Army to become a remarkably homogeneous force—and a homogeneous parade ground appearance has a strong attraction to the military mind. However, homogeneity carried the danger that there would be no firewalls to contain the rapid spread of dissent and disaffection through the army if issues arose that put Indian soldiers at odds with either their British officers or the Company Raj. The most likely source of such a development lay in the fact that the sepoys were high caste Hindus and the sowars were Muslim from a narrow region, while their officers were British and (however nominally) Christian.

The gap between the culture and beliefs of the soldiers and that of their officers was enormous. This had been obvious from the beginning. Once the decision had been taken (at Madras, before the rise of the Bengal Army) not to have Indians in command positions, it was obvious that the European officers would need, both to be very careful not to interfere with the beliefs and cultural norms of their Indian soldiers, and to learn their language (or, at least, the predominant language spoken in their army). Religious and cultural neutrality may have been easier for eighteenth-century Britons than for their nineteenth-century successors, shaped by the complex of values and attitudes we label Victorian as well as the more aggressive Christianity and triumphalism of the post-Waterloo years, but it was always understood by perceptive officers and Company administrators as essential to the functioning of the Company Raj. As the nineteenth century wore on, perceptiveness (or the number of the perceptive) was unfortunately diminished by bureaucratic routine, complacency and the tone deafness all too often bred by success. There was however one other institutional safeguard against the loss of touch with the sepoys' concerns and fears: the Indian 'officers'. Holding a position unknown in Western armies, they were not really officers at all in the Western sense, while being much more than non-commissioned officers. Positioned between white officers and brown soldiers, and lacking real command authority (they were outranked by the most junior white officers), they were nevertheless supposed to serve as bridges, advisors, even early warning systems. In practice the positions were filled, like those of the Company's European officer corps, on the basis of seniority, a reward for long service and good conduct. Age often then militated against effectiveness. Moreover, consigned as they were to a frustrating limbo, many Indian officers developed deep resentments that would finally surface in 1857.

If many of the arrangements for manning and controlling the Company's armies seemed anomalous by European norms, the way the Company's armies were supplied and moved was completely exotic. The armies inherited the logistic arrangements that served not only the Mughal armies but those of Indian states generally. Travelling bazars, armies of 'followers', reliance on a far-flung network of *banjaras* for provision and enormous numbers of animals—bullocks, elephants, camels, horses—were its hallmarks. To move a unit between stations in peacetime or in the field on campaign entailed managing a moving city. The Company's armies, like all Indian armies, moved slowly, surrounded by that moving city. Some of this was, of course, reminiscent of the armies of early modern Europe and of the armed hordes of the Thirty-Year War, but it would be a mistake to push this comparison too far. The logistic system of the Company's armies was an intelligent and effective adaptation of existing military systems in India. In the circumstances, there was no realistic alternative, and the effective management of this particular Indo–European hybrid (traces of which remained in the Indian Army of the Raj to its end), as readers of Wellington's Indian dispatches know, required the development of impressive managerial skill.

The skills required of the Company's officers were considerable and often underestimated, first by British regulars and then by posterity mesmerized by the lavish train of servants, the apparently comfortable colonial lifestyle, and by the undeniable fact that the largest of the Company's armies finally collapsed into a mutiny that shook British power in India to its roots, destroying the Company itself. However, it is important to remember the other side of the coin: the Company's officers were career-long, often lifelong, exiles in India. They had to learn not only one or more languages, but also much about a society which to them appeared alien and even incomprehensible. Some did this well, some less well, but the majority well enough that the Company's armies functioned effectively until 1857—and even then the Madras and Bombay armies continued to serve. The Company officers not only had to manage their troops, but the complexities of the hybrid Indo–European military system that provided their logistics. And if their lifestyle looks rather comfortable (allowing for the absence of both aspirin and air conditioning), it is necessary to bear in mind the well-filled European graveyards of India, where they, their wives and children all too often ended their Indian years.[8] In the last analysis, however, armies exist to fight battles and win wars. And it is on their record in doing so that any judgement on the Company's armies must ultimately depend. This raises the question of how effectively the Company's armies actually fought.

MILITARY EFFECTIVENESS

In most nineteenth- and early twentieth-century British accounts of the wars that accompanied the rise of the Company's power, the focus (as was then typical of military history) was on commanders and battles. Battle narratives tended to concentrate on the performance of regular British units, stationed in India continuously from Warren Hastings's time, and present at most major engagements. The Company's forces—who made up the vast majority of the troops engaged in nearly every battle and in all campaigns—were reduced in these narratives to supporting roles. Of course, there were Victorian-era narrative histories of the presidency armies, written by officers who had served Company and Crown, but they were mostly unread, indeed often unreadable, and in any case made little impact. In Sir John Fortescue's magisterial (and long taken as authoritative) thirteen volume *History of the British Army*, India is subdued by never-failing British infantry, with some support from Indian troops. True, Fortescue was writing about the British Army, but his unbalanced treatment—the narrative history counterpart of British regular officers' disdain for the Company's service—is symptomatic of an approach to the military history of the Company's Raj that is very misleading about the realities of warfare in India. It can often seem as if only with the 1857 Mutiny is the Sepoy Army (or, more precisely, that part of it which belonged to the Bengal Presidency) allowed to take centre stage.

The first of those neglected realities is that the Company became paramount in India on the shoulders of its sepoys. British regulars were few in number and only intermittently present until the 1780s. Even after they had become a continuing presence, their numbers were dwarfed by the size of the sepoy establishment. Seldom at full strength due to the ravages of climate, disease, and alcohol, British Army units were used sparingly both because of the cost involved and because of the further 'wastage' sure to result. The considerable amount of soldiering necessary to combat the many continuing challenges to the Company's authority throughout India—minor wars, insurgencies, 'pacification' efforts—was done by Indian soldiers. Small-scale pacification campaigns, or armed support for revenue collection, were unglamorous, arduous, and often deadly activities, not likely to win much attention from history. They were however essential to the smooth functioning of the Company's Raj.

One such episode in 1771 can stand for many. The Council of

Revenue at Patna in the Bengal Presidency asked for military support to bring a refractory landowner to order. The landowner in question possessed a fortress with inner and outer walls, a wet ditch, 5 cannons, and a garrison of 1,000 men. Another force was reported to be hovering in the vicinity to take any attackers in the rear. What began as a modest expedition—a few companies of sepoys and two guns—rapidly grew into a battalion-sized force (and sepoy battalions, at 1,000 strong, were roughly twice the size of comparable British army units) with substantial artillery support. There was a parallel civil-military argument over who got to negotiate the surrender of the fortress and, above all, to whom the windfall of loot would go. In the end, after some preliminary shelling, the fortress capitulated on terms (one of which was that women leaving it would be searched for valuables by a woman designated by the detachment commander, Lieutenant-Colonel Thomas Goddard, who on retirement took home over £100,000—tens of millions in today's values).

This sort of enterprise, as routine in the eighteenth and early nineteenth centuries as service on the North-West Frontier would later be, developed considerable logistic and tactical skills (not to mention the opportunities provided for enrichment). Yet, it was not without considerable costs. A similar revenue collection expedition by a Madras Army unit in the same year saw 18 of 20 Europeans fall ill, with 10 dying. A Company officer might develop his professional skills serving in a score of such operations for every major battle he saw.[9] Measuring professional performance in everything from small pacification expeditions to major wars in three armies over fifty years in a brief essay such as this is of course a matter of snapshots, and a few may serve to provide some sense of the Company's armies over the fifty years that separated Wellesley's wars from the 1857 Mutiny.

The wide variety of major military operations undertaken by the Company's armies over those decades break down into three broad categories: the consolidation of the Raj, its further expansion into contiguous territories, and finally 'power projection' based on India across the vast arc from the Middle East to East Asia, where Indian-based military power, given mobility by the Royal Navy, undergirded a growing network of British interests.

When Wellesley landed in India, two challengers to the Company's position remained. The Mysore Sultanate and the Maratha

Confederacy. The former—weaker perhaps than the British feared—was destroyed utterly. The latter, broken in the war that trained the future Duke of Wellington, remained on the Indian political landscape but not as a serious rival. Nonetheless, the final mopping up by Lord Hastings (Governor-General from 1813 to 1823) of the Marathas and their irregular Pindari allies in 1817–18 required a massive military operation that covered much of north and central India—a much more complex operation than anything that Wellington had had to manage in Spain: 100,000 men committed to a vast encirclement, an ambitious operation that was successfully completed. The troops involved were overwhelmingly Company sepoys. In a most remarkable feat of arms, the Battle of Sitabaldi (26–7 November 1817), a contingent of some 1,500 men that, apart from European officers, was an entirely Indian force, mostly from the Madras Army, first defended a position successfully against an attack mounted by a 20,000 Maratha force and then counter-attacked, scattering their assailants. After the Third Anglo–Maratha War, however, the Company's armies had few occasions to deploy within Company territory. Apart from the continuous low-level pacification and policing efforts, the focus shifted to the frontiers, where it confronted new enemies, real and imagined, and overseas ventures that posed new challenges to sepoy loyalties.

The border war with the Kingdom of Nepal (1814–16) was notable mainly because it led the Company to begin recruiting the tough mountaineers who became part of the legend of the Raj and whose descendants soldier on today in both the Indian and British armies. It is worth noting that the commander who brought the war to a successful conclusion, Major-General Sir David Ochterlony, was in many ways very typical of his generation of Company officers. The son of exiled American Loyalists, part of whose compensation for their losses was a Bengal Army cadetship for one of their sons, he landed in India in 1777. India became his real home, and he would end his life as British Resident in Delhi, an Anglo–Mughal grandee with some thirteen Indian consorts. Not all the Company's officers, of course, were as embedded in India as Ochterlony became, but many were, with a resulting grasp of their men's language and culture that became a component of the glue that bonded the army together. Unfortunately, Ochterlony's generation of officers were beginning to pass from the scene as a new set of demands on the sepoys began a slow erosion of that bond in the Bengal Army.[10]

Unlike the Nepal War, which ended successfully, the Afghan War (1839–42) was an unmitigated and avoidable disaster. It was undertaken rashly, an early 'Great Game' ploy to confront a (largely imaginary) Russian threat, on the basis of wishful thinking by the Company's 'politicals'. The politicals were Company officers, many of them hyper-adventurous junior army officers bored with peace-time regimental duties and slow promotion, who had gotten seconded to a quasi-diplomatic role with espionage and 'covert action' overtones. The resultant occupation of Kabul was incompetently managed by the local commanders and politicals and by their distant masters in Calcutta alike. Despite the ensuing debacle that saw the Kabul garrison destroyed, the Company's troops, when led competently, performed as well as ever. Yet the Afghan War was, the first unmistakable defeat the Company had suffered in over a generation. The subsequent success of Generals Sir Robert Sale and Sir William Nott in briefly retaking Kabul before withdrawing to India at the war's end did nothing to change the impression: the Company could be beaten.[11]

Although there would not again be a disaster as complete for the Company's arms as the loss of the Kabul garrison, another kind of fragility would surface in all the Company's subsequent wars: sepoy dissatisfaction that their terms and conditions of employment were being ignored. Already in 1824, the first of the Company's Burma Wars (1824–6) had produced the 'mutiny' of the 47th BNI at Barrackpur over the terms and conditions of deployment to and service in Burma, clearly beyond the Company's frontiers. As mentioned, the Commander-in-Chief, Sir Edward Paget, was a British Army officer known to be hostile to the Company's service, who turned a controllable situation into a bloody debacle. In fact, most of the Company troops used in Burma during the war and thereafter to garrison the Company's new Burmese territories were from the Madras Army, whose overseas deployment passed off without incident. In the aftermath of the Afghan Wars, the expansionists decided to annex Sind (1843). The military dimension of this was relatively uncomplicated but in the aftermath of victory special *batta* payments for service beyond the Company's frontiers were ended—Sind was, after all, reasoned the military bureaucrats in Calcutta, no longer 'abroad'. There was immediate discontent in many Bengal units and one, the 34th BNI, was disbanded as punishment. Even two Madras units, diverted from Burma, mutinied on learning that their expected overseas allowances would not be paid. In the end, Sind became part of the Bombay Presidency and therefore a 'home' commitment for the Bombay Army, an 'end run' around the *batta* issue. Another problem, however, surfaced in connection with Burma and Sind: the sepoys' growing concern that, with India conquered and (largely) pacified, they were no longer as important to the Company as they once had been. It was a fear that would grow in the Bengal Army as a result of the next series of wars.[12]

The two Sikh Wars (1845–6, 1848), following hard on the heels of the annexation of Sind, brought all these issues to a head. The Sikh state founded by Ranjit Singh became unstable after his death, but it still possessed the most formidable army that the Company had yet faced. In many ways it was a mirror-image of the Company's own army: well-disciplined infantry and gunners who had been trained on European lines for years, and were combat-experienced. When the almost inevitable clash came, the two brief wars saw some of the most ferocious infantry combat in the Company's history. The British commander in both wars was Major-General Sir Hugh Gough, a British Army officer undeniably gallant but with distinctly limited vision, whose sole tactical idea seems to have been the frontal assault. The Company's army won all the battles in both wars, but because of Gough's tactics the cost was very high. Had the senior leadership of the Sikh Army possessed the fighting qualities of their soldiers, the Company's army might very well have been defeated in the open field. As it was, the Sikhs demonstrated a weakness to be seen again during the 1857 Mutiny among the rebel commanders. Ranjit Singh's armies had been directed by European professionals who were long departed by 1845. The new Sikh senior officers, divided among themselves and mutually suspicious, were simply not as practised in commanding large formations. It was fortunate for the Company that this was the case, because cracks were beginning to appear in the foundations of the Bengal Army, and the next major conflict in which it would engage would be with the Company itself.[13]

WHY THE BENGAL ARMY FAILED

One of the notable features of the Sikh Wars was the poor performance of Bengal Army units in battle. The Bombay units were alleged to have been shaky in Sind, but in the Sikh Wars there was no question that Bengal units were 'sticky'—firing wildly and going to ground when ordered to advance. Gough, a far more unimaginative general than his much-traduced World War I successors, was at least perceptive enough to note that the morale of the Bengal Army had not yet recovered from Afghanistan when the Sikh Wars began. The morale and loyalty of the Bengal sepoys was then further compromised when, after the Second Anglo–Sikh War, the annexation of the Punjab brought with it a ruling from Calcutta that, as the Punjab was now Company territory, the foreign service *batta* was no longer payable. This was the same piece of blinkered economizing that, in the aftermath of the Sind War, had let to serious unrest among Bengal sepoys and the disbandment of one regiment. It is barely credible that the same mistake was again made only a few years later by the army's finance department, much less that it was compounded by the ruling's being made retroactive so that units serving in the Punjab were required to repay a month's allowance. The very predictable result of this act of ill-advised accountancy was a splatter of mutinies, another disbandment, and sentences of death, imprisonment, or lifelong exile passed on a number of sepoys. The Commander-in-Chief, India, Sir Charles Napier, a British Army officer, then rubbed salt to the wound by issuing a tactless order that the punishment of the rebellious units should be read out to all the units. It is perhaps no accident that Bengal units that served in the Sikh Wars all mutinied a few years later. As bad as all this was, the consequences of the annexation of the Punjab may in the long term have been worse.

Having taken over a large populous territory with a considerable population of professional soldiers, the EIC's administrators faced a very complex problem: how to structure and police their new territory. The decision was that it would not be administered like the 'regulation provinces' of the Bengal Presidency. There was, alongside, a decision to embody many ex-soldiers of the disbanded Sikh Army in new irregular corps. These units answered to the Punjab government, not to army headquarters in Calcutta, with its now heavily bureaucratized decision-making and rather disastrous commitment to cost cutting. Raised by individual British officers who had had themselves 'seconded' from their regiments (another example of the seniority system's adverse effect on good junior officers) and requiring far fewer European officers than line regiments, clothed in local rather than European style, and subjected to much less military routine while putting real responsibility into the hands of Indian officers, these units were an exceedingly cost-effective way of providing employment to many Sikh soldiers and giving them an incentive to loyalty. Jeremiah Brayser, for example, who had arrived in India in 1833 as a gunner in the Company's European artillery, won a commission in the First Anglo–Sikh War. He then raised a unit comprising of 400 Sikhs which came to be known as the Ferozepore Sikhs (or Brayser's Sikhs) who would remain loyal to the Company during the Mutiny, eventually becoming by 1947 the 1st Battalion of 11th Sikh Regiment. Such units, with their strong ties between officers and men, also conformed to suggestions about army reorganization being made by John Jacob of the Bombay Army, whose own irregular unit, the Sind Irregular Horse, had fought very successfully in the Sind War. Jacob criticized the rigid, bureaucratic structure of the Bengal Army. The Madras and Bombay armies of course were similar in structure, but neither had exhibited the same combination of poor performance in battle and rigid insistence on their financial entitlements as the Bengal Army in the 1840s. These irregular units also offered an alternative to it, and while the Bengal sepoys were almost certainly unaware of the professional arguments among Company officers about the best way to organize Indian units, they were aware of the implications of the emergence of an alternative army in the Punjab—made up of troops deeply hostile to the Hindu sepoys of the regular army. Might the Company now be planning to dispense with them, they wondered, the last of its serious Indian opponents having been dealt with?

All this occurred against a background of growing mutual incomprehension between officers and men in the Bengal Army. That army had become a vast, powerful, and remote bureaucracy as its officer corps underwent a sea change. Cadets arrived from Addiscombe with an outlook different from many of Ochterlony's generation. More assertively Christian, more triumphalist, they were more impatient with the 'natives'. Not all fit this generalization, to be sure, but enough did—especially given the drain of the bright, ambitious, adventurous and restless from regular line units into extra-regimental employment (like the Punjab Irregular Force)—to contribute strongly to a growing insensitivity to rising anxieties in the sepoy lines. What needs to be explored is the internal dynamics of the Madras and Bombay armies, whose officers had the same background but where, in the end, the armies held together.

The Bengal sepoys approached their service with a mindset not only radically different from that of their officers but from that of European soldiers generally. A generation ago Philip Mason pointed out that no Indian word existed that was an exact translation of 'mutiny'. The sepoys saw their service as contractual—when the contract was in their view breached, they felt justified in 'downing tools'. Something like this attitude had existed in early modern Europe: the sixteenth-century Spanish Army of Flanders mutinied regularly over pay, or its failure to arrive. But, all that had faded from the European military scene by the 1840s. The European sense of the obligation of a soldier under military law was coming into collision with something like the mindset of a powerful, assertive trade union that sees traditional workplace rules and practices being arbitrarily set aside by management, as in the case of the '*batta* mutinies'. Whether matters would have been handled differently had the commanders-in-chief been from the Company's service rather than rather scornful and uninformed British Army officers like Paget, Gough and Napier must remain an open question.

There is the issue of the caste composition of the Bengal Army and the deference Bengal officers paid to it. The homogeneity of the Bengal Army has been noted. The predominance of upper-caste soldiers had caused few problems prior to the 1840s, and it had certainly been army policy not to trespass on their sepoys' beliefs in this area. Many critics felt that by the 1840s this had been carried to absurd lengths and the sepoys had come to realize that much could be evaded or, conversely, done under the colour of the claim that caste required it. This is an area where certainty is probably unattainable. Sepoy beliefs were in all likelihood as dynamic as those of their officers. Just as the Christianity of Ochterlony's generation differed from that of the regimental officer of the 1840s and 1850s, so a sepoy of 1810 may well have had a different view of what his caste and beliefs demanded than his grandson serving in the 1840s. It is also true that as the bond between the EIC and its Indian soldiers weakened, this was one area where the sepoy still had unquestioned leverage.

Thus, even before the 1850s dawned, bringing Dalhousie's Governor-Generalship, the annexation of Awadh, the General Enlistment Act, and the new Enfield rifle with its notorious greased cartridge, the Bengal Army was showing signs of institutional failure. The events of the 1840s may be more important in the ultimate implosion of the Bengal Army than the much-canvassed events of the next decade. In a span of 10 years, the Bengal Army suffered a major disaster in Afghanistan and served in the Sind War, two Sikh Wars, and a campaign against the Maratha rump state of Gwalior (1843). There were two major episodes of disaffection, leading to courts martial, death sentences, and disbandments. Furthermore, there was a serious doubt about the army's 'will to combat' in the Sikh Wars. It is not surprising that outside observers, like John Jacob, became caustic about the Bengal Army or that the emerging 'Punjab School' of soldier-administrators put their faith in their new, largely Sikh, irregular corps.

Why did the Bengal officers not see that their army was becoming increasingly fragile? Pride and parochialism seem to be the heart of the matter. The Bengal officers had long regarded themselves as commanding a force superior to those of Madras and Bombay. This attitude of superiority would outlast the Company. Frederick Roberts, son of a Bengal Army general and himself a Bengal officer, would eventually be in a position, as Commander-in-Chief, India, in the 1880s, to give effect to his belief that south Indian peoples were no longer 'martial' and effectively bring the old Coast Army to an end. Furthermore, the Bengal officers had an established track record, going back to the 1790s, of beating off outside attempts to interfere with 'their' army. And, in any case, they surely felt, small upheavals were almost inevitable in such armies as the Company's and had always been weathered successfully, if messily. The army was still sound at heart.

Yet, by the end of the Sikh Wars the Bengal Army was not

sound. And then came a cascade of events in the 1850s. The annexation of Awadh, homeland to so many Bengal sepoys, had an adverse effect on their status. The General Enlistment Act (1856) impacted not only on the serving soldiers but also on their sons' prospects. Foreign service continued to cause problems for Bengal sepoys—the Second Burma War in 1852 again producing a reluctance to serve there, although this time there were no mutinies or disbandments. Interestingly, neither Madras troops ordered to Burma nor Bombay units involved in the 1856 Persian War exhibited any discontent. The other factors—discontented princes, aggressively Christian officers, unhappiness in the sepoys' home villages over British land revenue settlements—were aggravations, but were present in some form in the other presidencies without gravely unsettling their armies. The Bengal Army, both officers and rank and file, had taken a certain shape quite early and never thereafter changed. Few in that army felt it needed to restructure; those outside, who by the 1840s saw the problems clearly enough, lacked the power to do anything about them.

CONCLUSION

Two-thirds of the Company's armies proved perfectly serviceable in 1857. But, the disaffection of many Bengal units and the pre-emptive disbandment of others—especially in the Punjab, where the belief in the superior qualities of local recruits had already struck deep roots—opened the way for the 'Punjabization' of the post-Mutiny army with important consequences for not only the army but British policy for the duration of the Raj. Was 1857 inevitable? It can certainly look that way, but it may not have been. And here the 31st BNI's story again becomes relevant. In 1857, it was stationed at Saugor in the Central Provinces, part of a brigade made up of Company units—the only Europeans, officers apart, were a few gunners. There were no British Army formations at Saugor or anywhere near it. When the other infantry units present showed signs of unrest, the brigadier in command pulled all the European personnel into Saugor Fort, leaving the sepoy units to their own devices. Despite this, the 31st BNI remained loyal under its Indian officers, defending its absent officers' property, fighting an engagement with the disaffected 42nd BNI and 3rd Irregular Cavalry, and capturing their colours and some of their weaponry. As the 1st Battalion of 7th Rajput Regiment, the unit would still be on the *Army List* in 1947.[14]

It is impossible now to isolate and analyse the complex interplay of personal factors that produced the 31st BNI's behaviour at Saugor. It is enough to note both that the chemistry that had produced the remarkable episode at Bharatpur had not entirely evaporated from the Bengal Army. The events at Saugor are nevertheless a good gauge of what had either disappeared or been badly eroded in much of the army. Whether, in the face of changing attitudes in Britain itself and the changing nature of the Company Raj, that chemistry was doomed will doubtless remain an argued question, but it did not have to be—and in much of the Company's army was not. The failure of the Bengal Army in 1857 was, like an air crash, the result of a 'cascade of failure' over several decades and needs to be seen that way—not as something inherent in the very nature of the Company Raj and inevitably bound to occur.

NOTES

1. This is a work of synthesis, so there will be only occasional references to archival sources. There is no scholarly study of the Company's armies as a whole, and only the Bombay Army has been the subject of a relative recent history: Sir Patrick Cadell, *History of the Bombay Army* (London, 1938). Two quasi-official histories—Arthur Broome, *History of the Rise and Progress of the Bengal Army* (London, 1850) and W.J. Wilson, *History of the Madras Army*, 4 vols (Madras: Govt. Press, 1882) —are badly dated, and nearly unreadable. Philip Mason's *A Matter of Honour: An Account of the Indian Army, Its Officers and Men* (London: Jonathan Cape, 1974) could, perhaps, given the author's ICS roots, be considered another quasi-official history—at least from a British point of view. S.L. Menezes *Fidelity and Honour: The Indian Army from the Seventeenth to the Twenty-first Century* (Delhi: Viking, 1999) provides a perhaps complementary Indian perspective by a retired Indian lieutenant-general who began his career under the Raj. T.A. Heathcote, *The Indian Army: The Garrison of British Imperial India, 1822–1922* (New York/Manchester: Manchester University Press, 1974) is very good, although most of it falls outside the time period covered in this essay. A recent work—Daniel Marston and Chandar Sundaram (eds.), *A Military History of India and*

South Asia: From the East India Company to the Nuclear Era (Westport, CT: Praeger, 2007)—is an example of the sort of collaborative scholarship that may one day produce a full-scale history of the Company's remarkable army. The first two chapters cover the Company period.

2. D. Peers, *Between Mars and Mammon: Colonial Armies and the Garrison State in India 1819-1835* (London: I.B. Tauris, 1995) describes and analyses the Company's military-fiscal state.
3. It is worth emphasizing that tension between the two officer corps have never been given the attention they ought to have. They run, however, through the story of the British in India as an unbroken thread. This tension nearly provoked a mutiny by the Bengal officers in the mid-1790s—an episode whose traces may have been deliberately purged from the documentary record, so faint are its footprints in the Home Miscellaneous Series. See Raymond Callahan, *The East India Company and Army Reform, 1783-1798* (Cambridge, MA: Harvard University Press, 1972, p. 167, fn. 26).
4. There is a very good, if elderly, study of Jacob by another former ICS officer, H.T. Lambrick, *John Jacob of Jacobabad* (London: Cassell & Co., 1960). The Jacobs are a very good example of an Indian Army family, serving continuously in India for over a century. Using the Jacob Papers, courtesy of the late Lieutenant-General Sir Ian Jacob, I did a brief profile of the family's Indian service: 'Servants of the Raj: The Jacob Family in India, 1817-1926', *JSAHR* (Spring 1978), pp. 4–24. Further study of these families is much needed.
5. Charles Allen (ed.), *A Soldier of the Company: Life of an Indian Ensign 1833–1843* (London: Michael Joseph in association with the National Army Museum, 1988) is an abridgement of Albert Hervey's *Ten Years in India, or, The Life of a Young Officer*, 3 vols. (London, 1850). Hervey, a Madras officer who would die a major-general on the retired list, never heard a shot fired in anger, but his (very wordy) memoir gives a fine picture of the diurnal round of the Company's Madras Army as peaceful year succeeded peaceful year. Hervey was devoted to his sepoys—and very defensive about slurs upon them by unnamed (but almost certainly British or Bengal Army) critics. His memoir may help explain why the Madras Army remained loyal to the Company to the end.
6. Callahan, *The East India Company and Army Reform* discusses the confrontation between the Bengal officers and their London masters.
7. Callahan *East India Company,* pp. 16–43 examines the remarkable proliferation of allowances and perquisites. One of the most important was *batta*, basically a bonus, payable to both officers and sepoys (at very different rates) for any one of a number of reasons: for example, service at certain stations, service outside the Company's territories, or as a reward for outstanding service. Eventually much of the army was on some form of *batta* (half, full, or often double) much of the time.

Attempts to reduce or remove *batta* payments thus affected immediately the sepoys' standard of living—as well as their sense of how fairly they were being treated. It also affected officers' living standards, and the Bengal officers defended their *batta* as stubbornly as did their sepoys—with this difference: the officers' behaviour was never called mutiny.

8. Theon Wilkinson, *Two Monsoons* (London, 1976) is a fascinating tour of European—and mostly British—graveyards in India, vividly illustrating how short and precarious life could be for the Company's servants.
9. Menezes, *Fidelity and Honour*, pp. 124–43, devotes an entire chapter to 'Civil Disturbances and the Use of Troops in Aid of the Civil Power', a subject Mason avoids, but is in need of further study. Callahan's *East India Company*, pp. 215–20 covers Lieutenant-Colonel Goddard's revenue enforcement expedition. Goddard's expedition is unusual in that there is a full contemporary record which I was able to use: W.C. Macpherson (ed.), *Soldiering in India 1764–1787: Extracts from Journals and Letters Left by Lieutenant-Colonel Allan Macpherson and Lieutenant-Colonel John Macpherson of the East India Company's Service* (London: William Blackwood & Sons, 1928). While the Company records in the India Office Records, British Library, can tell us much, only the chance survival of personal papers can give us a real sense of what operations like this entailed—and yielded.
10. The Nepal War is covered by one of the few detailed modern studies of the Company at war, John Pemble's excellent *The Invasion of Nepal: John Company at War* (Oxford: Clarendon Press, 1971). There is no good study of Ochterlony, but he is one of the 'Anglo–Mughals' profiled in William Dalrymple's brilliant *The White Mughals* (London: Viking, 2006).
11. The First Afghan War has been much written about, but there is no scholarly study. The best introduction is Patrick MacCrory's *Signal Catastrophe: The Retreat from Kabul 1842* (London: Hodder & Stoughton, 1966). George MacDonald Fraser's remarkable historical novel *Flashman* (London, 1969) illuminates in a way that scholarly history often fails to.
12. Mason's *A Matter of Honour* is good on the Barrackpore episode (pp. 242–6) and on Sind (pp. 225–8). H.T. Lambrick, *Sir Charles Napier and Sind* (Oxford, 1952) is a full-scale, albeit dated, study.
13. No recent military historian has analysed the Sikh Wars. The relevant chapters in Saul David, *Victoria's Wars: The Rise of Empire* (London: Viking, 2006) are very traditional. Although the author of a very good study of the Mutiny—*The Indian Mutiny: 1857* (London: Viking, 2002)—David does not spend any time on the question of why the Bengal Army's performance was as weak as Gough's grasp of tactics.
14. The coming of the Mutiny is much written about, perhaps less well analysed. Mason, *A Matter of Honour*, pp. 219–68, and Menezes, *Fidelity*

and Honour, pp. 81–123, 144–60 cover it from quite illuminatingly different perspectives. The most recent general survey is David's *Indian Mutiny,* pp. 19–44. A brief survey is Raymond Callahan, 'The Great Sepoy Mutiny', in Marston and Sundaram (eds.), *A Military History of India,* pp. 16–33. Lambrick *John Jacob, passim,* discusses Jacob's pre-1857 criticisms of the Bengal Army as well as his approach to raising and leading irregular units. A good introduction to the 'Punjab School' of soldiers and administrators is Charles Allen's *Soldier Sahibs: The Men Who Made the North-West Frontier* (London: Viking, 2000).

CHAPTER 2

The Punjab Irregular Force, the North-West Frontier and the 1857 Mutiny

TIM MOREMAN

The raising of localized armed forces, often under the control of the foreign department of the Government of India rather than the military authorities, normally organized on the irregular pattern for the performance of specific duties was a recurrent feature of British rule in the later nineteenth century. Arguably, the Punjab Irregular Force (PIF) was the most famous and long lasting of these distinctive organizations remaining outside the control of commanders of the Bengal Army until 1886 and remaining localized for duty solely in the Punjab/North-West Frontier Province until 1903.[1] It had a highly specific and extremely specialized task to perform as part of the 'watch and ward' of the North-West Frontier and punitive operations in the nearby mountains.[2] On occasion, however, it was employed in a very different role. Thus, during the 1857 Mutiny, its units left the wilds of the North-West Frontier for north India. Although the actual numbers of 'Piffers', as its officers and men were popularly known, re-deployed from the Punjab when the Mutiny erupted may have been small, they played a crucial role at the decisive time and place—on the embattled Ridge outside Delhi and constituting the final assault on the strategic and symbolic centre of gravity of the Sepoy Revolt. Those military skills learnt in the border hills gave them a high level of combat effectiveness, and earned them considerable praise from British officers and men fighting alongside them during this campaign and later operations, including the assault on Lucknow. The rump of the PIF, meanwhile, played a key part in keeping the Punjab quiet as the Mutiny raged elsewhere and ensuring it played a vital role as a recruiting ground and pillar of strength to the beleaguered British administration. This chapter examines in depth the formation, specialized role, and tactics devised by the PIF for the performance of its duties in the watch and ward of the tribal areas, before going on to look at its contribution to the suppression of the 1857 Mutiny.

ORIGIN AND EARLY DAYS

Following the annexation of Punjab in March 1849 at the end of the Second Sikh War, the administration of British India became contiguous with the mountains and hills of the physiographic North-West Frontier of the Indian subcontinent. A new board of administration, headed by Henry Lawrence and assisted by John Lawrence and Henry Mansell, faced a formidable array of problems largely stemming from the endemic weaknesses previously displayed by the former Sikh regime in Lahore. Indeed, in many respects the former government had only exerted a weak hold over the trans-Indus districts and even less in the nearby hills, resulting in a situation of virtual anarchy. Taxation could only be collected, for example, in the border areas at the point of the bayonet with the assistance of large bodies of armed troops. Small forts studded the countryside from which local chieftains dominated the immediate area.[3]

The British from the first days of the board of administration were confronted with exerting some form of control along a lengthy and extremely difficult mountainous border across which lived fiercely independent tribes accustomed to warring amongst themselves and striking against the inhabitants of the lowland areas. The insistent military threat posed by an estimated 100,000 heavily armed Pathan fighting men to the security of the Punjab meant that other measures were also immediately undertaken to protect and control the inhabitants of the frontier areas. On 18 May 1849, Henry Lawrence was empowered by the Governor-General Lord Dalhousie to raise a force for the protection of the North-West Frontier and to ensure internal security while the strength and deployment of the permanent military garrison of the Punjab was determined. Ten regiments—five infantry (1–5th Punjab Infantry) and five cavalry (1st to 5th Punjab Cavalry)—were raised at stations throughout the Punjab during the summer and autumn of 1849, collectively designated as the PIF, intended for general service in Punjab and the trans-Indus districts. They were placed under the command of Brigadier John Hodgson, an experienced veteran of the Sikh Wars. Although not part of the new PIF, in many respects the Corps of Guides, raised in 1846, formed a model for these units in terms of organization and patterns of recruitment. After some initial uncertainty as to whether it should come under the command of the Bengal Army, the PIF was for its organization, training, and employment placed under the direct control of the board of administration of the Punjab. Writing in October 1850, Dalhousie explained that excluding the PIF from military control would deliberately secure for the local government the full and complete control of military means sufficient to effect any object which political consideration may, in their judgement, render it expedient to secure on that distant frontier. This decision to localize the PIF solely for duty in the Punjab gave the board of administration almost complete control of the troops stationed along the border, enabling it to quickly respond to raids or other developments without constant recourse to the central government for military support.[4]

The new infantry and cavalry units were organized and equipped on lines similar to other irregular regiments forming part of the Bengal Army. A British commandant and three officers—a second in command, an adjutant and a medical officer—were appointed to each regiment, selected from candidates drawn from the Bengal, Bombay and Madras armies, several of whom had served during the First Afghan War and had experience of the frontier tribes. All were young 'thrusters', with a proven track record, handpicked by Henry Lawrence. They were collectively destined for high rank, and included such distinguished soldiers as Sam Browne, Dighton Probyn, Charles Brownlow, Alfred Wilde, and John Vaughan. As one officer later explained: 'In my regiment each presidency has furnished an officer. A strange combination. A lieutenant, Bombay Army, commandant, a captain, Madras Army, 2nd in command; a cornet of Bengal Cavalry, adjutant.'[5] A wide degree of latitude was left to these relatively junior officers for raising, organizing and training their new charges, who only received pay and ammunition from central government. Indeed, each of the initial three regiments was raised on a different system of recruitment. The British officers-in-charge of these units also enjoyed wide autonomy as regards the uniform and equipment of the men under their command. Following service alongside a British rifle regiment the commanding officer of the 1st Punjab Regiment, for example, adopted a dark green dyed coat, trousers and *pugri* for his men that stood out while on service in the mountains. Unlike other units in the PIF, its men were also armed with rifled muskets with greater range and accuracy.

The annexation of Punjab had opened new recruiting grounds for this new force. The enlistment of Indians to fill the ranks of these new regiments was not problematic. Indian officers and non-commissioned officers were recruited from the families of local chiefs of noble birth on both sides of the administrative border. Each officer brought with him a number of dependants—brothers, sons and nephews—and followers, with personal allegiance to him, who were often paid out and equipped out of his private purse. Others were former Sikh officers thrown out of work following the disbandment of the durbar army or else from across the border in Afghanistan. The rank and file consisted of a mixture of Sikhs, Punjabi Muslims, Dogras and both cis- and trans-Indus border Pathans, organized in ethnically mixed companies, who willingly enlisted in large numbers attracted by regular pay, job security and prestige associated with military service. A large part came from the unemployed grizzled veterans of disbanded former Sikh/*Khalsa* regiments eager to continue a military career, who provided a valuable nucleus of already trained and experienced manpower for the new regiments. Other new sources were tapped. Pathan recruits from both sides of the administrative border also enlisted: indeed this soon became a central plank of frontier policy. As one officer later wrote:

> Thus it came about that the security of the troubled border was maintained by the descendants of the restless marauders who had roamed and plundered for generations and by their side fought Sikhs, their hereditary enemies still conspicuous for the discipline and daring with which Ranjit Singh had imbued their fathers.[6]

In July 1850, the five cavalry regiments totalled 273 Sikhs, 2,240 Muslims, 122 Brahmins, 215 Rajputs and 82 Hindus, while the infantry regiments totalled 455 Sikhs, 2,891 Muslims, 403 Rajputs, 731 Hindus and 6 Christians.[7] To ensure that these regiments were raised as soon as possible, recruiting officers were initially ordered not to be too particular about the age and size of potential new recruits; instead they should select 'stout, serviceable and young men whose best condition may be relied upon for full period of a soldiers service'.[8] A perceived imbalance in the different 'classes', however, caused some concern amongst senior officers, especially in terms of officers and non-commissioned officers giving some regiments 'an undesirable clique character and tone'. As a commanding officer wrote: 'In one Corps an unwise predilection as been evinced towards the Sheikhs [Sikhs], in another the Poorbas [Purbiyas] have been too much considered and in others the Mahomedans of the Country have been permitted to acquire undue weight and ascendancy.'[9] Class companies consisting of just one ethnic group were later formed in some units to improve efficiency.[10]

The organization of infantry and cavalry units reflected their different role in the defence of the border. Each infantry regiment, which shouldered the burden of hill warfare, had an established strength of four European officers. Each regiment was divided into eight companies, and each company had 1 subedar, 1 jemadar, 5 havildars, 5 naiks, 2 drummers and 100 sepoys. Each sepoy was paid Rs. 7 per month and provided with full arms, ammunition, and equipment by the government. A cavalry regiment was smaller in size than an infantry regiment. Each mounted regiment had a strength of 599 sabres, with each of its six sabre squadrons having 100 men. As one commanding officer wrote: 'My regiment consists of 4 British officers and 6 troops, each with its complement of native officers nearly 100 men, so that a corps is almost 600 strong....'[11] A very different system was employed in raising and equipping cavalry units. Instead of equipment being provided, each sowar was paid Rs. 20 a month out of which he had to provide his own clothing, equipment, and arms (swords and in some cases lances). Unlike other irregular cavalry units, each sowar of the cavalry regiments of the PIF had a light percussion carbine fastened to the saddle while on duty. Each officer and enlisted man was required to provide and maintain his own mount, chiefly imported from Afghanistan and Persia, from the pay provided by the government. The death of his horse, however, could quickly terminate a military career.[12]

The irregular regiments making up the PIF differed from the

outset in one major important respect compared to line (regular) units of the Bengal Army. To carry out its highly specialized duties on the watch and ward of tribal territory, each infantry and cavalry regiment was given a complete permanent establishment of ponies, mules, camels, and followers, as no organized commissariat system existed west of the river Indus. As Brigadier Hodgson explained:

> The grant of mules and camels will enable the troops to act with advantageous activity on all emergencies and if continued would afford the means of employing that description of carriage best adapted to the character and peculiar difficulties of the country in which military operations will be required.[13]

About 40 mules and 20 camels, for example, were given to an infantry regiment for carrying camp equipment and ammunition in the field, as well as trained attendants to look after them. This decision materially increased their effectiveness by enabling them to respond at an hour's time to internal unrest or tribal raids.

This new force was bolstered by the permanent addition of three light field batteries, raised from former Sikh Durbar horse artillery, each equipped with six conventional 9-lb smooth-bore guns and a 24-lb howitzer. These were led by officers of the Bengal Artillery, who had distinguished themselves during the Sikh War and manned by Sikh officers and gunners. Two other garrison companies manned fixed defences along the border.[14]

THE 'WATCH AND WARD' OF TRIBAL TERRITORY AND THE CONDUCT OF HILL WARFARE

The newly raised PIF was given full responsibility for the 'watch and ward' of the administrative border stretching between Kohat and Mithunkote. Two infantry regiments, one cavalry regiment, and an artillery battery were garrisoned in each district and were held in instant readiness to stop tribal incursions and prevent outlaws from taking refuge in the nearby hills. A chain of mud forts and outposts was steadily constructed along the length of the border between Dera Ghazi Khan, Dera Ismail Khan, Bannu, Kurram, Kohat, Asni and Bahadur Khel. They were linked by a new military road running parallel to the border that allowed troops to be shifted rapidly from area to area in response to tribal incursions. Cavalry regiments, supported by small detachments of infantry, were dispersed in a chain of small mud forts, blockhouses, and outposts that blocked valleys, ravines or other covered lines of approach used by raiding gangs. The intervening ground between these posts was systematically patrolled by cavalry detachments to deter raids, gather intelligence, and attempt to intercept parties of marauders. Although reasonably effective, these detachments were too few and too heavily encumbered to effectively police the line of the poorly defined border. So, the Indus border could not be totally sealed against tribal incursions. Outpost duty provided valuable practical training denied to the rest of the regular army requiring considerable initiative, resourcefulness and physical fitness. Many of the duties involved in the watch and ward of the border were civil rather than military in character, involving PIF troops in a range of tasks supporting the local civil administration that considerably strengthened the latter's authority. The infantry regiments garrisoned frontier cantonments and forts, guarded treasuries and jails, furnished escorts, safeguarded cattle and livestock, and protected the lives and property of British subjects living near the border. The local magistrates were empowered to call out troops in the event of tribal raids or local discontent. United under the orders of the local government, close cooperation was ensured between civil and military officers in the pacification of the trans-Indus areas. Indeed, military and police duties were synonymous during the 1850s and the denial of safe refuge in the surrounding hills to outlaws escaping British justice always formed an important part of the PIF's duties. Several commandants were assigned civil duties in addition to their military work. Captain John Coke, for example, was both Deputy Commissioner of Kohat and Commanding Officer of the 1st Punjab Infantry. As a result of this constant service along the border, the officers and men of the PIF steadily acquired a detailed knowledge of the tribes, their language, and customs which proved of inestimable value to the performance of their joint political and military duties.

Peshawar district, located at the mouth of the Khyber Pass, was the only part of the frontier defence entrusted to regular British and Indian troops of the Bengal Army stationed in the

Punjab, who were primarily responsible for defence against attacks by the conventional Afghan Army. As these duties were of a more regular nature, large numbers of conventionally organized, equipped and trained troops were permanently garrisoned in the area and were retained under the control of the commander-in-chief in Bengal. During the 1850s, forts were constructed and garrisoned by troops of the large Peshawar Brigade at Abazai, Michni, Shabkadr and Fort Mackeson. Unlike further south the immediate defence of the border of Peshawar was entrusted to the civil police, distributed in a line of small towers and outposts, while the Corps of Guides was made responsible for protecting the border from raiding by the Yusufzai tribe.[15]

The political authorities, the PIF, and the Bengal Army garrison at Peshawar, however, proved unable to provide complete security against raids along the lengthy and poorly defined border, despite a defensive system consisting of 15 forts, over 50 outposts and over 12,800 irregular and 10,821 regular troops in 1855. The sheer length of the uninhabited border, the broken scrub-covered terrain in the foothills, the close proximity of tribal territory and the location of many villages and areas of cultivated land well in advance of the outposts meant that a system of passive defence never had a real chance of securing success. It proved difficult to safeguard the local inhabitants as the administrative border between tribal territory and the plains was ill-defined and because many of the Pathan tribes owned land and lived on both sides of it. Skirmishes regularly occurred between hostile tribesmen and British troops and villagers, who raided the lowland areas as they had done under the previous Sikh regime, burning villages, stealing property, seizing hostages, and murdering several British officers. In many cases the political authorities successfully curbed these activities by suspending payment of financial allowances, punitive fines, the seizure of hostages and economic blockades of tribal territory. However, the ultimate sanction available to the board of administration in dealing with particularly recalcitrant tribal sections rested on force of arms to restore order and maintain British prestige.

During the 1850s, the PIF and the regular troops stationed in Peshawar district, mounted a succession of counter-raids and punitive 'butcher and bolt', 'harry and hurry' and 'tip and run' punitive expeditions across the administrative border into the hills in response to serious tribal incursions, resulting in a state of near continuous warfare. A total of fifteen expeditions were carried out between 1849 and 1855 against the Kohat Pass Afridis, Mohmands, Miranzai tribes, Utmanzai Waziris, Hassanzais, Ranizais, Utman Khel, Bori Afridis, 'Hindustani fanatics', Shiranis, Kasranis, Michni Mohmands, Aka Khels, and Orakzais, as punishment for offences committed in British territory and to demonstrate the ability of imperial troops to penetrate their hills at will.

It became clear during these operations that the conduct of expeditions in tribal territory posed a range of difficult operational and political problems. The Indian columns had to operate in virtually unknown country without the benefit of maps or reliable guides and initially with minimal intelligence regarding the fighting strength of the tribes. It proved particularly difficult to identify an objective that would enable Indian troops to achieve a decisive victory and thereby secure a lasting settlement: for no organized government, capital city, or town existed in tribal territory. The fighting strength of a tribe or their villages represented the only tangible objective for an Indian column. However, when Indian troops approached, the local inhabitants normally abandoned their homes and dispersed into the surrounding hills, leaving their fighting men to conduct guerrilla warfare making it impossible for Indian troops to inflict serious casualties and thereby compel them to surrender. The proximity of Afghanistan and other neutral tribes, moreover, provided sanctuaries for women, children, and livestock and areas where fighting men could rest and re-group. Additionally, the independent tribes were often given active support by Afghan and neighbouring tribes with food and fighting men. As a result, Indian troops were forced to exact punishment by seizing livestock and destroying villages, fortified towers, water tanks, buried reserves of food and standing crops, or else to remain in temporary occupation of an area until hunger, exposure, or the necessity to sow crops compelled the tribes to pay fines of money or weapons. Such measures departed from the accepted principles of 'civilized warfare' and gave hill warfare a distinctive character very different from 'proper' operations carried out by British and Indian troops in the plains.

The rugged mountainous terrain in tribal territory was the main factor that dictated the conduct of hill warfare by causing a range of tactical, logistical and administrative problems. The steep and precipitous hillsides, interspersed by a succession of knife-edge ridges, rugged spurs, cliffs, and precipices, were impassable to organized bodies of men equipped with wheeled transport and cavalry. Indian columns were compelled to advance along narrow, winding, boulder-strewn riverbeds and valleys overlooked from vantage points in the surrounding hills. Valley floors were usually broken and intersected by deep ravines and the troops frequently had to cross rivers and streams. During most of the year, the water courses did not present an obstacle, but during winter after sudden heavy rainfall when in spate they were capable of sweeping men and animals away. An absence of roads, broken terrain and scarcity of water made the movement of large bodies of troops difficult and time consuming and meant that the maximum distance a column could march in a single day was severely restricted. The few existing tracks through the hills were usually only narrow pathways, winding through defiles and over difficult mountain passes often requiring considerable improvement by sappers and miners or pioneers before they could be used.

The PIF columns operating in tribal territory had to carry large quantities of stores, food and fodder as only small quantities of meat, corn, rice, straw, grass, or firewood could be foraged from the barren hills. Hardy pack mules and camels were the only form of transport capable of moving across the broken terrain, but they placed severe administrative and logistical constraints on expeditions that were in many respects a more serious check on operations than tribal resistance and dominated the conduct of operations in the hills. Slow-moving columns of pack animals were normally forced to advance in single file lengthening the line of march, causing continual stoppages and delays while being difficult to protect. Casualties amongst the transport animals by enemy action or disease, were often sufficient to impede or bring to an end military operations. A large proportion of the carrying capacity of pack transport, moreover, was devoted to carrying forage for the animals themselves, whose protection, care, and management were of particular importance as troops were completely dependent upon them during a hill campaign.

As there was a limit to the number of men and pack animals that could be moved over one road in daylight, large forces normally had to be broken into several columns and moved by separate routes. The movement, protection and supply of columns dependent on pack transport limited the maximum strength of a particular column to no larger than four or five battalions, a mountain battery and a company of sappers. Such a force moving in single file normally stretched over nine miles in length and required approximately 5,000 mules to supply it in the field for only a short period of time. Indeed, transport and supply difficulties made it imperative that no larger a force than was absolutely necessary was employed in the mountains.

Endemic diseases and the harsh climate also hamstrung the conduct of military operations in tribal territory. Sickness and mortality rates amongst imperial troops and followers from malaria, sandfly fever, dysentery, etc., were often greatly in excess of the casualties inflicted during the course of fighting. Heat-stroke during the summer and intense cold with heavy snowfalls during the winter dictated when and where operations could take place and led to heavy casualties that could incapacitate entire units. Animal transport upon which the columns depended was also highly susceptible to disease. Scarcity of water also acted as a powerful constraint that limited the areas in which British columns could operate and the length of time they could remain in the hills.[16]

The military characteristics, techniques and arms used by the Pathans also determined the tactics employed by Indian troops. Tribal society lacked any formal military organization in a European sense. However, when an external threat overrode the internal divisions that normally prevented the tribes from acting together, the fighting strength of a Pathan tribe or section would unite to form a *lashkar* whose characteristics reflected the loose social and political organization of tribal society. The *mullahs* settled internal differences and arranged truces between individuals or families at feud, allowing a tribe to decide a plan of campaign, the number of men to be provided by each section, a rendezvous and date of assembly and to choose a leader. The size of *lashkars* varied widely from small parties to several thousand men, although the capacity of the surrounding area to support a force dictated its maximum size. A *lashkar* normally lacked regular leadership, discipline, organization or any form of organized transport or supply arrangements. Command normally devolved on a charismatic individual or religious leader with sufficient influence or personal leadership to weld the fighting men together. The acephalous and egalitarian nature of Pathan society, however, precluded effective leadership over any extended period of time. Individual tribesmen would arrive equipped with their own arms, ammunition, blanket and food at a chosen place to form the *lashkar*, which would also be accompanied by unarmed men and boys who carried food, ammunition and wounded and acted as reinforcements employing discarded weapons when men were killed or wounded. A *lashkar* was incapable of maintaining itself in the field for a period longer than ten days and, once the supplies carried by individual tribesmen were exhausted, they either returned home or forcibly requisitioned supplies from the local villages. It would also lose what limited cohesion it possessed if defeated, as its discredited leaders lost all authority and were unable to rally the tribesmen or organize further opposition. In such a scenario, the *lashkarwallas* would disperse to their homes carrying their dead and wounded, mourn their losses, and wait while tribal *jirgas* deliberated the need for further action. These factors meant that the strength of a *lashkar* was liable to fluctuate wildly in accordance with its mercurial morale, the state of its provisions and the success of the fighting in progress. Despite these inherent defects, the lightly equipped *lashkars* enjoyed a considerable tactical and strategic advantage over Indian troops as they were less circumscribed by supply and transport difficulties.[17]

The martial skills developed and refined by individual tribesmen during years of feuding and inter-tribal warfare were the tribal *lashkars'* main source of strength. Accustomed to fighting from youth, individual Pathan tribesmen were physically fit, skilled at skirmishing, fieldcraft and the use of arms and were inured to local diseases. Unlike imperial troops, tribesmen were intimately acquainted with the local terrain, paths, and resources. Tribal clothing—*chaplis*, baggy trousers, flowing grey shirts normally bound with leather ammunition belts and untidy *pugris*—and their skill in utilizing the broken hillsides for cover and concealment made it difficult to spot the tribesmen skirmishing over the hills. Tribal tactics were particularly well adapted to the terrain and to their own military characteristics. The *lashkars* normally attempted to hold defensive positions at ridges or passes which were heavily fortified with *sangars* sited to allow frontal and flanking fire on the probable line of advance of an attacking force, where they would mount a determined resistance. Each man fought according to personal judgement once fighting began, exploiting the terrain for cover and concealment, advancing or retiring as an engagement developed. Pathan tribesmen would seldom remain to fight at close-quarters with the assaulting troops and, if their flanks, rear or line of retreat were threatened, would disperse into the surrounding hills before an organized pursuit could be mounted. The *lashkars* excelled at desultory hit-and-run guerrilla warfare, attacking isolated parties of troops, raiding convoys on the lines of communication, sniping foraging parties, and attacking rearguards at the end of each day's operations. When the situation offered a prospect of success, they would attack with élan and engage in hand-to-hand combat. Their speed and mobility across the rough, precipitous terrain, effectively enabled the *lashkars* to ebb and flow around Indian columns and easily evade attacks by organized bodies of troops giving them the freedom to choose the time and place for an attack and to keep the initiative.

The PIF's tactics were also dictated by the locally manufactured long knives, swords, and firearms employed by trans-border Pathan *lashkars*. The vast majority of the tribesmen initially encountered by British forces were armed with a variety of swords, knives, and shields, making them reliant on combat at close quarters. Following the First Afghan War (1839–42), the Pathan tribes had steadily acquired a large number of matchlock or flintlock long barrelled *jezails* (crudely manufactured muzzle-loading rifled muskets) whose range and accuracy outclassed the Brown Bess percussion muskets initially employed by Indian troops.[18] They gave tribesmen a distinct qualitative advantage in small arms, allowing the *lashkars* to harass British columns from out of range without effective reply. The procurement of such firearms steadily altered tribal methods from reliance on shock tactics and hand-to-hand combat, to guerrilla warfare against the Indian columns. However, *jezails* were not as highly effective as many officers and men against which they had been used believed. Tests on two *jezails* purchased in the Khyber Pass in

1875, by the adjutant-general for musketry indicated that both weapons were crudely manufactured, inaccurate and had an effective range of only 300 yards.[19]

The officers and men serving in the PIF quickly learnt 'on the job' that hill warfare had special characteristics of its own and that conventional tactics, training, and equipment devised for operations on the Indian plains against similarly armed, organized and trained troops, were of little use in tribal territory. Indeed, it was soon apparent that military operations against the trans-border Pathan tribes represented a distinctive form of warfare requiring the development of operational principles and specific minor tactics for each arm of service. Fortunately, the ranks of PIF regiments at the beginning included several officers with prior experience of the tribes, dating from the First Afghan War, who could provide initial guidance in the tactics of mountain warfare against a tribal opponent. This was complemented by advice and local knowledge provided by locally recruited officers, non-commissioned officers, and men already accustomed to fighting in mountainous terrain.[20]

The frontier regiments soon learned that the tribal *lashkars* were unwilling to engage in a stand up fight with Indian troops. As Major John Nicholson, Deputy Commissioner at Bannu, noted in September 1853: 'It is not the policy and never has been the practice of any of the tribes on this frontier to meet our troops openly in the field. Any operations in which this force has been engaged have been skirmishing of greater or less magnitude, on broken or hilly ground.'[21] As a result the infantry bore the brunt of fighting in tribal territory and quickly learnt to employ light infantry skills in place of ponderous formal battalion drill, with its reliance on discipline and close-order line and column formations that dominated training in the regular Bengal Army. It was impossible to maintain close-order infantry formations or exploit disciplined massed firepower across the broken hill sides making it essential to employ loose, flexible, skirmishing tactics utilizing the ground for cover and concealment, modelled on those used by their Pathan opponents. This also meant they had to develop the individual skills of marksmanship and fieldcraft and be sufficiently fit to move quickly over the hillsides carrying their arms, ammunition and equipment. A direct corollary of such dispersion on the battlefield was that officers and men had to be self-reliant, well-motivated, and capable of exercising considerable individual initiative in comparison to those serving in the regular army. Such duties required particular martial skills that many officers believed only the local inhabitants possessed. As one senior officer noted, it was apparent that: 'The superior adaptation of the Pathans and indeed of all the races in the Punjab and trans-Indus territory had for hill fighting and the rough and constant work of the Derajat.'[22]

To carry out their role as light infantrymen, changes were made in arms and equipment issued to frontier regiments. Personal equipment was reduced to a minimum light marching order and men frequently wore *chaplis* in place of boots to increase their mobility. A less conspicuous khaki drab or brown uniform was adopted by all infantry regiments in January 1853 (with the exception of the 1st Punjab Regiment's dark green uniforms), instead of the heavyweight, uncomfortable and easily noticeable scarlet clothing used in the Bengal Army that had hitherto been worn. The khaki uniform provided effective camouflage against the brown backdrop of the arid border hills.[23] The smoothbore percussion musket, with which the majority of the infantry regiments were initially equipped, also proved unsuitable for fighting in the hills. A combination of its short range, inaccuracy, and heavyweight placed the Indian troops at a marked disadvantage when opposed by lightly equipped tribesmen armed with *jezails*. During fighting in the hills bordering the Derajat, the marked superiority of 1st Punjab Infantry's rifles—a regiment with arms, green uniforms and equipment modelled on the 60th King's Royal Rifle Corps (which had served at Peshawar in 1849–50)—was quickly demonstrated. In May 1853, Brigadier General Hodgson requested that the light companies in each infantry regiment should be armed with similar weapons, so that they could be brigaded together to form a corps of riflemen in event of an emergency and place them on equal terms with the armed tribesmen equipped with *jezails*.[24] Although it was felt that a small proportion of muskets should be kept in case of a major incursion into the plains or hostilities with Afghan troops, Hodgson's request was widely supported by political and military officers accustomed to tribal tactics.[25] As Major J.D. Macpherson, Military Secretary to the Punjab Government, pointed out: 'The drill also of Rifle Corps give the men a great superiority over soldiers trained to the Battalion exercise. In the one case the men are taught to act singly, to take advantage of all cover, to rely on the excellence of their weapon.'[26] Two regiments were completely re-armed with two-grooved Brunswick Rifles so that rifle regiments could be stationed permanently at Kohat, and in the Upper and Lower Derajat, in addition to the flank companies of the remaining units. Although slow and difficult to load in comparison to the musket, the greater accuracy and range of 200–300 yards enabled the Indian troops to oppose tribal *lashkars* on equal terms for the first time.[27] The number of Brunswick rifles issued to the infantry steadily increased until, by 1856, four complete infantry regiments and the light companies of the remaining four had received this weapon.[28] With rifled small arms judged as of such importance in hill warfare that as soon as Enfield Rifles became available in the subcontinent, the PIF officers requested they be issued the first examples for service on the North-West Frontier.

It also proved impossible to employ conventional horse-drawn wheeled road-bound field artillery in the mountainous areas devoid of roads. Two specialized mountain artillery trains, modelled on units improvised during the Anglo–Nepal War and the First Afghan War, were raised by the Bengal Army during the early 1850s and equipped with the following types of ordnance—3-lb guns, 24-lb howitzers and 4.5-inch mortars—capable of being broken down and carried in small loads by pack mules. Those guns that equipped the Peshawar and Hazara Mountain Trains were capable of coming quickly in and out of action in the hills at very restricted positions.[29] They rapidly demonstrated their utility during the Hassanzais Expedition on the Black Mountain prompting a request by Brigadier Hodgson in October 1852, that a mountain train should be added to the PIF, but instead two 3-lb mountain guns were attached to the light field batteries stationed at Kohat and Bannu.[30] The relative immobility of mountain batteries when compared to infantry units and the strain they placed on transport and supply arrangements, meant that they normally formed a small component of any force operating in the border hills. The paucity of guns, lack of shell power and the difficulty of ammunition supply meant the main fighting had to be carried out by the infantry, with mountain guns tasked to provide invaluable close fire support in both the attack and defence. An absence of opposing artillery and the short range of tribal *jezails*, however, allowed the mountain gunners to break a battery into two gun divisions that operated in close proximity to the forward troops. Artillery enjoyed an unprecedented moral superiority over the tribesmen unaccustomed to its employment, magnifying the normally limited physical impact of its small calibre shells that were often unable to dislodge defenders entrenched behind *sangars*, or to engage tribesmen hidden behind hill crests. Indeed great care had to be taken not to employ artillery batteries too early in a battle for fear that they would drive off the tribesmen and prevent a general engagement with a *lashkar*.[31]

Unlike units of the two other arms, the PIF's cavalry regiments were seldom employed in punitive expeditions due to the vulnerability of horsemen in the mountains, except for an occasional detached squadron to safeguard the line of communications, escort convoys, and for orderly work. Cavalry had a valuable moral effect on the tribesmen out of proportion to its physical impact since the majority of the hill tribes were unaccustomed to horses. An opportunity to use the *arme blanche* in hill warfare was rare and the cavalry were relegated primarily to the duties of watch and ward of the administrative border during which they developed considerable mobility and skill at moving over difficult ground. On several occasions, small bodies of horsemen successfully dealt with large raiding parties operating out of the safety of the hills.[32]

The regiments and batteries of the PIF quickly adapted to local conditions and devised specialized tactics to conduct an attack in the hills, protect columns on the march, protect columns when halted at night and to govern the conduct of withdrawal in contact with hostile tribesmen that were dominated by the twin principles of offensive action and the maintenance of security. The maintenance of the offensive throughout operations against the tribes was accepted as a basic principle of hill warfare, to exploit the *lashkars*' lack of cohesion, demoralize its members, and take advantage of the superior discipline and training of Indian troops. Attacks on a large scale were an exception, except at the beginning of a campaign when tribesmen normally occupied strong defensible positions blocking a line of advance into the hills. A combination of a frontal attack with an enveloping movement on one or both flanks was frequently employed to force tribesmen out of strong defensive positions when they stood to fight and to inflict heavy casualties on a retreating *lashkar* which normally bolted when its line of retreat was threatened. Initially, the short range of Pathan matchlocks and *jezails* meant flanking attacks had only to cover relatively short distances with little loss of life. Attacks or retirements were made in bounds up the spurs or along the ridges by dispersed infantry who carefully avoided low ground or re-entrants where they could be fired upon from above or surrounded. Reserves and supports moved closely behind the firing line, providing covering fire as an attack progressed and using flanking fire to clear the *sangars* and the breastworks. A close-order line was still required shortly before an enemy position was reached in case the Pathan swordsmen counterattacked *en masse*. Hill warfare normally necessitated the dispersion and the decentralization of command and control to give Indian columns the degree of flexibility required when operating across difficult terrain. Most fighting frequently devolved into a series of separate unrelated skirmishes, rather than a formal set-piece encounter under the direct control of senior officers.

The Indian columns operating in tribal territory otherwise seldom encountered serious resistance from the *lashkars*. Instead, opposing tribesmen normally concentrated on attacking and harassing Indian columns as they marched through tribal territory. The comparative immobility of Indian columns relative to the tribal *lashkars* exposed the former to attack from the flank and rear, and directly against the vulnerable pack transport which made ensuring all-round security of the transport animals a matter of special importance. The essence of the tactical problem lay in ensuring the security of the main body of a column and protecting its long, vulnerable train of pack transport from attack from the surrounding hills. It was quickly discovered that the key lay in controlling the flanking ground and dominating the surrounding area by 'crowning the heights' on either side of the route of march with small parties of troops who occupied all high ground or tactically important terrain features within effective *jezail* range of a column (300 yards). The tribesmen were seldom prepared to attack uphill and were wary of moving in the vicinity of piquets, as these positions were normally fortified with *sangars* that protected against sniping or direct assault. A ring of piquets provided all-round defence to the main body of the column as it moved along the valley floor denying positions from where tribesmen armed with *jezails* could fire on the troops, blocking nalas and covering lines of approach to the valley below that could be used by swordsmen to approach to close quarters unseen. Piquets protecting the flanks of an advancing column would rejoin the main body once the rear guard had passed out of effective range of their position, which could then be safely abandoned to the enemy. The evacuation of a piquet was often the point of greatest danger as tribesmen sought to seize the vacant position and attack the retreating detachment. During a withdrawal the main body of the piquet would retreat downhill with speed, leaving an officer or non-commissioned officer and a handful of men who would make as much noise as possible and flee as soon as the rest of the piquet had rejoined the main column. If casualties were suffered, it became axiomatic to immediately counterattack to recover the dead and wounded and to reoccupy the position. Piqueting required a high degree of physical fitness, drill, co-ordination, intelligence, and personal skill if the 'crowning' of the heights along the line of march was to proceed without impeding a column's progress and ensure complete security. The selection of the tactical features that needed to be piqueted and the routes by which detachments should advance across the intervening ground, required an officer with a practised and skilful eye in the advance guard. The posting and withdrawal of piquets led to the development of elaborate codes and drills by the PIF to prevent tribal attacks on imperial troops or undue delay for columns on the march. The premature evacuation of a piquet, for example, could endanger the security of an entire column or the other piquets and necessitate rapid counter-attacks to recover the position from the enemy that might delay an entire operation.

The protection and security of British encampments at night was based on similar principles as those used to protect a column on the march. The mountainous terrain forced troops, followers and pack animals to encamp on the valley floors, where the ground was sufficiently level and water was available, but such locations were vulnerable to sniping as they were always commanded by the surrounding hills and the low lying ground was often poorly suited to defence. The surrounding heights dominating a camp were held by small detachments of troops, occupying *sangars*, and were ordered to hold the position overnight to deny the tribesmen sniping positions and dominate lines of approach to the encampment below. During the hours of darkness, piquets could not provide complete protection from sniping at close range, attacks by tribesmen who infiltrated the outer ring of defences, or thieves intent on stealing rifles or equipment from Indian troops. The defence of the main body from a surprise attack was ensured by the construction of elaborate field defences encompassing the limits of the encampment. A perimeter wall or breastwork, built with rocks, stores, or bales of fodder, and backed by a trench would stop tribesmen rushing a camp, provide cover from sniping, prevent rifle thieves from infiltrating an encampment, and provide shelter for the sleeping troops. Infantry units were deployed along the length of the perimeter while the central area was reserved for the transport, cavalry or other non-combatant units. Within its walls, messes, and sleeping places were often dug down into the ground or surrounded by *sangars* to protect against sniping into the densely packed perimeter camp. The construction of such elaborate defences was time consuming and meant that the columns had to encamp long before nightfall in order to allow sufficient time for their completion while it was still light. Despite these serious drawbacks, the importance of such perimeter defences was demonstrated on numerous occasions when large parties of swordsmen penetrated the surrounding ring of piquets and launched desperate attacks on the troops in the valley below.

Withdrawal from contact with hostile tribesmen, an operation that occurred frequently, was the most difficult phase of an expedition in tribal territory during which the heaviest fighting normally occurred. A *lashkar* normally interpreted a withdrawal as a sign of success causing the scale and intensity of attacks to dramatically increase. The superior mobility of tribal skirmishers and local knowledge gave them an advantage in pressing a retirement which normally left the commanding positions in tribal hands from where heavy fire could be delivered on the withdrawing imperial troops. As a rearguard gradually retired, it had to be covered by infantry and artillery in successive layback positions until out of effective range of the tribesmen. Such operations required considerable skill, in order to be achieved without loss. Mountain artillery normally acted as the mainstay of a withdrawal leap-frogging back from successive firing points in the same manner as the infantry. The brutality which the tribesmen often meted out to British or Hindu prisoners exerted a powerful influence on hill warfare. The mutilation of the dead bodies of imperial troops was commonplace, while captured soldiers were liable for castration or otherwise disfigured before being put to death. Any dead and wounded left behind during operations necessitated rapid counterattacks as a result to recover casualties before they fell into tribal hands. As the numbers of wounded increased, so the pace of the retreat slowed as men were encumbered with the dead, the wounded and rifles which were not to be allowed to fall into tribal hands.

These principles and minor tactics devised by the PIF to conduct what became known as hill warfare were a practical, pragmatic and highly effective response to local conditions. From the outset, the units of the PIF quickly earned praise from senior officers for the performance of their arduous duties on the north-west frontier. Writing in 1850, the commander-in-chief wrote to Lawrence after seeing the 1st Cavalry Regiment and the 1st Infantry Regiment in action:

> I have great pleasure in saying that they are excellent regiments, I really have seen none better. We all know that it takes more time to form a cavalry regiment than an infantry regiment, and Daly has got his wild horsemen into excellent order, his regiment is perfectly pliable and handy, he has made wonderful progress.... As to Coke's I have seen nothing superior to it in drill. It is admirable and both you and I saw how this brave corps fought under its excellent leader, in the five days campaign. In short I am more pleased with these two commanders than I can well express.[33]

During the 1850s, the PIF's regiments carried out the majority of hill campaigns alone, giving it experience and an unrivalled practical expertise in mountain warfare. By 1857, some of its units had participated in no less than twenty different skirmishes with the trans-border tribes. As it was free from the overall direction and straitjacket of the regular military authorities, its units were able to quickly adapt their arms, equipment, and training to meet the specialized local military requirements of mountain warfare. A permanent establishment of regimental pack transport proved critical in ensuring the success of military operations in which so much depended on transport and supply, allowing PIF units to move quickly and with comparative ease through the border hills. As a result of the PIF's permanent commitment to the watch and ward of the border, both officers and men out of necessity also gained an intimate knowledge of tribal territory and its inhabitants. During such operations and while on outpost duty British and Indian officers learnt to exercise a degree of initiative and self-reliance unknown in the regular army. A high state of efficiency was maintained under Brigadier-General Hodgson, who ensured that its regiments and batteries frequently exercised their men and transport in full marching order near their cantonments as if engaged against hostile tribesmen.[34] The resulting close cooperation and mutual understanding that developed between its regiments and batteries, high standard of training and *esprit-de-corps* within the force that developed added considerably to its effectiveness. Isolated from the mainstream of military life in India by distance and the Indus, and relieved only between the border cantonments its officers and men developed a high standard of professionalism devoted solely to local political and military requirements. Indeed, despite the harsh conditions in the border cantonments, the unrivalled opportunities for active service and its growing reputation meant competition was fierce amongst officers to serve in its regiments and batteries.

In comparison, the regular Bengal Army regiments and British units that garrisoned Peshawar district, trained solely in conventional operations, lacked knowledge of tribal tactics or suitable transport, equipment and training adapted to the exigencies of mountain warfare. Armed with muzzle-loading muskets, clothed in scarlet uniforms and accompanied by large quantities of baggage, regular troops proved highly vulnerable in the hills. Knowledge of mountain warfare could only be acquired through close contact with the PIF in the field or had to be bought by experience by the successive commanders and regiments posted to Peshawar district at a high cost in lives, reputations and prestige. Columns composed of regular troops employed in the hills lacked a similar degree of mobility as PIF units, as prior to 1861 no standing transport was maintained by regular units during peacetime and it had to be improvised before each campaign. The collection of sufficient animals, carriage, and followers in the Punjab often delayed operations for several weeks. As S.S. Thorburn later observed:

> In hill fighting the garrison was only strong through numbers and discipline. In fact, no troops in the Bengal army were adapted for guerrilla warfare in the mountains: Britishers and Hindustanis alike were plainsmen, not cragsmen, and neither moved unless accompanied by immense baggage trains. Owing to these disabilities expeditions launched from Peshawar were infrequent, and when undertaken were very costly, formal, and ineffective campaigns carried on close to a base within our border than the rough-and-ready sort of marching customary in the Derajat.[35]

The periodic relief of units, carried out every two or three years within the Bengal Presidency, militated against the assimilation or dissemination of local knowledge regarding tribal territory and its inhabitants as well as practical experience of mountain warfare. Any information gained through practical experience was soon lost before it could be passed on to the rest of the regular army as units returned to the mainstream of professional soldiering in India with its emphasis on conventional warfare.

The success with which the frontier regiments and batteries policed the administrative border and conducted punitive operations in tribal territory was reflected in 1855, when the PIF, commanded by Brigadier Chamberlain from February 1855, assumed responsibility for the watch and ward of the border between Mardan and Abbottabad, with Peshawar district intervening between its existing garrisons at Kohat and in the Derajat. To carry out these duties the strength of the force was, during the 1850s, steadily augmented to five regiments of cavalry, six regiments of Punjab infantry, the Queen's Own Corps of Guides, four regiments of Sikh infantry, three light field batteries, two mountain trains, and a garrison battery.[36]

THE PIF AND THE INDIAN MUTINY OF 1857–1858

By the 1850s the board of administration had made remarkable progress in bringing order to the Punjab and a semblance of it to the trans-Indus districts. Much work, however, remained to be done, with the tribesmen remaining an insistent threat to the security of the Punjab. Other matters, besides, quickly became more pressing. The outbreak of the Mutiny at Meerut in May 1857 sent shockwaves that, thanks to the post and telegraph, quickly reached the frontier cantonments.

The drive, resolution and willingness to act that was displayed by British administrators and soldiers in the Punjab played a key part in the rapid disarming of Bengal Army regiments in the Punjab and the ruthless elimination of a handful of units that had mutinied. Indeed, this action quickly won the support of the frontier chiefs, who previously had supported the British against the Sikhs, and kept the tribal areas quiet. As a result they provided a vital pool of manpower for new recruits during the course of 1857. The PIF played a crucial role as one of the few available bodies of loyal 'native' troops available that year to British commanders for retrieving Delhi and then in subsequent operations in the North-West Province and Awadh. A direct result of the separate system of military administration, the isolation of the trans-Indus areas, and sheer distance from the cradle of the Bengal Army in Awadh and the different patterns of recruitment was that the PIF regiments were largely inured from efforts by mutineers to suborn them. They had little or no common ground with the Hindu rank and file of the Bengal Army infantry regiments. Indeed, the fact that that PIF regiments would prove actively loyal and 'true to its salt' was assumed by Sir John Lawrence, who immediately ordered several of its highly experienced regiments to form a key part of a Movable Column commanded by Brigadier Neville Chamberlain, that was eventually sent out on 25 May 1857 from Wazirabad towards Lahore.

As the PIF began its steady progress throughout the province, disarming suspect regiments and overawing the populace, its regiments were quickly hived off (and replaced by British units) as the situation demanded reinforcement of the beleaguered British and their few loyal Indian troops at the strategically and symbolically important city of Delhi. The recapture of Delhi was correctly judged as the key to political and military success in suppressing the Mutiny. The best corps of the PIF—the Queen's Own Corps of Guides, 1st Punjab Infantry and 4th Sikh Infantry—quickly reached the beleaguered British forces outside Delhi after carrying out a series of forced marches, despite the searing summer heat and, for its Muslim troops, having to fight during the month of Ramazan. The march made by the Corps of Guides, commanded by Henry Daly, was truly remarkable—580 miles in 21 days—in full marching order, carrying arms and equipment. These hard-bitten infantrymen and cavalrymen made an immediate impression on one officer:

> The Guides Corps is a sight to see. Their dress is highly peculiar and the men are chiefly of two sorts, viz., the tall, powerful and swarthy Afghan, and the short, muscular, olive-skinned Gurkha. They are the admiration of the camp.[37] When asked when his men would be ready for action, Captain Henry Daly replied: In half an hour.[38]

Without further ado its sowars went into action, repelling a carefully concerted rebel attack from the city, albeit at heavy cost. For some time the Guides and the Sirmoor Battalion of Gurkhas were the only loyal Indian troops fighting alongside British troops in Delhi. Former elements of the Movable Column arrived from Punjab in dribs and drabs during the summer, as soon as they could be spared, with its main body eventually reaching Delhi on 14 August 1857 after successfully overawing the Punjab. Eventually the troops of the PIF despatched to Delhi, after giving assistance in the Punjab, included: a squadron of the 1st Punjab Cavalry, a squadron of the 2nd Punjab Cavalry, a squadron of the 5th Punjab Cavalry and the 2nd and 4th Punjab Infantry and 4th Sikh Infantry.

The experience and morale earned by the PIF on frontier service and the skills learnt on the North-West Frontier during the watch and ward of the tribal areas made them a vital and highly effective addition to the relatively small body of loyal Indian troops available for the suppression of the Mutiny. Indeed, its training, experience and light infantry skills proved ideally suited to operations on the Indian plains, refuting claims that troops trained solely to mountain warfare were incapable of holding their own in conventional toe-to-toe battle on the Indian plains. The PIF units greatly distinguished themselves in the fighting that followed, albeit at a heavy cost in dead and wounded. Around Delhi the Guides suffered 319 killed out of an initial strength of 550. Coke's Rifles had 664 effectives and lost 208 killed or wounded. Following the fall of Delhi, the squadrons of Punjab Cavalry, the 4th Sikhs and the 2nd and 4th Punjab Infantry, formed part of the column which joined Sir Colin Campbell at Lucknow and took part in the relief of the city.

The discipline, and efficiency of the rump of the PIF that remained behind in the trans-Indus areas of the Punjab also paid dividends. They played an important role in maintaining law and order and in helping to raise and organize new irregular horse and other levies from the border tribes that filled the breach and kept the border quiet in this newly conquered province. This policy of co-opting the trans-border tribes in their own defence proved highly successful. Only one punitive operation of note took place during the Indian Mutiny in the area north-west of Rawalpindi beyond the Indus. Following various disturbances along the border the garrison at the Fort at Mardan, which consisted of the 5th Punjab Infantry and 2 mountain guns of the Peshawar Mountain Battery under the command of Major J.L. Vaughan, mounted several small-scale punitive operations, with the support of the 2nd Punjab Cavalry, against the so-called Hindustani fanatics at Sheikh Jana and then Narinji in July-August 1857. Following an attack on the British assistant commissioner encamped at Sheikh Jana, another punitive operation was required during the spring of 1858. Under the command of Major-General Sir Sydney Cotton, a much larger force composed of PIF and regular units, advanced into the hills and destroyed villages at Chinglai, Panjtar, and Mangal Thana. Following a pitched battle near Sitana, the back of the resistance was broken, with Enfield rifles, used for the first time in hill warfare, conferring a decisive advantage on Anglo-Indian troops against tribesmen armed with close quarter weapons.[39] The official report stated that:

> The services ... rendered by that portion of [the PIF], which was left behind Trans-Indus—cannot be considered of less value than the services rendered by their more formidable comrades, who had an opportunity of earning the many honors they attained in fighting the battles of empire in Hindustan. The peace of the border was of vital importance to the peace of the Punjab, and it is known that the peace of the Punjab was then of the utmost moment for the safety of the empire.[40]

This may well be an understatement. Behind the shield provided by the PIF, the Punjab became the main British recruiting ground for new infantry regiments that were modelled on the PIF and numbered consecutively after its units.

The uprising of 1857 to a large extent 'made' the PIF, establishing and then greatly enhancing its reputation. It led to a marked change in attitude towards its 'benighted' officers and men and their onerous duties on the North-West Frontier. As Vaughan later wrote: 'If our brethren of the regular Sepoy army had once viewed us with pity as condemned to permanent service on the frontier scantily provided with makes service pleasant in an ordinary Indian station, the tables were now turned, and our lot was regarded as enviable.'[41] Indeed, it was so successful that it later formed the model on which the whole 'native' army was reorganized during the 1860s.[42] Belief in the supposedly superior military qualities of 'martial' Sikh, Pathan and Punjabi Muslim troops was also firmly entrenched in the minds of a new generation of British officers.

The PIF, however, perhaps paradoxically did not escape criticism in discussions about the organization of British arms in India during the aftermath. The independence of such a large number of men outside the jurisdiction of the commander-in-chief was questioned during the ensuing reorganization of the Indian Army.[43] In defence, Brigadier-General Sir Neville Chamberlain, the PIF's current commander, emphasized the joint political and military role of the force, and stressed the importance of localization to maintain an intimate knowledge of the frontier and its inhabitants. He argued that its men had become accustomed to mountain warfare by repeated operations against the trans-border tribes and that in its methods of organization, recruitment, and training, the PIF was now ideally fitted for conducting military operations against the hill tribes. The Commissioner of Peshawar, Captain W. James, effusive in his support, emphasized the unique character of the fighting in which it was employed. One officer noted:

> Everyone who has been engaged on expeditions on this frontier must admit that it is a peculiar kind of warfare, requiring special training of officers and men. Independent of the harassing duties attendant on campaigning everywhere, there are peculiar difficulties to be encountered in the hills on the border, and which are overcome by practice only. I have no hesitation in saying that troops freshly and indiscriminately brought to the work must fail; even physically they would break down. I can assure the Government that I have seen sepoys of the Regular Army shot down and cut down on the hill side perfectly helpless, whilst

their comrades of the Irregular Force have been driving the enemy up a neighbouring hill; and if we look to smaller matters (which in truth make up the efficiency of the whole) we shall see how the Irregular of the Punjab Force excels his comrade of the Regular Army.... It is necessary to occupy many points, and to keep up communications with them all; this involves the detachment of many parties, and Native Officers and Non-Commissioned Officers are frequently Commanding small but important posts, in which intelligence, care, and prudence of mind, and knowledge of the enemy's tactics to extricate themselves from. Such incidents are unobserved generally, but the enemy is acquainted with them, and they frequently tend, as much as more open signs of power and skill, to the successful result of the day; and to establish a wholesome fear of our men.[44]

Such whole-hearted support for the PIF contrasted sharply with the biting criticism he reserved for regular Bengal Army regiments:

Conceive a General had never before seen an expedition of the kind, with a force which found itself on the frontier in ordinary course of relief!! Supposing the General and his Officers to be even superior to the ordinary men;—we require no prophetic skill to calculate the rest—not aware of the style of the enemy's warfare, of the nature of the country he is about to penetrate, of the arrangements found by experience to be required for the efficiency and comfort of his men, of the weak points of our organisation under such circumstances, of the manner in which the enemy can most readily inflict loss on us, of the arrangements for the wounded, and above all of what men can and what they cannot do, it would be a miracle if he avoid a disaster.... Nothing which I have said can, I trust, be considered in any way disparaging to the officers of the other divisions of the army. I simply assert that, while the main principles of war must be the same anywhere, yet its details are necessarily dependent on the character of the enemy and that these can be mastered only by experience and practice: any attempt to theorize will prove abortive, and just as peculiar training is necessary for the various departments of the same profession in civil life, so it is essential in the Army.[45]

Despite objections, the PIF remained under the orders of the Punjab government.[46] Although major changes were implemented in the regular Indian Army during the 1860s, the organization of the PIF remained essentially unaltered, apart from a reduction the strength of its regiments and their attendant transport.[47] It remained first and foremost responsible for the watch and ward of tribal territory, but as later events would show, it provided a valuable reserve of trained and experienced manpower.

CONCLUSION

The policy of maintaining localized armed forces organized for a specific task in the trans-Indus areas of the Punjab proved highly successful. The PIF proved itself a remarkably effective means of control over the unruly trans-border tribes in the first eight years of British rule in the Punjab. It continued to do so until it was finally amalgamated with the Bengal Army in 1886. When it was formed, no one had realized just what an important part the PIF would play in the maintenance of British rule in India. The officers and men of the PIF later demonstrated to the Indian military authorities its high level of military efficiency and morale. Without its highly effective and decisive contribution to the pitched fighting in and around Delhi in 1857, the British task of quelling the outbreak would have been far more difficult. Its regiments also played an important role in later operations around Lucknow and to a lesser degree in central India. Many Indian officers and men returned to the Punjab laden with the spoils of war, while other British and Indian officers were awarded honours and decorations during the fighting, including several Victoria Crosses. The part played by those regiments left behind on the watch and ward of the North-West Frontier and aiding in maintaining law and order in the newly-conquered Punjab itself is arguably no less significant. Its officers and men played an important part in disarming suspect Indian regiments of the Bengal Army, overawing otherwise hostile elements in the local population and more importantly within tribal territory and freeing-up other British and Indian regiments for service elsewhere in the subcontinent. Under the security umbrella provided by its units, Punjab became a major new recruiting ground and a pillar of strength that enabled the British to pacify the subcontient.

NOTES

1. For general histories of the PIF (later Punjab Frontier Force) see R.S. Dey, *A Brief Account of the Punjab Frontier Force from 1849 to 31 March 1903*

(Calcutta: W. Newman, 1905) and R. North, *The Punjab Frontier Force: A Brief Record of their Services* (Dera Ismail Khan: Commercial Steam Press, 1934).

2. See T.R. Moreman, *The Army in India and the Development of Frontier Warfare: 1849-1947* (London: Macmillan, 1998).
3. For background see C.C. Davies, *The Problem of the North-West Frontier 1890-1908, with a Survey of Policy since 1849* (London, 1932).
4. Major G. Hutchinson, offg. Secy. to the Govt. of Punjab, MD, to Major-General Sir R.G. Birch, Secy. to the GoI in the MD, 1 October 1860, P/191/44, IOR, BL, London.
5. Charles Allen, *Soldier Sahibs: The Men Who Made the North West Frontier* (London: Viking, 2000), pp. 209–10.
6. Lieutenant-General Sir H. Daly, 'The Punjab Frontier Force', *Journal of the Royal United Service Institution,* vol. 28 (June 1884), p. 912.
7. Captain W.A. Mayhew to Major R. Wylie, offg. Secy. to the Govt. of India, MD, 25 July 1850, F/4/2393, IOR.
8. H. Elliot, Secy. to the GoI with the Governor-General to the board of administration for the affairs of the Punjab, 16 May 1849, H/761, IOR.
9. Brigadier J.S. Hodgson, Commanding PIF, to Major H. Burn, Deputy Secy., Lahore, 25 March 1851, P/42/56, IOR.
10. J.L. Vaughan, *My Service in the Indian Army – and After* (London: Archibald Constable, 1904), p. 45.
11. Allen, *Soldier Sahibs*, pp. 209–10.
12. Daly, 'The Punjab Frontier Force', pp. 911–12.
13. Brigadier Hodgson, Commanding Punjab Irregular Force, to Major H.A. Burne, Deputy Secy. to the board of administration, 5 December 1850, P/42/55, IOR.
14. For an overview see Moreman, *The Army in India and the Development of Frontier Warfare*, pp. 1–6.
15. Ibid., pp. 6–8.
16. *Military Report on Waziristan* (Simla: G.S.I., 1924), pp. 119–21; *Military Report on Tribal Country between Khyber and Kurram* (Simla: G.S.I., 1930), pp. 17–18; *Military Report on the Mohmand Country* (Simla: G.S.I., 1926), pp. 13–14.
17. J.W. Spain, *The Pathan Borderland* (The Hague, 1963), pp. 76–7, and A.S. Ahmed, 'Pukhtun Tribes in the Great Game', *Asian Affairs,* vol. 11 (1980), pp. 139–40.
18. Lieutenant-Colonel W. Gordon, Chief Inspector of Musketry, to the Adjutant-General, 4 December 1867, L/MIL/3/784, IOR; R.O. Christiansen, 'Conflict and Change Among the Khyber Afridis' (University of Leicester, Ph.D., 1987), pp. 286–7; Major-General J.G. Elliot, *The Frontier: 1839–1947* (London: Cassell, 1968), p. 111.
19. Major W. MacKinnon, 'Jezail Experiments', *Proceedings of the United Service Institution of India,* vol. 20, no. 4 (1875), pp. 201–3.

20. Elliot, *The Frontier*, p. 27.
21. Major J. Nicholson, Deputy Commissioner, to Major J.D. Macpherson, Military Secy. to the Chief Commissioner, 4 September 1853, F/4/2549, IOR.
22. Major J.D. Mcpherson, offg. Secy. to C. Allen, offg. Secy. to the GoI, FD, 31 May 1853, P/200/32, IOR.
23. *Selections from the Records of the Government of India (Foreign Department), No. VI Report on the Administration of the Punjab, Territories, comprising the Punjab Proper and the Cis and Trans-Sutlej States, for the Years 1851–52 and 1852–53* (Calcutta: Calcutta Gazette Office, 1854), pp. 36–7 (hereafter *Selections from Records No. VI*), V/23/1, IOR.
24. Brigadier J.S. Hodgson, Commanding PIF, to Major H.D. Macpherson, Military Secy. to the Commissioner, 29 April 1853, P/200/36, IOR.
25. Lieutenant-Colonel Mackeson, Commissioner & Superintendent Peshawar Division, to Major J.D. Macpherson, Military Secy. to the Chief Commissioner, 2 September 1853; Captain J. Coke, Commanding 1st Punjab Infantry to Major J.D. Macpherson, 22 December 1853, F/4/2549, IOR.
26. Major J.D. Macpherson, offg. Military Secy. Chief Commissioner Punjab, to Lieutenant-Colonel R.J. Birch, offg. Secy. to the GoI in the MD, 11 October 1853, F/4/2549, IOR.
27. Minute by the Governor-General, 3 November 1853, Lieutenant-Colonel R.J. Birch, off. Secy. to the GoI in the MD to J. Lawrence, Chief Commissioner Punjab, 9 November 1853, F/4/2549, IOR.
28. *Selections from Records No. VI*, p. 37; *Report on the Administration of Public Affairs in the Punjab Territories from 1854–55 to 1855–56 Inclusive* (Calcutta: Official Press, 1856), pp. 94–5, V/10/2, IOR.
29. Brigadier-General C.A. Graham, *A History of the Indian Mountain Artillery* (Aldershot: Gale and Polden, 1957), pp. 4-6.
30. Brigadier J.S. Hodgson, Commanding PIF, to Major N. Chamberlain, Military Secy. to the board of administration, 5 October 1852, and C. Allen, offg. Secy. to the GoI to the board of administration for the affairs of the Punjab, 10 November 1852, P/43/63, IOR.
31. R.H. Scales, Artillery in Small Wars: The Evolution of British Army Doctrine 1860–1914 (PhD Dissertation, Duke University, 1976), p. 80.
32. See *History of the 1st Punjab Cavalry* (Lahore: Govt. Central Gazette Press, 1887), *History of the Second Punjab Cavalry* (London: Kegan Paul, Trench, 1888) and *History of the 23rd Cavalry (Frontier Force), late 3rd Regiment, Punjab Cavalry* (no imprint, *c.* 1910).
33. His Excellency the Commander-in-Chief to Colonel Lawrence, 23 July 1850, F/4/2427, IOR.
34. Brigadier-General J.S. Hodgson to Major H.D. Macpherson, offg. Military Secy. to the Chief Commissioner, 10 March 1853, P/200/25, IOR.

35. S.S. Thorburn, *The Punjab in Peace and War* (Edinburgh and London, 1904), p. 294.
36. *Report on the Administration of Public Affairs in the Punjab Territories from 1854-55 to 1855-56 Inclusive*, p. 97.
37. Saul David, *The Indian Mutiny* (London: Viking, 2002), p. 161.
38. George Younghusband, *The Story of the Guides* (London: Macmillan, 1908), p. 73.
39. Captain H.L. Nevill, *Campaigns on the North-West Frontier* (London: John Murray, 1912), pp. 39–43.
40. Maj. G. Hutchinson, offg. Secy. to Govt. of Punjab, MD, to Major-General Sir R.G. Birch, Secy. to the GoI in the MD, 1 October 1860, P/191/44, IOR.
41. Vaughan, *My Service in the Indian Army*, p. 90.
42. A.H. Shibly, 'The Reorganisation of the Indian Armies, 1858–79' (University of London, Ph.D., 1969) p. 124.
43. Ibid.
44. G. Hutchinson to R.G. Birch, 1 October 1860.
45. Ibid.
46. Major-General R.J. Birch, Secy. to the GoI, MD, to the Secy. to Govt. of Punjab, MD, 19 November 1860, and Memorandum by Sir John Lawrence, 8 December 1860, Lawrence Papers, MSS.EUR.F.90/23, IOR.
47. *General Report on the Administration of the Punjab and its Dependencies, for 1859-60* (Calcutta: Bengal Printing Company Limited, 1860), pp. 40–1, V/10/13, IOR.

CHAPTER 3

Artillery in India: 1800–1857

R. BALASUBRAMANIAM
RUTH RHYNAS BROWN

The political and military developments in the first half of the nineteenth century were crucial to the establishment of *Pax Britannica.* These developments were, in one manner, related to the effective use of artillery by the British. This was one of the important factors that created British paramountcy in India and a comparison of the state of artillery of the British and the states that they defeated is necessary for the historians of the period. This task is difficult because most of the references in the literature usually tend to view the historical events and political developments without analysing the impact of technology on the ability of the adversaries to wage war. Therefore, if the subjugation of the Indian subcontinent by the British is to be properly understood, one has to critically look at the period prior to the upheaval of 1857. The great outbreak of 1857 has been one of the episodes that scholars of Indian history have regarded with interest and, usually, some prejudice. It is not the aim here to debate the true character of the movement but to understand the state of technology as revealed by remaining artillery pieces of this period, primarily of the Indian states. The available artillery pieces of the Indian states of this period have not been critically analysed from the perspective of British *versus* Indian warfare.

The design of Indian fortifications and their vulnerability to the British cannon fire has been explored. Detailed analysis of artillery of the Marathas and Sikhs reveals that the cannons of the 'native' Indian powers were not simple imitations of the European types, but intelligent adaptations of European artillery, set to Indian standards of weights and measures. Information regarding British artillery during this period has been documented and therefore, the focus will be primarily on the artillery of the important Indian states. Nevertheless, a brief background on the guns of the EIC follows.

THE GUNS OF THE EAST INDIA COMPANY

Before the battle of Plassey, the EIC's requirements for cannons were relatively small, but the growth in the size of its possessions and the army meant that small contingents of field guns and garrisons guns needed to be stationed all over the country. This requirement grew during the first half of the nineteenth century, with the EIC's overseas expeditions to Burma, Afghanistan, and Persia, as well as campaigns within the subcontinent against the Marathas and the Sikhs.

By 1857, the EIC had a well-established network to supply its forces with guns and carriages. A foundry had been built near Calcutta, while there were three gun carriage manufactories, one in each presidency. A typical EIC cannon from Cossipore Gun and Shell Factory (in Calcutta) dated to 1854 is seen in Figure 3.1. The name of the then superintendent of the factory, Captain Broome, is mentioned on the surface inscription. In addition, there were series of arsenals and depots attached to cantonments and British settlements. Of these, during the course of 1857, the EIC lost control of two major arsenals in Delhi and Kanpur and the Gun Carriage Manufactory at Fatehgarh. When Colin Campbell re-took the Fatehgarh Manufactory in 1858, he found that it had been used as gun foundry by the rebels for casting bronze cannon.

As the military needs of the EIC grew, its demand for artillery increased. The EIC needed both iron and bronze guns for its service—bronze for the mobile field units and larger calibre iron guns for garrison and siege trains. For much of the eighteenth century, the EIC acquired its guns from England, usually from the bronze founders in London, such as Richard Gilpin or Francis Kinman, and its iron guns from established suppliers such as the Harrison family and later, the Carron Company. However, there had been pressure to set up a manufactory in India. A gun foundry was erected towards the end of the eighteenth century at Fort William. This was done in order to able to respond more

FIGURE 3.1: TYPICAL EIC BRONZE CANNON CAST IN THE COSSIPORE IN 1854. THIS IS AT PRESENT IN THE MEHRANGARH FORT IN JODHPUR.

quickly to the EIC's needs, since orders put through the Court in London took more than a year to arrive in India.

Even with the creation of the gun foundry in Calcutta, the EIC continued to order many guns from London. However, the situation became more acute in 1825 with the death of Francis Kinman, the last independent gunfounder in London who had supplied the EIC with many guns over the years. Now the only bronze gunfounders left were in Woolwich Arsenal, which as a government facility could not automatically supply a private body like the EIC adequately. It was imperative for the EIC to have its own source. A decision therefore was taken to move the foundry and rebuild it in the old gun carriage yard at nearby Cossipore.

Captain Hutchinson, the Superintendent, went on a tour of Europe to visit foundries and the Woolwich Arsenal, to investigate the latest technologies and to order machinery. Based on this tour, he produced a plan and built the new foundry. In its prosperous years, the foundry could produce about 100 guns a year, few of which failed proof. These tended to be the lighter calibre guns, howitzers and mortars. When asked in 1857 about how many guns he could produce, the then director reported about 15 guns a month. This could be doubled by working day and night, but at the cost of quality.

There was some dispute about the quality of guns cast at Cossipore. Some reports compared the guns favourably with those cast at Woolwich Arsenal, while others suggested the Cossipore cannons were both more expensive and of inferior quality. At some points in its existence, the rate of production plunged to a few guns a month, with very poor proof rates. Much depended on the quality and enthusiasm of the foundry director. It is an irony that one of the great British heroes of 1857 was Archdale Wilson, who as a lieutenant had been responsible for one of the more productive periods of the Cossipore Foundry. During the siege of Delhi, he may well have been fighting rebels equipped with cannons cast during his own period of office, bearing his own name.

The guns which came from the London founders were based on patterns produced for the Board of Ordnance and the Royal Artillery. The India artillery officers argued that they needed slightly different guns for their own use, rather than slavish copies of Woolwich Arsenal products. Once production was initiated in India, they could control the designs of their cannons more closely. The EIC also needed larger calibre cast-iron guns for the garrisons and for siege trains. These still had to be shipped out infrequently as they were produced in limited ironworks in Great Britain. These were the Yorkshire Furnaces of Low Moor and Bowling and the Midland Works of Bailey, Pegg and Company, and the Walkers. A number of guns from the Cossipore Foundry have survived. Some are in the collections of Great Britain, some in the Royal Armouries and the Museum of Artillery, Woolwich, and others in collections in various parts of India.

During this period, all the guns were smoothbore muzzleloaders. The smallest calibres were the lighter field guns: 3, 6, 9 and 12-pounders, which were the weapons of the horse artillery, mobile guns which could be quickly moved by horse. The howitzers were also light guns, but they threw larger shells and were therefore much feared by both sides. There were also larger field guns and mortars which had to be moved by bullock or elephant. The field guns, howitzers, and smaller mortars were of bronze, while larger guns, like the 18-pounders and upwards and larger mortars were of cast-iron. The large iron guns and mortars formed the slow-moving siege train. At this time, there was only one siege train available to the EIC forces in the Bengal Presidency, consisting of about 24 guns of which half were the small 5.5-inch mortars. This siege train was used for the recapture of Delhi in 1857, where it played a vital role.

The EIC's artillery were not the only British guns in India at this time. There were also several companies from the Royal Artillery and more arrived in the course of the emergency. They were armed with bronze light field guns cast at Woolwich Arsenal and larger calibre iron siege guns and mortars, cast in British ironworks. The guns used by Captain Maude of the Royal Artillery during Henry Havelock's advance to Kanpur were cast in England. This was the period when, following the unsatisfactory performance of the British troops in the Crimea, the authorities were experimenting with rifling and breechloading, but these guns were still in their experimental stage in 1857.

The ammunition at this time was a mixture of solid round shot of cast iron, canister and grape shot for antipersonnel use. Both the canister and grape involved smaller types of solid shot and shell (hollow shot filled with explosives). During some of the longer-lasting actions, such as at Lucknow (1857–8), the participants regularly risked life and limb recovering undamaged shot for re-use. Again, this indicates that both sides were using the same types of gun with interchangeable ammunition.[1] The horrific damage inflicted by such shot and shell has been captured in photographs taken in the immediate aftermath of the sieges, particularly those of Delhi and Lucknow.

The specific use of artillery by the Indian 'mutineers', does not warrant a detailed discussion. Those Indian gunners who went to the rebel side used the standard equipment. The Number 3 & Number 5 companies of Number 4 Bombay Artillery Battalion and 6 foot companies and Number 4 Troop of the Bengal Artillery revolted. There is no detailed reference to 'native' manufactured artillery being used in the conflict in standard accounts. However, there are a couple of indications of their manufacture—first at the Gun Carriage Manufactory at Fatehgarh and second, in a fort at Kalpi where about 4 foundries were discovered. There is a reference to a battery of 6 miniature guns discovered after the relief of Lucknow, which had been made for the Nawab of Awadh. However, these appeared to be princely toys and not functional pieces of ordnance. The Royal Armouries of Awadh had a pair of small howitzers cast by Claude Martin in 1780s. In effect, 1857 was a civil war, since the antagonists were originally on the same side and trained and equipped in the same manner. They all served their guns with such competence and bravery that, thereafter, Indian crews were not employed to man guns until 1935. This appears to be an important effect of the uprising on the organization of artillery in India.[2]

While it would be difficult to analyse the state of artillery technology of all the Indian powers who fought against the British in the period prior to 1857, it is important to focus on the most important states, whose defeat ultimately allowed the EIC to establish its supremacy. The developments of artillery technology during the first half of the nineteenth century had far-reaching consequences in regions such as Ceylon, Afghanistan, and Burma. The military developments in those regions were also related to the effective use of British artillery.

The main focus as regards the artillery of Indian states, would be that of the Marathas and Sikhs. The available artillery pieces of Tipu Sultan, spread across several continents, need a critical technical analysis, to understand the impact of European technology on his cannons. Some of the important questions that need to be answered are, whether the designs of Indian cannons of this period were 'blind' copies of the European varieties, or were there some inherent differences. We are lucky in this regard when it comes to Sikh artillery because we have at our disposal a large amount of data that allows us to draw some conclusions regarding the state of Maratha and Sikh artillery.

ARTILLERY AND FORTS IN PRE-BRITISH INDIA

It is important to understand the design of Indian forts and their vulnerability to artillery fire. With the advent of gunpowder and cannons, several new design philosophies of fort construction evolved. Several forts were redesigned. In some cases, an outer line of fortification was added to existing forts (from the second half of the fifteenth century onwards) to make it difficult for cannons to destroy the strategic buildings within the main fort.

In Europe, it was realized that high walls and towers could be susceptible to cannon fire. Therefore, the fortifications were built at much lower level behind a deep ditch. Utilizing this method, the fortifications were not too high and therefore, were not easily breached by cannon shots. Therefore, with the introduction of gunpowder and siege guns in medieval Europe, we notice the building of so-called *trace italienne* type forts. This gave rise to the concept of bastion, a projecting artillery tower which eliminated dead zones and allowed cannon and hand guns of the defenders within the fort to sweep the entire ground in front of the wall.[3]

Most research on Indian forts has been addressed from the point of view of aesthetics and art historical aspects rather than function. The art historian did not bother too much with defence problems. However, there are some exceptions. Sidney Toy first addressed the security functions of several Indian forts.[4] J. Deloche has provided valuable inputs on the defence systems employed in Hindu and Muslim forts of Deccan. He has also studied the role of cannons in the forts of Deccan. In the Indian context, some drastic changes in fortification designs included additional embrasures with better covering, as well as levelling of towers and walls to make room for the installation and movement of cannons. These were developments intended to weaken the besiegers. In fact, the provision of gun platforms on bastions is considered a unique Indian feature. However, all the forts were not dramatically modified bearing in mind the *trace italienne* pattern. While alterations in Indian fort designs were implemented quite quickly in the early medieval era, this was not so during the later medieval ages which witnessed the progress of cannon technology in western Europe. The early medieval forts long continued to dominate the Indian skyline and were susceptible to cannon fire. While European forts lowered their walls, the Indian forts builders continued to increase the height of the forts. The Indian forts were built with high and massive enclosures until the end of the eighteenth century. Several possible reasons have been cited for not adopting the *trace italienne* design: artillery was not powerful, Indian forts were situated on high hills and in thick jungles, which in turn made it difficult for the besiegers to invest. Further, the political culture of *fitna* made investments in fortifications superfluous, as Indian cities and forts were of the disposable kind and therefore not worth the expensive defence. Forts charged hands through negotiations backed by force rather than through the conduct of decisive sieges. Deloche opines that the shots fired from the Indian cannons were not powerful enough to breach the fortifications. One possible reason for this could be the widespread use of stone balls rather than metallic shots in cannons, between the sixteenth and eighteenth centuries. It could also imply that the high ramparts may have been useful to prevent the approach of the enemy towards the fort.[5]

The Mughal commander of Ausa Fort sent a report in 1671 to Aurangzeb (the artillery was always under the direct command of the Mughal emperor from the time of Babur), requesting him to purchase iron cannon shots using the already sanctioned amount for purchase of stone balls, because he understood the effectiveness of metallic cannon shots.[6] It may be relevant to point out that the development of cast iron technology in Europe in sixteenth century permitted large-scale production of cheap cast iron cannon balls. The use of cast iron for cannon ball manufacture was one of the first major applications of cast iron in Europe. Unfortunately, Indian rulers did not pay much heed to developing this technology, and cannon balls were primarily made of stone. This may explain the ineffectiveness of Indian cannon fire in breaching fortifications. Overall, the non-adoption of the *trace italienne* design resulted in relatively easy take over of these forts by British artillery bombardments, during the wars that were fought in the first half of the nineteenth century.

The Mughals effectively used artillery in maintaining their military hold on their empire. The *Ain-i Akbari* emphasizes the importance of artillery in the Mughal military doctrine.[7] Well known among the successor states were those of the Marathas and the Sikhs. To a great extent, they acquired political power by utilizing good artillery. However, there are not many Sikh and Maratha cannons extant: most cannons captured by the British were melted down after the Anglo–Maratha and Anglo–Sikh wars. Some of the light artillery pieces were preserved, but shipped to England as war trophies. The same is the case with some of Tipu Sultan's cannons. In the forts that were captured by the Europeans, the original indigenous cannons were dismantled and melted down. For example, we know that a large number of indigenous guns, both the bronze and forge welded iron varieties, were pulled down by the French in Ginjee in 1751, then transported to Pondicherry and destroyed there.[8]

MARATHA ARTILLERY

The Marathas rose to prominence with the revolt of Shivaji during the second half of the seventeenth century and were a major power in northern India in the eighteenth century. Their sphere of influence extended from western India into central India and down south. There were different families that later controlled the Maratha empire, namely the Bhonsles of Nagpur, Holkars of Indore, Gaikwads of Baroda and the Sindias of Gwalior. In all these locations, cannons were stationed for the protection of forts. Overall, however, European observers were dismissive about Maratha artillery. In their view, the Maratha cannons were never made of any precise calibre, but cast differently in various diameters and the ball was afterwards adapted to the bore. Europeans commented that instead of cast shots, the Marathas used forged shots and therefore their cannon fire lacked the precision which characterized British artillery. Maratha military culture was blamed for this shortcoming. Lieutenant Moore noted that when a gun was loaded, all the people in the battery sat down, talked, and smoked for half an hour; when it was fired, if it knocked up a great dust, that was thought to be sufficient.[9]

The Maratha mode of warfare emphasized speed and stress was laid on cavalry. Even firearms were integrated within the overall ambit of mobile warfare. The Marathas also used mounted infantry by placing two men on a camel; one to drive the camel and the other to fire a wheel-lock musket capable of throwing a 3 oz. ball.[10] These firearms were deployed by the Marathas during the First Anglo–Maratha War which lasted from 1774 to 1783. The Second Anglo–Maratha War began in 1803 and Arthur Wellesley commanded the EIC force in Deccan. Wellesley had with him 5,000 allied cavalry (2,000 of Nizam and 3,000 belonging to the Peshwa), 1,900 cavalry and 4,000 infantry, 1,000 gunners, plus 34 guns.

That the Marathas matched the European powers in military hardware, became clear during the Battle of Assaye in 1803. On the Maratha side, Daulat Rao Sindia deployed 18,500 cavalry, 500 matchlock men, 35 pieces of heavy artillery and 170 light guns, in the region south of Narmada. He was supported by Raghuji Bhonsle, who had 20,000 cavalry, 6,000 irregular infantry, 35 artillery pieces, 500 camel guns and 500 rocket men.[11] Just before the onset of hostilities, Lieutenant-Colonel John Collins warned Wellesley in the following words: 'I tell you, General, as to their cavalry, you may ride over them, wherever you meet them; but their infantry and guns will astonish you.'[12]

The forces under Wellesley clashed with the Marathas on 24 September 1803 at Assaye. The artillery doctrine of the Marathas surprised the British. The Marathas after altering their position resorted to heavy cannon fire from the village of Assaye when the British troops were crossing the Kaitna River. The British 74th Regiment lost almost 60 per cent of its officers and soldiers. Wellesley agreed with Collin's assessment of the Westernized artillery and infantry of Sindia and wrote on 24 September 1803 that 'the action was very brisk indeed, the fire from the enemy's cannon the hottest that has been known in this country for some time; and our loss in officers and men has been very great.... Sindia's infantry behaved remarkably well, and stood to their guns to the last.'[13] The Marathas were known for their speed of operation. The strength of their field artillery became clear during the confrontation between the British forces and the Marathas during the other battles of the Second Anglo–Maratha War. At the Battles of Assaye and Laswari in 1803, the British were shocked and horrified at the potential of the Maratha artillery.[14]

The EIC mobilized the largest army during the Third Anglo–Maratha War (1817–18). About 1,20,000 men, including 81,000 infantry were brought to the field. In contrast, during the Second Anglo–Maratha War, the EIC had mobilized only 55,000 infantry.[15] It appears that the superior artillery of the British was instrumental in its victory over the Marathas. Jagadish Narayan Sarkar asserts that the artillery pieces in the Peshwa's forts were ineffective, stating that the cannon pieces were cleaned only once a year.[16] This cannot be completely true because the Marathas knew the importance of artillery. We shall soon study a fine specimen of Maratha light artillery, which is still maintained in pristine condition. Let us however look at some extant guns.

The Marathas not only used firearms, but also manufactured

them. Baji Rao I established his own foundry in 1739. Several different types of cannons were manufactured. It is said that the cannons were named after gods and painted in a fantastic manner. Indore was the centre of the Holkar's dominion. At the Central Museum in Indore, 35 small and big cannons are preserved. Out of these, 7 cannons have a similar shape and weight, and most of the inscriptions on them are in Persian. On one heavy cannon, inscriptions are in Urdu and on another, in Hindi. S. Bhatt has described this in detail. Based on a letter that was written by Malhar Rao to Maharani Ahalyabai, it is known that four big cannons were sent from Delhi to Ahalyabai at Indore when the Marathas raided Delhi.[17] In 1857, several cannons were cast by Raja Holkar and were given to the rebels. A large number of Maratha cannons can be seen at the Central Museum in Chennai. A significant specimen is a cast iron cannon of Holkar that was captured during the Battle of Mehidpur (19 December 1817). Interestingly, the design of this cannon is unlike the typical European cast iron cannon.[18] Similarly, Pune also has a good collection of Maratha cannons. For example, the Regiment of the Artillery Association possesses light cast iron pieces showing an interesting elongated cascable design.[19] These pieces offer evidence of the ability of Indian states to manufacture cast iron cannons, keeping them in a serviceable and useful condition, however crude their designs were.

Unfortunately, not many pieces of Maratha field artillery are extant because the British melted most of the light bronze cannons, after their victories. Some of the captured Maratha light ordnance was transported to England, to be presented as war trophies. Therefore, some examples of the wonderful bronze cannons of the Marathas are available in England, such as one in the Rotunda Museum. A wonderful example of Maratha light cannon is available at the Royal Artillery Historical Trust collection. This has been called the Malhar Rao Howitzer. The British captured this howitzer at Kadi in Gujarat in 1802, just before the Second Anglo–Maratha War. The gun was one of the 58 pieces captured from the army led by Malhar Rao. The cannon has been described as a hybrid of a mortar and howitzer [see Figure 3.2(a)]. It could fire explosive shells in field battle like an howitzer and at higher trajectories like a mortar. The excellent construction of the carriage is to be noted. The intricate construction of the cannon and its mounting is a good example of the engineering skill of the Marathas. The rear view of the cannon [Figure 3.2(b)] gives us an idea about excellent engineering of the cannon. Notice particularly the plumbline, which ensured that the cannon was placed horizontally and therefore, accuracy of fire was ensured. The other tools that were carried with the cannon carriage can also be noted in Figure 3.2(b). Iron spikes found on the rear of the carriage trail helped in stabilizing the cannon [see Figure 3.2(b)]. During firing, these would have dug into the ground on recoil. This wonderful artillery piece clearly disproves the disparaging remarks made by some European observers that the Maratha gun carriages were clumsy. The Marathas manufactured excellent field artillery pieces, designed to ensure speed of movement during field battles.

When Holkar turned to Ranjit Singh (not to be confused with Maharaja Ranjit Singh of Punjab), the Raja of Bharatpur, for supply of money and arms, he was assigned the Dig Fort. However, with the fall of Dig on 23 December 1804, the remnants of Holkar's army took shelter in the Bharatpur Fort, constructed in 1732 by Raja Suraj Mal. Lake began the Siege of Bharatpur on 7 February 1805. One of the prime causes for his failure was an inadequate battering train at his disposal. During the first siege of the fort by the British in 1805, four abortive assaults cost 3,100 casualties. The fort was defended by a train of artillery manned by 8,000 persons. After this siege, a treaty was signed with the ruler of Bharatpur, that allowed peace to prevail for the next twenty years. The British came prepared the next time they laid the siege in 1825, after the death of Ranjit Singh. A large force was sent to Bharatpur under Lord Combermere, who brought with him 27,000 men, along with 154 artillery pieces. A breach was affected by bombardment from the artillery and by laying underground mines. The Bharatpur Fort was taken by assault on 18 December 1825. A cannon that was captured from Bharatpur during this campaign is now located in Fort William, in Calcutta (Figure 3.3). Inscriptions on the surface indicate that it was manufactured in 1819. It appears to have been used in action against the British in 1825. The name of this cannon is Samburan. It is a muzzle loading smoothbore made of brass alloy. The inscription on the surface indicates that it was manufactured

(a)

(b)

FIGURE 3.2: MARATHA LIGHT CANNON, MALHAR RAO HOWITZER, NOW IN THE ROYAL ARTILLERY HISTORICAL TRUST MUSEUM: (a) FULL VIEW AND (b) DETAILS (PHOTOGRAPHS, R.D. SMITH, COURTESY OF THE ROYAL ARTILLERY HISTORICAL TRUST).

FIGURE 3.3: CANNON CALLED SAMBURAN FROM BHARATPUR CAPTURED BY THE BRITISH IN 1825 AND NOW LOCATED AT FORT WILLIAM IN CALCUTTA.

under the supervision of one Nahar Singh, during the reign of Maharaja Prithvi Inder Sawai Jawahar Singh Bahadur of Bharatpur. There are several other cannons still present on the ramparts of Bharatpur Fort. Obviously, the cannon technology available to the Jats was not inferior to that of the British. However, the lack of cast iron cannon technology appears to have caused some disadvantage since costly copper alloys needed to be used.

THE CANNONS OF THE SIKHS

The Sikhs fought the Mughals and later, the British. In 1799, Ranjit Singh consolidated the small Sikh states into a strong unit and built a powerful kingdom. It has been said that the Sikhs did not implement a systematic and scientific method of warfare, but fought, keeping individual valour in mind. Although they did not invent any new weapons, they utilized the available weapons with deadly effect.[20] The early artillery of the Sikhs was limited in scope, as the *Sirdars* could not collect sufficient guns. Their early carriages and cannons were clumsy and of primitive design. A commentator called Forster mentions that 'the artillery of the Sikhs were awkwardly managed and its use ill-understood'.[21]

However, Maharaja Ranjit Singh realized the important role played by artillery in field warfare. He took great care to maintain a powerful artillery. It is interesting to note that in 1838 Lord Auckland presented Ranjit Singh with a battery of elaborately decorated cannons cast in Cossipore. Some of them were taken back after the Sikh Wars and they are now in the Armouries and Woolwich. Under Ranjit Singh, Sikh artillery was completely overhauled and was organized on the European pattern. We hear about some dignified and high-sounding names for cannons of the Sikhs: *Fateh Jung* (Victory in Battle), *Jang-i-Bijli* (Thunder of Battle), *Sher Dahan* (Roaring of Lion), etc. These large cannons were inscribed in Persian with the name of the gunfounder, the place and the year of manufacture. The *Fateh Jung* was one of the largest field guns of the Sikhs and shot projectiles weighing 39 pounds. It was cast either by Muhammad Hayat in 1824 (according to a Persian inscription) or by Sudha Singh, Suba Singh, and Gobind Singh in 1827 (according to a Punjabi inscription). It was depicted in an engraving in the *Illustrated London News* of 20 March 1847, resting on a massive split trail carriage with numerous reinforcing straps and thick studded wheels. N. Carleton comments that it was a massive construction with no dolphins or lifting rings visible and there is no visible backsight or foresight. Unfortunately, the present whereabouts of this cannon are unknown, although it is known that it was placed outside Government House in Calcutta in 1942.[22]

Ranjit Singh progressively assembled a massive artillery establishment. Between 1799 and 1808 the total number of his cannons, inclusive of all calibres, is estimated to have been between 35 and 40. By 1845, the Sikh army possessed about 250 cannons. Ranjit Singh initiated the manufacture of cannons in Punjab by setting up a factory in Lahore, in 1807. A foundry was established in 1807 at Amritsar, where gunpowder and fuses were also manufactured. In the same year, he set up two departments for handling *topkhana* (heavy cannons) and *topkhana khurd* (light cannons). The cannons were placed on specially prepared carriages of sissoo wood and carpenters were specially brought in from Delhi for their construction. A whole host of workshops grew around the foundries to satisfy the almost insatiable demand for high quality metalwork. The workmanship seen in Sikh artillery further testifies to the employment of a variety of skilled workmen to manufacture these pieces. In several cases, the carriages and limbers are made of padouk, a form of Burmese teak. The Maharaja clearly paid a lot of attention in obtaining materials from afar, for his artillery. By 1808, Ranjit Singh had acquired about 100 *shuturnals* and established another office under the *Daroga-i-Zamburkhana* (Superintendent of Swivels). Forty to fifty buffaloes were required to pull each heavy cannon. In order to obtain some idea of the Sikh heavy cannon, let us look at two examples from Patiala. The first is called Kurrah Khan. The original cannon was depicted in Smyth's Plans of Ordnance and this shows the way the cannon was mounted on top of the carriage. Another Sikh heavy cannon located at Qila Mubarak in Patiala possesses a muzzle shaped like a dragon. In 1810, Ranjit Singh created horse-drawn artillery. There is an interesting story that on 22 December 1810, Gopal Singh Zamadar brought two pieces of cannon drawn by horses and Maharaja Ranjit Singh immediately ordered that a separate branch of artillery be created. The horse-drawn artillery branch was inaugurated in 1811 under the supervision of Mir Mazher Ali Beg. Several light cannons of the Sikhs are seen in Patiala Palace and these have been described in detail by R. Balasubramaniam.[23]

Continuous expansion and modernization of the artillery branch occurred under Ranjit Singh. The workshops at Lahore, Amritsar, and Kotli Lorahan were expanded in 1813 and special craftsmen were invited from Delhi to manufacture cannons on the British pattern. In the same year, a new kind of cannon, a mortar called *gubarah*, was added to the artillery. With these improvements, the quantity and quality of cannons swelled and it has been reported that in 1821, Ranjit Singh possessed 200 cannons and 200 *zamburaks. Zamburaks* were swivel cannons mounted on tripods. With the capture of more forts, he was able to add another 64 cannons by 1823. By this time, there were two *derahs* (battalions) for large cannons and two for swivel cannons. The *Derah* Ilahi Baksh possessed 15 cannons and consisted of 395 men, while *Derah* Mazhar Ali Beg comprised of 6 cannons and 159 men. The number of guns swelled to 370 cannons and 370 *jinjals* (a type of swivel cannon) by 1831. The artillery was again re-organized and now consisted of four divisions. The *topkhana jinsi* (mixed batteries) consisted of *gavai* (bullocks-drawn), *phili* (elephant-driven), *shutari* (camel-drawn) and *habath* (howitzer section derived from French hobit cannons). The second division was the *topkhana aspi* (horse batteries). The third was the *zamburkhana* (swivel batteries). In addition to these divisions, a separate division was established for the exclusive use of the Maharaja, called *topkhana-i-mubarak* or *topkhana-i-khas*. This was further divided into *topkhana kalan* (heavy guns) and *topkhana khurd* (light guns). The condition of Ranjit Singh's artillery earned the admiration of Captain Burns, who commented that 'the guns were well cast and the carriages in good repair; they had been made in Lahore and cost him Rs. 1,000 each'.[24]

Gajnal and *hathnal* were swivel cannons carried on elephant back. The number of cannons in the royal armoury rose to 192 by 1838–9. Another 100 guns were located in different forts of the kingdom. The number of *zamburaks* were almost 500. W.L. McGregor witnessed a *Dussehra* parade, where he personally saw 500 camels loaded with swivel cannons.[25] Moreover, there were long duck-like guns in the possession of Ranjit Singh and these were called *bharmar* guns. By 1839, about 4,490 people were employed in the artillery department, for which the monthly expenses were about Rs. 33,346.

In order to further strengthen his firepower, Ranjit Singh purchased material from outside his kingdom. In 1835, he sent a mission to Calcutta to purchase 1,100 muskets and 500 pistols and in 1836, he acquired Rs. 40,000 worth of arms from the French. Such were the developments and acquisitions of Ranjit Singh that his artillery was on a par with the artillery strength of the EIC. Henry Fane commented that Ranjit Singh transformed his artillery and musketry to perfection, the latter being nearly as good as those of the EIC, with the advantage of being lighter.[26] In 1836, two English observers, MacNaughten and Osborne, witnessed Sikh artillery in action in the bombardment of Dinanagar. They commented that there was not much difference between the Sikh artillery and that of the British, except that the quality of the gunpowder was a little inferior, since it was produced in Indian factories. All the powder was manufactured in the state foundries at Lahore, Amritsar, Kotli Loharan, Kashmir, and Wazirabad. Ranjit Singh was quite proactive in introducing the latest technologies. Significant improvements were brought about in the sphere of ammunition. Innovations such as spherical cases and iron shrapnel were adopted. The noted engineer Lehna Singh Majithia was heavily involved not just in cannon manufacture, but also in the development of shrapnel shells (1831) and other ammunition types.

After the death of Ranjit Singh in 1839, deterioration set in the Sikh Army. However, the artillery establishment actually grew under the successors of Ranjit Singh. A huge supply depot was established at Busean, between Ferozepur and Ambala. The number of cannons under Ranjit Singh had been 192 and the artillery branch had employed 29,168 employees in 1839. The establishment grew to 232 cannons with 50,065 employees in 1843, under Maharaja Sher Singh. In the following year, Raja Hira Singh employed 50,805 employees to handle 282 cannons. The record of 1845 under Sirdar Jawahar Singh, notes that the number of employees had grown to 72,370, with a corresponding increase in the number of cannons to 381. The annual expense in this period increased from Rs. 382,088 in 1838, to Rs. 852,696 in 1845. The cannons mentioned above do not include the pieces under the various *jagirdars*. In fact, the increased quantum of artillery has been suggested to have had an harmful influence, in that it resulted in fiscal breakdown and the ultimate disintegration of the Sikh Kingdom.

The Sikhs employed fairly sophisticated cannon manufacturing technologies in the construction of their cannons. Ranjit Singh transformed the Sikh Army into a modern organization, based on the model of Napolean's army. Instructors and advisors were recruited from the former Maratha armies and from Europe. We hear of two influential generals, Jean Francois Allard and Jean Baptiste Ventura, who served in Napoleon's Army and were recruited by Ranjit Singh. Interestingly, another prominent military advisor, General Claude Auguste, worked closely with the Sikh engineers and they were able to revolutionize cannon manufacture and mass produce cannons along the lines of the EIC cannons.

Similar to the case of Maratha cannons being destroyed after battles with the British, most of the Sikh cannons were dismantled/ melted down after the British victory in the Anglo–Sikh Wars. The Cossipore Foundry was able to melt down captured artillery and used them to manufacture cannons for the EIC. About 256 guns were captured in the First Sikh War. These included a majority of brass cannons. There were also howitzers, mortars and iron guns. Guns in the field army not already captured were surrendered under the terms of the subsequent Treaty of Lahore (9 March 1846), in order to make further organized resistance impossible. However, it is clear the British had little idea of the true number of Sikh guns. The Sikhs still managed to mobilize over 100 cannons only two years later. On 3 March 1847, the captured guns were paraded with great ceremony in front of Government House in Calcutta. This was a carefully orchestrated public relations exercise designed to dispel rumours of defeat at the hands of the Sikhs and overawe other Indian states. Even though their final fate is still unclear, it seems that the majority of guns were melted down at the EIC's Cossipore Gun Foundry. A few probably remain in India and Pakistan, but further research is needed to account for all of them. A handful of the most ornate pieces were dispatched to Europe and presented to institutions and persons linked with the British campaign against the Sikhs. These became known as 'Sutlej Guns' after the campaign. A pair of cannon were even sent to Berlin and presented to Prince Waldemar of Prussia. The Sutlej Guns are distinct pieces, different from other Indian ordnance. They combined a modern, functional barrel design with a handsomely decorated block trail horse artillery carriage. The carriage design is supposed to have been based on the model of Congreve, who designed such carriages for the EIC. Despite the elaborate and highly decorative appearance, they were fully functional weapons that were captured in the heat of battle. In all, over twenty Sutlej Guns have survived, half of which are on their original carriages and many with limbers and gun tools.[27]

Four Sutlej cannons were taken to Britain by Governor-General Henry Hardinge. Two of these were presented to Queen Victoria and displayed at Windsor Castle in 1848. The Windsor guns were described in detail in an article in the *Illustrated London News*, dated October 1848. The *Illustrated London News* described the Windsor Guns as beautiful specimens of oriental art. In the early 1900s, they were moved from Windsor to the Tower of London, before being finally transferred to Woolwich in September 1927, to become catalogue objects II.273 and II.274.

The Sikh cannon now at Woolwich, which is catalogued as II.193, is a bronze 8.33-pounder (7 *seers*) of 4.1-inch calibre. It was probably cast in Lahore in the late eighteenth or early nineteenth century. This is one of several cannon produced between 1760 and 1825, based on the *Zamzamah* or Kim's gun, which was cast in Lahore in 1755–6. (In fact, most of the guns cast in Sind possessed similar designs.) It is a fine example of the Mughal casting tradition already prevalent in Punjab, before the Sikhs came to power. Similar pieces have been dated to as late as 1825. The barrel is decorated in the Mughal style with palmette borders and a vase and flowers motif. The button is decorated with a lotus flower and dolphins in the shape of *makaras* (mythical water demons). By the mid-1820s, ornate cannon of this type were being replaced by simpler, more streamlined types which were both lighter and easier to produce. The closest contemporary British equivalent, a brass 9-pounder, introduced in 1719, weighed almost 531 pounds less and was a foot shorter. At some point in its service life, probably in the 1820s, the barrel was remounted by Sikh engineers on a Napoleonic-style split trail carriage and aiming was improved by attaching a strap around the button connected to a capstan elevating screw.[28]

The cannon shown in Figure 3.4 is catalogued as II.274 in the Royal Artillery Museum. It is a 6-pounder (5 *seer*) and cast around 1838 in Lahore. Its calibre is 3.25-inches (i.e. 5.5-pounder). This cannon is one of the finest surviving examples and shows the exceptional technical and artistic expertise of the Sikh foundries and workshops. The barrel, produced in Lahore in 1838, is based on the British light 6-pounder; the carriage on the Bengal Artillery pattern introduced in 1823, but lavishly decorated with brass, copper, steel and pearl inlay. This cannon was almost certainly captured from Aliwal, where four guns attributed to the work of the prominent Sikh military engineer, Lehna Singh Majithia, were singled out for specific mention. It may have been made for the *Fauj-i-Khas*, the elite brigade of the Sikh Army. Commanded by his best French officers, using French drill and imperial flags and eagles, it was also known as the 'French Brigade' or the 'French Legion'.[29] The Sutlej Guns have many similar features in decoration, most notably the use of applied and inlaid copper, brass, and

FIGURE 3.4: HORSE DRAWN CANNON (*ASPI*) OF THE SIKH ARTILLERY, PRESENTLY IN THE COLLECTION OF THE ROYAL ARTILLERY HISTORICAL TRUST IN ENGLAND (CATALOGUE NO. II.274). IT WAS CAST AROUND 1838 IN LAHORE. (PHOTOGRAPH, R.D. SMITH, COURTESY OF THE ROYAL ARTILLERY HISTORICAL TRUST.)

steel with common decorative themes to the fittings. Some interesting inlay work on II.274 can be noted. Neil Carleton and Buck point to the excellent design of the port-fire cutters cast in the form of peacocks with fishtails. The excellent design of the trail of the carriage and the limber hooks cast as elephant heads deserve notice. Even small fittings such as lifting handles and the armrests on the gunners' seats, are cast in elaborate animal forms. None of the paired carriages are identical. There is variation throughout, from the general shape down to the smallest fittings, demonstrating that many craftsmen were involved. It is thought that the carriages are manufactured as part of preparations for the marriage of Prince Nau Nihal Singh in the same year. It was intended mostly for the *Fauj-i-Khas* and later assigned to a regular *aspi* brigade.

It is stated by Europeans that throughout Maharaja Ranjit Singh's reign, Sikh engineers had access to EIC patterns and workshops, as well as diplomatic gifts of cannon periodically. These accelerated artillery development to such an extent that by the late 1830s, Sikh artillery rivalled that of the EIC in both quantity and quality. However, the local ingenuity and the engineering ability of the Sikhs must be appreciated, in that they did not blindly copy the pieces but studied them carefully and adapted them to the local conditions.

Careful drawings of the captured Sikh cannons were made by Captain Ralph Smyth of the Bengal Artillery. The inscription that accompanied a set of twelve such cannons, ascribes their manufacture to 1838 and they were manufactured by Bagi Khan for General Kushal Singh. It has been stated that the design of these cannons is based on a Bengal Artillery horse cannon gifted to the Sikhs in 1831. The Punjabi engineers and craftsmen modified this piece of hardware to effect major changes in their foundries, producing ordnance in ever-increasing quantities. It must be appreciated that there are technical differences between the British and Sikh varieties, with the Sikh ones being slightly heavier in the barrel. This shows that the British gifts were not simply copied but that the designs were closely studied and adapted for Sikh usage.

There is this story of an interested British Captain (Ralph Smyth of the Bengal Artillery) who took careful measurements of the captured Sikh cannons. His illustrations and data are now proving crucial to our understanding of the Sikh artillery. He compiled technical information on all 203 brass cannon and 33 howitzers, 5 mortars and 11 iron guns. (Unfortunately, four guns were lost en route from the Punjab.) He identified 96 distinct types, took weights and measurements and drew plans of the barrels and elevations of the more interesting carriages and limbers. His data not only illustrates what these cannon looked like but enable us to make a direct comparison between Sikh artillery and its European counterparts. Far from being dominated by large and heavy cannon as stated in most contemporary accounts, the majority of guns he recorded were 6-pounders (almost 90 per cent of these of just one pattern). The other most numerous types were between 6-pounder and 12-pounder in size, then the most common sizes for field artillery and again dominated by only a few patterns.

An important observation by Carleton on the Sutlej Guns may be mentioned here. It was assumed that since Ranjit Singh had French military advisors, the barrels must have been French or based on French designs. However, the dimensions did not match and when Carleton examined Ralph Smyth's data on the

Type I, he found that the weight too did not match British examples. They were actually 5.5-pounders and not 6-pounders as previously thought and the proportion of gun metal to shot fired was slightly more than that used in British types (more like 116 lbs/1 lb shot fired instead of the ideal 112 lbs/1 lb). The clincher was discovering that the unconventional shot weights recorded by Smyth converted very neatly into *seer* weights, across the entire range of types captured during the First Sikh War. This also convinced Carleton that the Sikh guns were not slavish copies of European types, but produced to their own set of weights and measures. When Ralph Smyth compiled data on the Sikh guns around 1846–8, he recorded the width across the muzzle and base ring, length from muzzle to vent, as well as overall length and width of bore. Based on these data, Carleton compared the proportions of the piece (as we know, older guns tended to be about 3 calibres wide at the muzzle) and the length in calibres. This, Carlton proposes, gives an indicator of its relative efficiency. Carleton has used these diagnostic tools in the past, since cannon tended to become lighter and shorter over time as engineers realized that they could achieve the same result using less metal. The British aimed for an ideal of around 100 lbs or 1 cwt (112 lbs) per 1 lb shot fired. Thus, the barrel of a British bronze 6-pounder should be somewhere in the region of 600 to 672 lbs. Carleton claims that the most efficient Sikh pieces came close to achieving this by about 1838.

There are several other examples of Sikh horse drawn cannons located in England. These have been catalogued by Carleton. Another type of cannon captured by the British was the heavier Mughal type. An interesting example of Mughal-type Sikh cannon is presently located at Zeughaus in Berlin. This has been described by Carleton and Buck. Two such pieces were presented to Prince Waldemar of Prussia, by Henry Hardinge in 1848. One was dated to 1817 while the other to 1829 and called *Fateh Jang*. It mentions that it was cast in Lahore by Muhammad Hayat, under the supervision of Mian Qadir Bakhsh. These two engineers were instrumental in casting a large field cannon by the name *Fateh Jang*, in 1827. It was originally mounted on a three-wheeled Indian carriage based on Mughal design. However, the surface of the cannon was devoid of ornamentation and also there were no dolphins, clearly indicating the European influence in the manufacture of this cannon. Interestingly, one of the engineers, Mian Qadir Baksh, was provided a stipend by Ranjit Singh to study EIC workshops in Ludhiana. He later wrote a book in Persian titled *Mifta ul Qila*, on the subject. We have some Sikh cannons at Patiala. Another notable example is a large bronze cannon of the Sikhs, which was captured by the British after the Anglo–Sikh War and now located at Fort William in Calcutta. This is seen in Figure 3.5 and offers visual proof of the engineering excellence of the artillery of the *Khalsa* state. After analysing the guns, it seems that lack of artillery was not a critical factor that led to the subjugation of the Sikhs. An analysis of the large and light cannons of the Sikhs confirms that Indian engineering skills were much evident in the production of artillery in the period prior to the establishment of British power in the Indian subcontinent.

FIGURE 3.5: LARGE SIKH CANNON CAPTURED BY THE BRITISH AFTER THE ANGLO–SIKH WAR AND NOW LOCATED AT FORT WILLIAM IN CALCUTTA.

CONCLUSION

A critical analysis of the artillery of the Indian powers in the period prior to the upheaval in 1857 has been presented in this paper. The artillery of the major Indian states, like the Marathas and the Sikhs, were quite advanced as attested by available artillery pieces of these powers. Indians successfully adopted several European techniques with necessary changes to suit the local conditions. Hence, the military success of the British prior to 1857 was certainly not based on firepower superiority.

ACKNOWLEDGEMENTS

R. Balasubramaniam acknowledges the cooperation and permission of the Archaeological Survey of India and the Indian Army in the study of Indian cannons.

NOTES

1. H. A. Young, *The East India Company's Arsenals & Manufactories* (Oxford, 1937); see also http://www.brown.edu/Facilities/University_Library/collections/askb/beato/beato.html.
2. R.R. Brown, 'Taming the Tigers: An East India Company Gun from Museum Bronbeek, Arnhem', *JOS*, vol. 16 (2004), pp. 67–74.
3. Jos Gommans and D.H.A. Kolff, 'Introduction', in Gommans and Kolff (eds.), *Warfare and Weaponry in South Asia: 1000-1800 AD* (New Delhi: Oxford University Press, 2001), pp. 34–6.
4. Sidney Toy, *The Strongholds of India* (London, 1957), pp. 18–19, 33–4.
5. J. Deloche, 'Études sur les fortifications de l'Inde: III. La fortification hindoue dans le Sud de l'Inde (VIc-XVIIIc siècle)', *Bulletin de L'École Française d'Extrême-Orient*, vol. 88 (2001), pp. 77–134; 'Études sur les fortifications de l'Inde: IV. La fortification musulmane dans le Dekkan méridional (XVc-XVIIIc siècle)', *Bulletin de L'École Française d'Extrême-Orient*, vol. 89 (2002), pp. 39–106; 'Gunpowder Artillery and Military Architecture in South India (15th–18th Century)', *IJHS*, vol. 40 (2005), pp. 573–96.
6. *Selected Documents of Aurangzeb's Reign (1659–1706)*, ed. Yusuf Husain Khan (Hyderabad, 1958), pp. 90–1.
7. I.A. Khan, *Gunpowder and Firearms: Warfare in Medieval India* (New Delhi: Oxford University Press, 2004), pp. 91–127.
8. J. Deloche, *Senji (Gingi), ville fortifiée du pays tamoul* (Paris/Pondichery: EFEO, 2000), pp. 131–2, 225–9.
9. Kaushik Roy, 'Firepower-Centric Warfare in India and the Military Modernization of the Marathas: 1740-1818', *IJHS*, vol. 40 (2005), pp. 597–634; Edward Moore, *A Narrative of the Operations of Captain Little's Detachment of the Maratha Army* (London, 1794), pp. 66–8.

10. W. Egerton, *Illustrated Handbook of Indian Arms* (1880, rpt., Bangkok: White Orchid Press, 1986), p. 32.
11. R.G. Burton, 'Battles of the Deccan: Assaye', *JUSII*, vol. 20 (1891), p. 166.
12. *Wellington at War: 1794–1815: A Selection of His Wartime Letters* (ed. and Introduced by Antony Brett-James (London: Macmillan, 1961), p. 80.
13. *Wellington at War: 1794–1815*, p. 81.
14. R.G.S. Cooper and N.K. Wagle, 'Maratha Artillery: From Dabhoi to Assaye', *JOS*, vol. 7 (1995), pp. 58–78; N. Carleton and M. Buck, 'Guns of the Rajahs: Indian Artillery from the Mughals to the Sikhs', *JOS*, vol. 16 (2004), pp. 57–66.
15. Valentine Blacker, *Memoir of Operations of the British Army in India during the Maratha War of 1817, 1818 & 1819* (London: Black, Kingsbury, Parbury and Allen, 1821), p. 29.
16. Jagadish Narayan Sarkar, 'Limitations of the Art of War in Medieval India', *Journal of the Bihar Research Society*, vol. LIX (1973), p. 109.
17. Shashikant Bhatt, 'Inscriptions on the Cannons Conserved in Central Museum, Indore' (Translation of the original Hindi Article 'Kendriya Sangrahalaya Indore Mein Sarankshit Topoein Par Utkeern Lekh'), personal communication, 2006.
18. R. Kannan and R. Balasubramaniam, Documentation of the Cannons in the Government Museum Chennai (Madras) (Commissioner of Museums, Government Museum, Chennai, 2000), pp. 8–9.
19. S.K. Chatterji, *Vintage Guns of India* (New Delhi: Macmillan, 2001), pp. 69–75, 102-13.
20. G.N. Pant, *Studies in Indian Weapons and Warfare* (New Delhi: Army Educational Stores, 1970), pp. 181–211.
21. G. Forster, *A Journey from Bengal to England*, vol. 1 (London: R Fauldoer, 1798), pp. 332–3.
22. N. Carleton, personal communication, 2006; N.H.V. Symons, *The Story of the Government House* (Calcutta, 1935). See Chapter 3.
23. R. Balasubramaniam, *The Saga of Indian Cannons* (New Delhi: Aryan Books International, 2002).
24. A. Burns, *Travels into Bokhara*, vol. 1 (London, 1831), p. 59.
25. W.L. McGregor, *History of the Sikhs*, vol. 1 (London, 1846), pp. 240–3.
26. Henry Fane, *Five Years in India*, 2 vols. (London: Henry Colburn, 1842), vol. 1, pp. 159–65.
27. N. Carleton, http://www.sikhspectrum.com/112005/artillery_maharaja_ranjit_singh.htm.
28. Ibid.
29. Carleton and Buck, 'Guns of the Rajahs: Indian Artillery from the Mughals to the Sikhs', pp. 57–66.

CHAPTER 4

Delhi Before and After 1857

IQBAL HUSAIN

The British after the suppression of the 1857 revolt were not satisfied with the punishment inflicted on the rebels. Their wrath also fell on the monuments and other buildings including residential houses. Their destruction was allowed in the name of military operations and urban development. In this paper, an attempt is made to identify the buildings which existed just before the outbreak of the rebellion and to see how they were demolished afterwards. Efforts have also been made to identify the present locations where once these buildings existed. Most of the buildings chosen for the present study were located within the walled city then known as Shahjahanabad. Some buildings and gardens located near the walled city have also been included for the present paper as they were used both by the 'rebels' and the British forces as fortifications.

As is well known, the rebellion broke out in Delhi on 11 May 1857 when a number of rebel soldiers arrived from Meerut.[1] Soon British rule in the city disappeared and a rebel government was formed with an unwilling Bahadur Shah Zafar, the last Mughal Emperor, as nominal head. The British after having been driven out of the city with considerable loss of life and property, had taken shelter at Alipur, nearly 10 miles north of Delhi. From here they consolidated their scattered forces and, strengthened by fresh arrivals, subsequently launched a counter-offensive. The first important encounter between the two rival forces took place at Badli ki Sarai on the night of 8 June 1857. We know very little about the history of Badli ki Sarai. It was in all probability a Mughal *sarai* built some time in late seventeenth century. Like other *sarais*, it had a square building, with four towers, a courtyard, and a well in the middle. It had numerous little chambers for the use of the travellers, with loopholes opening to the outside.[2] The *sarai* was situated on the Delhi–Karnal highway[3] and had a very strong gate. After the battle the British forces destroyed the *sarai* as the rebels had made their fortifications there. The gate through which the Grand Trunk Road originally passed, now stands to remind us of the historical past.

Between 8 June and 17 June 1857, the rebels made a series of attempts to check the advance of the British forces.[4] In the process, Hindu Rao's *kothi*, originally built by Edward Colebrook, the Resident of Delhi and later on occupied by William Fraser until his murder in 1835, and subsequently bought and renovated by Hindu Rao Ghatke, suffered heavily. Hindu Rao was the brother of Baira Bai, the favourite wife of Daulat Rao Sindia. Hindu Rao shifted from Pune to Delhi and lived in this *kothi.* Hence, its earlier name (Rekka House) was forgotten and it became popular as Hindu Rao's *kothi.*[5] Due to continuous combat, Metcalfe House, *Edgah*, and the Flag Staff Tower suffered considerable destruction. The *Edgah* is also known as Kothi Jahan Numa Syed Ahmad Khan. It was built either in 1828 or in 1835. The crest of the northern part of the Ridge near the University of Delhi is occupied by a circular tower which originally surmounted a flag staff and is known as the Flag Staff Tower.[6]

The British forces led by Brigadier Wilson were not as strong numerically as the rebels but more disciplined and organized. Despite continuous attempts by the rebels to check the British advance towards the city, they could not succeed. Marching cautiously, the British forces descended from the northern Ridge, crossed the land which now has the vast campus of the University of Delhi, reaching the Qudasia Garden on the bank of river Jamuna and raised a strong battery there in the teeth of cannon fire from the rebels at Kashmir Gate and walls of the city. To counter rebel fire, the British forces entrenched themselves in the Qudasia Garden. The Qudasia Bagh had been built by Udham Bai, the favourite wife of Badshah Muhammad Shah (died 1748). When Syed Ahmad Khan compiled the *Asar-us Sanadid*, the Qudasia Bagh had a beautiful tower, a *baradari*, and a mosque. Its lofty western gateway still survives.[7] Being in the close proximity of Kashmir Gate, Qudasia Garden became very important from the military point of view. Its capture by the rebels could have lead to a complete rout of the British. Foreseeing the gravity of the situation, the British concentrated a large part of their forces here and put enormous pressure on the rebels. In this conflict the British emerged victorious but destroyed a large part of the garden to raise batteries and levelled the adjoining buildings of Kashmir Gate. The garden is now occupied by the Inter State Bus Terminal and tourist camp site. The gateway, the mosque and the pavilion survive.[8]

It would be observed that destruction of monuments and buildings took place both inside and outside Delhi during the progress of the war in 1857. Delhi city suffered heavily during 1857. The buildings that stood to 1850 may be recovered from the contemporary writings and a very interesting and important map of Shahjahanabad of 1850, published by Kraff and J. Malik of the University of Bonn in 1992.[9] A comparison of this map with that published by the Archaeological Survey of India (1969) indicates that a large number of buildings do not exist. Let us now discuss some of the buildings and *mohallas* that existed in the 1850s.

The Red Fort had a number of magnificent buildings and gardens. Built in 1650, it had a length of almost 6,000 m from wall to wall and is octagonal in shape.[10] Its walls are about 8 m high and 3.6 m wide with 27 towers, each 9 m in diameter. Originally, it had 13 gates: Delhi Gate, Rajghat Gate, Khizri Gate, Nigambodh Gate, Kehlaghat Gate, Lal Gate, Kashmir Gate, Badru Gate, Kabuli Gate, Pather Kali Gate, Lahori Darwaza (then not in use), Ajmeri Gate, and Turkman Gate. The Calcutta Gate was built by the British.[11]

If we look at the map of Shahjahanabad of 1850 and enter the Red Fort from Lahori Gate, we find that a garden had existed on the left side. A number of other unidentified buildings, a mosque, a *baradari*, *nazarat* (office), and *rath khana* existed there. Straight ahead from the Lahori Gate was a passage with vaults on both sides up to Chatta Gate. Just after crossing the Chatta Gate, we came to a vast courtyard on the right side of which stood the *Naz haveli.* In the middle of the courtyard was a tank connected with a canal connected with the Jamuna River. This canal also supplied water to several other parts of the city. To the right of the canal, there was Delhi Darwaza Bazar (facing the western side) and the Darwaza Nau Mahal (facing east). Further west of the Delhi Darwaza Bazar was the garden of Mirza Gauhar. And further east of the Darwaza Nau Mahal was the Mina Bazar. On the eastern side of the courtyard and the tank was the Gate of Naqqar Khana which opened on the vast courtyard called as Chowk Diwan-i Am. The Diwan-i Am stood on the east of the courtyard.[12] Adjacent to it on the eastern side lay Rang Mahal or Imtiyaz Mahal, also known as Musamman Burj,[13] a bath, and other apartments. To the left of Rang Mahal was an extensive courtyard. Its western part had a gate which opened on to another courtyard that in turn lead to the gate of the Jawahar Khana (jewellery house) on the left.[14] On going further left to the Jawahar Khana was an extensive garden and in its eastern corner stood the Moti Masjid. In the middle of the garden was situated the Zafar Mahal or Jal Mahal. The garden known as Hayat Bagh had been built by Muhammad Shah in 1742. In the middle of the garden was built a tank of red sandstone with a marble platform.[15] On the right side and almost in the middle of the Chowk Diwan-i Am was a gate leading to Deorhi Hawa Sira (spelt *Diwar-i Hawa Sira* in the Bonn publication of the map of Shahjahanabad 1850) which was connected to the west with the courtyard of Nau Mahal. Nau Mahal or nine palaces were the residence of the princes. They lived in abject poverty and cried from the roof tops for help.[16] On the left side of the Chowk Diwan-i Am, was a small mosque whose door opened on to the Mahtab Bagh lying in neglect and close to it on the south and east were two other gardens. On the extreme left were stables and a passage to the Salimgarh Road leading to Salimgarh Fort. On the right side of Rang Mahal and Darya Mahal was situated Chota Rang Mahal. Its construction was originally started by Islam Shah, the son of Sher Shah around 1546, who died before its completion. Murtaza Khan, a noble of Akbar, built a bridge before the gate of the fort, which then was called Noorgarh.[17] Between the Rang Mahal and the Chota Rang Mahal stood Darya Mahal. Just outside the fort walls on the right hand side was situated an extensive garden known as Buland Bagh Badshahi and further away was a *dharamshala*, Mohalla Mahilahi on the corner of which stood the *haveli* of Ghulam Jilani which extended up to the Rajghat Gate.[18]

A look at Delhi Guide Map of 1969 indicates that the Red Fort buildings and gardens have been brutally vandalized over the years. The northern and southern parts of the fort, which once had extensive gardens and residential houses, were destroyed by the British under the pretext of military exigencies.[19] Fergusson tells us that all the courts of the palace were destroyed for the construction of the British barracks; he angrily criticized those who had carried out this fearful piece of vandalism. Today, in the Red Fort only the entrance hall, the *naubat khana*, the Diwan-i Am, Diwan-i Khas, Rang Mahal, Moti Masjid, Saman Burj and the bath survive. The British soldiers constructed barracks in the middle of the fort and these were in use of the Indian Army until a few years ago. The northern and southern parts had also been under the military occupation.[20] The barracks (as they stood till recently) were built in Hayat Baksh Bagh. Syed Ahmad Khan tells us that once there was an attractive garden there. It had several beautiful structures. In the middle of the garden, there was a tank of 60 × 60 yards with 49 fountainheads with silver plates. Around the tank were another 112 fountainheads which functioned all day and night due to six wide canals made of red sandstone. None of these structures exist any more.[21]

Let us now have a look at Shahjahanabad. Starting from the Red Fort and descending from Lahori Gate, there were two roads. Going by the right hand road, there were a number of buildings on the right side of it, with an extensive garden. On the left corner stood a mosque and on the right hand side of the mosque was the *mohalla* known as *chob farosh* (iron nail sellers' locality). And further right existed a *dharamshala* and other residential houses. Further right to the *dharamshala* stood a *pani chakki* (water mill) which was connected with the Jamuna, through a canal from Nigambodh Ghat. To the west of it stood a mosque, and further west another mosque known as the Kuan Wali Masjid, and further west a number of residential houses, *kucha kaghzi mohalla*, *chapa khana*, and north of the *chapa khana* the *haveli* of Mansur Ali Khan (Safdar Jang, the founder of Awadh Nawabi). Further right in the easterly direction there were residential buildings, traditional baths, and the magazine. Last came a very large garden with a graveyard. Most of these buildings have vanished.[22] The reason for such a large scale disappearance of buildings is ascribed to the introduction of the railway line which even now passes through this area. In place of the gardens and post offices stand the General Post Office, the railway yard, the Delhi Junction Railway Station, and its vast complex of buildings. The railway yard was used by the army units stationed in the Red Fort.

The left side of the road from the Lahori Gate which connected Chandni Chowk did not have many buildings. It was said that the street from Lahori Gate to Chandni Chowk was 36 m wide and 1,368 m long. Chandni Chowk, also known as Lahori Bazar, had been built by Jahanara Begum, daughter of Shah Jahan, around 1648–50. In the middle of the chowk flowed the canal built by Ali Mardan Khan with rows of trees on both sides. The canal has been filled.[23] Chandni Chowk was built on an octagonal plan. Around it were constructed beautiful shops.[24] The bazaar had attained the position of an international shopping centre (besides being a centre for social and cultural activities) when Nadir Shah invaded India.[25]

On the left side of the Lahori Gate stood the Sunahari Masjid built by Javed Khan, the eunuch of Muhammad Shah.[26] Left of this mosque was an open space, a big water tank called Chashma Lal Diggi, and beyond that stood the building of Syed Bhore Shah. Going further west from the cross-road leading to Chandni Chowk, there was a canal in the middle of the street leading to Chandni Chowk. Some of the important buildings on the right side of the road were a mosque, Kothi Ali Khan, Kocha Mehjabin, a number of other buildings and gardens. Then came the *kothi* and garden of Begum Samru. In the middle of the garden there were some rooms. The garden had a gate opening on the main road of Chandni Chowk known as Darwaza Begum Samru. Further west were Kucha Munna Lal, a *dharamshala*, Kucha Kirki and Kucha Manik Chand. Most of the buildings and gardens have vanished and a few remain but under new names. It must be admitted that most of the buildings in this area were not destroyed by the British. The rebels, making defensive preparations to save the city, razed some of the buildings and gardens. And the rebel soldiers took position in the Chandni Chowk and there they fought a fierce hand to hand battle with the forces of the EIC. Yet many other buildings later faced the wrath of the British on the suspicion of providing defensive positions to the rebel soldiery.[27]

Soon after entering the Chandni Chowk from the Lahori Gate side, there were several buildings, an elephant stable, Kucha Bulaqi Begum, Haveli Salatin, Kucha Dharamsala, Kucha Chawdi,

Kamra (room) of Garden Sahib, Gulab Rai Mir Chandar, Kucha Latu Shah and further west to it was the Chabutra Kotwali[28] and also a *madrasa*. A little above the Chabutra Kotwali on the west stood Sunahari Masjid built by Raushan-ud-Daulah. Further west were buildings like Shish Mahal, Kucha Hakim, Katra Ashrafi, etc. And on the extreme west stood the Fatehpuri Mosque and on its left across the road was *Tawaif Kucha*.[29] There were some more buildings on the left side of Chandni Chowk extending up to the northern gate of Jama Masjid.

In sum, numerous buildings existed between the Red Fort and Jama Masjid. The main road linking the mosque and the fort emanated from the Delhi Darwaza, which was frequently used, as the Lahori Darwaza was closed. In front of the Delhi Darwaza was an open space. The road to Jama Masjid passed through an octagonal crossing. To its right side were Kucha Mirza Hakim Beg, and a little towards the west existed Kucha Bulaqi Begum and the palace of Nawab of Jhajjar. North of the road were buildings like Imambaras, Thakur Darwaza, Bagh Kolin and a little above that, the *katra dhobi* (washermen's quarters), adjacent to which stood the Sarmast Khan ka Katra. On the left side of the octagonal chowk was the Gate of Khan-i Dauran leading to the *haveli* Khan-i Dauran, and a little above the *haveli* to the west stood a number of buildings. Most of the buildings on both sides of the road have now disappeared. The British after recapturing Delhi in September 1857 destroyed most of the buildings (with a few exceptions like the *dargah* of Khwaja Kalimuddin Chisthi) and converted the urban landscape into an expanse of waste land. Later Edward Park was built on the destroyed structure, which has since changed its name to Subhas Park. It is in this area where now stands the mausoleum of Maulana Abul Kalam Azad and the markets.[30] The destruction of historical buildings also took place around Turkman Gate and Ajmeri Gate which were centres of resistance against the British. The list includes Haveli Khairati, Ganj Mir Khan near Turkman Gate, and Kucha Mir Khan and Haveli Qamruddin Khan near Ajmeri Gate.

A populous city full of architectural marvels was vandalized by a 'civilized' nation. The time has come not only to make a detailed study of Delhi but also of Lucknow, Bareilly, Kanpur, Jhansi, and Allahabad to find out how many historical buildings suffered during and after the 1857 Uprising.

NOTES

1. Abdul Latif, *1857 ka Tarikh-i Roznamcha*, ed. K.A. Nizami (Delhi, 1958), p. 55.
2. G.W. Forrest, *A History of the Indian Mutiny*, vol. 1 (London: William Blackwood and Sons, 1904), pp. 71–2.
3. Y.D. Sharma, *Delhi and its Neighbourhood* (Delhi, 1982), p. 138; H.C. Fanshawe, *Shahjahan's Delhi: Past and Present* (n.d., rpt., Delhi, 1978), p. 78; Forrest, *History of the Indian Mutiny*, p. 78; Reverand J. Cave Brown, *The Punjab and Delhi in 1857*, vol. 1 (n.d., rpt., Delhi, 1970), p. 320.
4. T. Metcalfe, *Two Narratives of the Mutiny in India* (n.d., rpt., Delhi), pp. 120–1, 124.
5. T.W. Beal, *Oriental Biographical Dictionary* (n.d., rpt., Delhi, 1971), p. 166; *Poona Residency Correspondence*, vol. 14, *Daulat Rao Sindia's Affairs*, ed. Jadunath Sarkar (Bombay, 1951), p. 253; Percival Spear, *Delhi, Its Monuments and History*, updated and annotated by N. Gupta and Sykes (Delhi, 1994), pp. 18–19; Forrest, *History of the Indian Mutiny*, pp. 78–9.
6. Spear, *Delhi and its Monuments*, pp. 134–5; H.C. Fanshawe, *Shahjahan's Delhi: Past and Present* (n.d., rpt., Delhi, 1979), pp. 77–8, 82, 123; Forrest, *History of the Indian Mutiny*, pp. 82–3; Syed Ahmad Khan, *Asar-us Sanadid* (n.d., Delhi), p. 348.
7. Khan, *Asar-us Sanadid*, p. 348; Forrest, *History of the Indian Mutiny*, pp. 87–8.
8. Spear, *Delhi, Its Monuments and History*, p. 16.
9. I am grateful to J. Malik, University of Bonn for providing this map. This map is hereafter cited as Map of Shahjahanabad 1850.
10. Bernier identifies this as semi-circular. Bernier, *Travels in the Mughal Empire*, ed. V.A. Smith (Delhi: E.A. Constable, 1983), p. 241.
11. Khan, *Asar-us Sanadid*, p. 133.
12. Map of Shahjahanabad 1850; James Fergusson, *History of Indian and Eastern Architecture* (n.d., rpt., Delhi, 1967), pp. 310–11.
13. Khan, *Asar-us Sanadid*, p. 108.
14. Map of Shahjahanabad 1850; Fergusson, *Indian and Eastern Architecture*, p. 311.
15. Khan, *Asar-us Sanadid*, pp. 350–1.
16. Syed Ahmad Khan, *Sirat-i Faridia* (Agra, 1896), pp. 23–4.
17. Khan, *Asar-us Sanadid*, pp. 96, 107.
18. Syed Ahmad Khan identifies it as *Khas Mahal* or *Chota Mahal*. Khan, *Asar-us Sanadid*, p. 107.
19. Map of Shahjahanabad, 1850.
20. Fergusson, *Indian and Eastern Architecture*, p. 312.
21. Ibid., pp. 312–13.

22. Ibid., Khan, *Asar-us Sanadid*, p. 124; Fanshawe, *Shahjahan's Delhi*, p. 23; Map of Shahjahanabad, 1850.
23. Map of Shajahanabad, 1850; Bashiruddin, *Waqiat-i Darul Hakumat Dilli* (Delhi, 1919), p. 96.
24. Delhi Guide Map, 1969; Khan, *Asar-us Sanadid*, p. 314.
25. Bashiruddin says that it was built in CE 1600. See *Waqiat-i Darul Hakumat Dilli*, p. 96.
26. *Dargah Quli Khan, Muraqqa-i Delhi*, ed. Nurul Hasan Ansari (Delhi, 1982), pp. 1320–33.
27. Khan, *Asar-us Sanadid*, pp. 133–5, 335. There existed another Sunahiri Masjid near the Chabutra Kotwali built by Raushan-ud-Daulah Zafar Khan, a noble of Muhammad Shah.
28. Lord Roberts, *Forty One Years in India: From Subaltern to the Commander-in-Chief* (London), pp. 246–7; James Leasor, *The Red Fort: An Account of the Siege of Delhi in 1857* (1956), pp. 336–8.
29. Khan, *Asar-us Sanadid*, p. 709.
30. Map of Shahjahanabad, 1857; Khan, *Asar-us Sanadid*, pp. 133, 709; Delhi Guide Map 1969.

CHAPTER 5

Mutiny, Rumour, and Gun Runners of Calcutta: A Journey Back to 1857

ANASUA DATTA

1 Chowringhee Road, is the present address of the East India Arms Company. The present proprietor, Ananta Kumar Biswas, now over eighty years, ushers me into his old house near Shyambazar (a locality in Calcutta). His big bright eyes lit up, he greets me with a smile. A deep resonating voice gets into the mood of *adda* and his copper complexioned battle worn face looks excited as he unwinds into an anecdote about the history of 'natives' entering the arms trade during the Company Raj. He narrates, 'The Biswas family, originally from village Nasibpur, district Hugli, in 1840 initially got involved with the gunpowder trade which graduated into arms! By, profession this family was of farmers.' The story goes that with only 10 *annas* in the pocket, Krishna Chandra Biswas and his elder brother D.N. Biswas walked all the way to Calcutta from their ancestral village. Once in the city, a neighbour got it into their minds that if they could appease the First Lady of the Company, the chances of the Governor-General taking notice of these two village bumpkins would become bright. And he could possibly offer them their wish.

Ananta Kumar Biswas failed to recollect the exact date as well as the name of the Governor-General during whose tenure this particular incident had taken place. He admits that his ancestors K.C. Biswas and D.N. Biswas did not maintain any personal diary related to the events or to significant dates in their lives and business. Whatever is available is in the form of anecdotes and stories that have survived because of the oral tradition that has been handed down in the Biswas family. If we consider this event to have taken place approximately ten years from the date of the establishment of their concern, then we can surmise that the Governor-General was Lord William Bentinck. As luck would have it, the Biswas siblings greeted the First Lady with a simple bouquet of flowers at the Fort William rampart when she took her daily morning walks! She was moved and impressed by the gesture and prevailed on her husband to offer the Biswas brothers work as launderers of army uniforms in Fort William. With this modest beginning the Biswas brothers felt confident to venture into the trade of gunpowder and arms when the EIC administration allowed Indians to do so.

THE GUN DEALERS OF BRITISH BENGAL

This story of the rise of an Indian family in the firearms business in the heart of Calcutta is indeed remarkable. Initially, the Biswas brothers imported gunpowder and muzzle loader guns from England. In those days no letter of credit was required by the importers. Faith and belief in the parties were the foundation of such trade. The exporter received his payment after his consignment was sold by the importer. As was the norm of such times, a 'letter of recommendation' from the Governor-General was sufficient to establish a business in arms trade. In 1840, the Biswas brothers named their establishment D.N. Biswas & Company and their office address was 2 Hare Street, Calcutta. Unfortunately, at a later date the younger Krishna Chandra broke away from his elder sibling to start his own enterprise, K.C. Biswas & Company at 1 Chowringhee Road. This company changed its name again, to East India Arms Company, some time during the Second World War.[1]

The story of Indians venturing into the gunpowder and arms trade in the 1830s also includes the Daw family, inhabitants of Kotolpur village in Bankura district. They belonged to the *Gandhobanik* subcaste of traders who knew the art of making gunpowder with a mixture of sulphur, saltpetre, and charcoal. Nrisingha Daw started a modest establishment in Rishra along the Hugli (Ganga) and had access to the settlements of the Portuguese (Chinsurah), French (Chandannagar), and Dutch (Srirampur).[2] His son Narahari and grandsons Sibnarayan and Madhusudan migrated to Calcutta in 1835. Sibnarayan's third son Narasingha Chandra Daw managed to get the Governor-General's

'Letter of Recommendation' to start his fire arms shop named N.C. Daw & Company at 56–57 China Bazar Street. This piece of history was narrated to me by Samarendranath Daw in his silken voice. Being the present owner of N.C. Daw & Company at 9 B.B.D. Bag East, he is proudly reminiscent of the bygone era and these facts are corroborated by his nephew Alokekumar Daw of A.T. Daw & Company located at 2 Lenin Sarani.[3]

In those pre-'Mutiny' days along with the spread and establishment of business and commercial interest, the British traders worked overtime with the ulterior motive of acquiring territorial supremacy. In the process, the EIC was also careful to get the backing of the influential Indian gentry. In 1793, Governor-General Lord Cornwallis proclaimed the Permanent Settlement Act, creating an alliance with 'new zamindars' and 'jotedars'. Some of the older zamindars fell in with the EIC's scheme of things and compromised to retain their status. During the Santhal Rebellion of 1855 and the general rebellion of 1857, this new class of EIC's allies came out openly for the British. It is chronicled that the Burdwan Maharaja, Mahatab Chand, permitted the EIC army to use the roads in his territory. He also supported the British forces with elephants and bullock carts. In addition, he also provided cavalry and provisions to the EIC troops during the Mutiny of 1857.[4]

The other set of powerful elements in the eighteenth-century politico-economic scenario were the 'native princes'. The EIC maintained diplomatic relationships with them by posting its political agents or Residents at the respective *durbars*. The EIC's expansionism was expressed vigorously, especially through Lord Wellesley's policy of Subsidiary Alliance (1798–1805) and Lord Dalhousie's Forward Policies (1841–57). The consequences of these policies and alliances were felt during the revolt of 1857. It has been found that the territories under direct EIC rule were harder hit than in those under indirect rule or where the EIC had less territorial interest. The rulers of Gwalior, Hyderabad, Patiala, and Tripura, who were not under direct EIC rule, extended their hands to the British to check the uprising. Nevertheless, the Mutiny was the final nail in the EIC coffin and a new approach was initiated in the relationship with Indian princes by the British Crown.[5]

The Crown's representatives in India were prone to give a taste of their omnipotent power to the 'native' princes, but at the same time they were also keen to make these 'true representatives of Indian tradition and true leaders of Indian people' their allies. As a result, the 'true leaders' were honoured in the imperial *durbar*. F.L. Halliday in his *Annual Report of the Police Administration of the Town of Calcutta and Its Suburbs* noted that instructions had been given to the police on the occasion of the reception of the Maharaja of Gwalior at Government House. A list of roads would remain closed for public thoroughfares from 3 p.m. to 5.30 p.m. No carriage would be allowed to stand on the streets except those belonging to parties attending the *durbar*.[6] Mahatab Chand Rai of Burdwan had already been honoured with the title of 'Maharajadhiraj Bahadur' on 30 August 1833 by Governor-General Bentinck. This probably explains the Burdwan ruler's loyalty during the stormy days of 1857. As a reward for active loyalty during 1857–8, Queen Victoria granted permission to Mahatab Chand and his successors to keep his own contingent of armed sepoys. He was honoured with a 13-gun salute in the Grand Imperial Durbar of 1877.[7]

The fate of some leading families of Calcutta was also inseparably linked with the increasing power and authority of the EIC in socio-economic and political scenario from the first half of the nineteenth century. Certain families loyal to the Mughals had no scruples in changing their allegiance to the British in order to flow with the tide. Among them was Raja Nabakrishna Deb, his nephew Raja Radhakanta Deb of Shobhabazar, Raja Tarakhnath Kanungo of Dinajpur, and Radha Govinda Singh of Kandigram in Murshidabad. In fact, Raja Nabakrishna Deb acted as a political agent of the EIC and had stood by its side during the significant years of 1756–67.[8] Raja Radhakanta Deb received Queen's honour in 1859. The Mughal authority of Delhi had honoured Sukhdeb of Dinajpur family with the title of 'Raja' due to his efficiency in administration. The same tradition was followed by the EIC and the title of 'Maharaja Bahadur' was to be bestowed on Tarakhnath of the Dinajpur family for its support during the Mutiny, the Bhutan War, and the Santal disturbances, but the papers were lost on the way to Calcutta.

Apart from traditional bania groups like Seths, Basaks, and Dhooratiyas (who used to take part in salt auctions) merchant families like the Palchowdhuris of Ranaghat and the Deys of Srirampur[9] and some *subarnabanik* families also profited from their linkages with Portuguese, Dutch, French, and British as purveyors of goods, lenders and changers of money, and as go-betweens. Among them were the Malliks of Sinduria Patti, the Malliks of Pathuriaghata and Chorbagan, and the Roy family of Posta.[10] Some of them started to invest their profits from commercial transactions in land, and vice versa. They represented a group of urban zamindars. Charbagan's Mallik family was praised for its respect and loyalty to the British Crown during the coronation of George V. They organized *kirtans* in their household temple and offered prayers for the well-being of the new emperor. A grand Imperial *Durbar* was held on 1 January 1877 in the city of Calcutta to honour Queen Victoria. She was bestowed with the title of *Bharateswari*. The Governor-General presented a *sanad* of honour to Rajendra Mallik. In 1878, Lord Lytton venerated him with the title of Raja Bahadur for his generosity and strength of character. The Raj permitted these families to keep armed retainers and freed them from the provisions of Arms Act Regulations.[11]

Reputed Europeans, 'English Nabobs', high-ranking British bureaucrats and officials, new Indian zamindars, local rajas, and compradors formed a sizeable portion among the clientele of the Indian gun dealers. These aristocrats within their own concept of space tried to utilize their romantic attachment to traditional ways and means through which their power and status could be projected. Many zamindars, and princes saw themselves as successors of the Mughals, and adopted spectacular forms of hunting, popular among the Mughals, as a distinct way of displaying their power, status, and prestige. Their European brothers followed suit. The European hunters followed the same paternalistic attitude in colonial India as they did in their own country, of defending the lower orders from dangerous beasts. So, hunting provided a common base of interaction for European military officials, civilians, and local aristocrats. It also served as a form of recreation for both the sahibs and their Indian counterparts. The British deliberately used hunting as a shared enthusiasm to build a bridge with the Indian aristocracy. While the English 'Nabobs' were adopting the hunting tradition of the Indian aristocrats, their Indian counterparts were also keen to gain proficiency in 'the more distinctively British hunting sports'. Though before 1800 European elites took part in the hunting session of the Indian princes as mere spectators; their role gradually changed to active participation. Joint hunting sessions became a regular feature. For hunting, muzzle loading guns, rifles, and shot guns were used. After 1857, the British authorities tended to regularize their relationship with the princely states and Indian aristocrats, the main proxy of their power. Although Lord Dalhousie's 'Forward Policy' ousted the Nawab of Awadh from power in 1856 and he was sent to Calcutta, the 'great elephant borne hunts' of Awadh were emulated with enthusiasm by the British. Daniel Johnson graphically describes the fireworks of the 'Great Hunt' practised by the Nawab of Awadh. He used to take 40 to 50 double barrel guns, besides a number of single-barrel long guns, rifle and pistols out to the hunt.[12] British control over every sphere of Indian life was increased and regularized from 1870 onwards. The British policy makers were inclined towards reclamations of forest lands as these were now considered to be rich revenue yielding areas. The motive to maximize revenue brought the white rulers into direct conflict with wild animals which make *shikar* more important than before. Viceroys Ripon, Dufferin, Curzon, and Minto were also seem to have taken part in 'Great Hunts'.[13]

When N.C. Daw and D.N. Biswas started their business, muzzle-loading guns were in great demand. The guns, the spare parts, and the gunpowder were imported from Britain, Belgium, and Germany. The foreign companies who supplied the Indian arms sellers were Holland & Holland, C. Pavy & Sons, C.G. Bonehill & Company of England, Webley & Scott Company and Smith & Wesson's of U.S.A., Bernadelli of Italy and Belgium's Jenson Fills & Company.[14] The Paradox of Holland & Holland Company and Wesley Richard's Explora were well-known shotguns. The Maharaja of Cooch Behar used .465 Cordite Rifle on his *shikar* expeditions.[15]

Meanwhile, the second son of N.C. Daw, Asutosh Daw, started his own business. He started his career as an employee of an English shop owner at 40 Chandni Chowk. This shop used to sell saddles and all kinds of items required by a horse rider. Before leaving this country the owner handed over his shop to Asutosh Daw. It was this English owner who had also procured permission for his business in guns. During Christmas and New Year a large number of Europeans clients from different parts of the country crowded these shops. These shops also catered to the 'native' aristocrats like the maharajas of Burdwan, Cooch Behar, Tripura, Gobardanga, Jhargram and others from inside and outside Bengal.[16]

Mention must be made of indigenous Mungher guns and the guns manufactured at Ramnagar. It is difficult to find out the exact date when gun manufacture began in Mungher, but during Siraj-ud-daullah and Clive's tenure, Mungher was already an indigenous arms-producing centre. The Maharaja of Ramnagar had in his possession single-barrelled breech-loading rifles presented to him by the Duke of Brabant in 1890. Prior to this gift, a percussion elephant rifle (dated 1850), and a Belgian Pin Fire Sporting Rifle had been presented to him by the Duke in 1865. A number of double-barrelled hammer rifles possessed by the royal family of Ramnagar has the tag, 'Made in Ramnagar'. The Ramnagar royal family had guns from Thomas Bland & Sons of 430, West Strand, London.[17]

During the early nineteenth century, Indian manufactured guns had became dated in comparison to the European flintlock guns. In spite of this not all the indigenous firearms were crudely made. Some were costly pieces of craftsmanship, often gifts from one ruler to another, or part of the personal ornament of a raja. The barrels could be chiselled with arabesques and the muzzles adorned with animal heads. Gold and silver decorations were applied to the breech and lock which were often studded with rubies and emeralds. The stocks were either inlaid with enamel plaque or painted with hunting scenes or *nautch* girls. In course of time other indigenous centres manufacturing double-barrel guns also emerged in Tawai, Manipur, Gauhati, and other places.[18]

However, the Indian firearm businessmen faced direct competition from foreign companies. As early as 1793 a left-handed gun is advertised by Peter Augier, Cutler and Armorer, Arlington & Company, of Number 51, Cossitollah, 3B, Tank Square, Calcutta. Messrs R.B. Rodda and Company of Birmingham, manufacturers of huge elephant guns, had already established a branch in Calcutta in 1830, at Dalhousie Square. In 1900 they shifted their business to 2 Wellesley Place.[19] Another advertisement for various firearm products including guns, rifles, and pistols appeared in the *Bengal Harkaru* and the *India Gazette* on 20 May 1857. The advertisement contained the name of the makers (described as first-rate) as well as the prices (publicized as moderate) of the respective products. It spoke of Samuel Colt's revolvers, a double-barrel Minie Rifle by T.K Baker with a bore of 18 inches, with apparatus comprising of powder flash, bullet mould, cleaning rod, extra nipples, nipple wrench, turnscrew and woollen cover. The cost came to about Rs 575. The advertisement also mentioned a double-barrel self-priming gun by Charles Smith of King William Street, London in a mahogany box and all the apparatus with a price of about Rs 400. In addition, Monte Christo guns and pistols by Barnes & Company, London were also available for sale. The pistol was described as 23 inches barrel length in an oak case, complete with cleaning rod, oil bottle, and turnscrew. The price came to about Rs 125.[20] Various Judicial Proceedings of 1857–8 name the establishment of Messrs Manton & Company, of 13 Old Court House Street. Manton often came out with regular advertisements of their products in *Bengal Harkaru* and *India Gazette*. It had a shooting gallery at 6, Cossitollah. The advertisements between 1857–8 also featured the name of Army & Navy Cooperative Society Limited.

The *Annual Reports of the Police Administration of Town of Calcutta and its Suburbs* by F.L. Halliday, Commissioner of Police, Calcutta (for the years 1907, 1908, and 1910) provide the names of following gun dealers: Messrs Manton & Company, R.B. Rodda & Company, Walter Locke & Company, Lyon & Lyon Company, A. Hartman & Company, Manager, Army & Navy Cooperative Society Limited. Among the indigenous dealers were Messrs N.C. Daw & Company, D.N. Biswas & Company, K.C. Biswas & Company, A.T. Daw & Company, Coondoo & Company, and N.C. Dutt & Company.[21] They are mentioned in connection with the statement of arms and ammunitions imported by sea during the year 1909 by each dealer of the town of Calcutta.

A magazine for the reception of gunpowder from vessels proceeding up the river, was erected at Mayapur. On 18 July 1801, Fort William ordered that all powder should be landed at Mayapur instead of Achipur from 1 June 1803.[22] On May 1850, the Collector of Customs at Calcutta informed Messrs Manton & Company of this. Messrs Manton & Company had stakes in the

Howrah Magazine and appealed to the Board of Customs for a compensation of Rs 1,900. The amount was subsequently settled at Rs 1,000.[23]

Meanwhile, under the initiative of the EIC, gun manufacturing began at Cossipore near Calcutta in 1801. The first gun was manufactured in Gun Carriage Agency, Cossipore. There was also a small arms factory at DumDum.[24] The ordnance factories in India mainly manufactured small brass guns till the 1840s. Iron guns with shot and shell were mostly imported from Britain. The factories of South Asia merely undertook their repair. The entire process was time-consuming and costly. Moreover, supply depended on 'secure sea-lines of communications'. After the assault on Delhi in 1857, the British realized the utmost importance of artillery in siege warfare. As a result, the post-Mutiny period witnessed a corresponding emphasis on improving the production facilities for these weapon systems in India.[25]

1857 MUTINY, PANIC, AND THE GUN DEALERS OF CALCUTTA

The price of a gun reached its height and the Calcutta gun dealers made huge profits during the 1857 Mutiny. All Englishmen and 'native' Christians were anxious to possess guns for their own defence. Calcutta was gripped with fear, indiscipline, and helplessness. Spine chilling rumours threatened day-to-day life. During the month of July 1857, rumour spread that the sepoys of Barrackpur, joined by the 'natives' living in the suburbs, were coming to Calcutta and together would soon loot and murder the entire English population! The rumour spread that the dethroned Nawab of Awadh was already walking the streets of Garden Reach along with his companions with the intent to loot. T. Rice Holmes spoke about Panic Sunday, 14 June 1857, when a rumour spread that the mutinous Barrackpur sepoys had reached Calcutta, and, reinforced by armed retainers of the Nawab of Awadh, were ready to finish their slaughter of the entire Christian population. Holmes continues:

> Members of council and government secretaries barricaded their doors, or abandoned their homes in terror or to take refuge on board of the ships in the river. Inferior officials, scampering wildly across the plain from Chowrangi to the Fort! The frenzied activity saw families of . . . high officials and other Englishmen making a beeline for the Fort

hoping to get shelter at least under the cannons mounted at the entrance of the Fort William. Eurasians rushed out of their houses in the suburbs to seek refuge from an imaginary foe. The streets were thronged with the carriages and palanquins of the fugitives, while their deserted homes lay at the mercy of the "*budmash*".[26]

The *ferangis* of Kasaitala, Chunogalli, and Chowringhee who could not even imagine touching a trigger, were now practising how to shoot. Such fear also prevailed in official circles when John Grant, an English official, pointed out the 'dangers to which the capital was exposed from the Mohomedan population, the *budmashes*, the armed retainers of the Nawab of Awadh, the disaffected native regiments within its precincts or at neighbouring stations'.[27] Panic stricken councillors and secretaries to the Governor-General were seen running helter-skelter, each of them were doing different things like loading pistols, bolting doors, and repairing their door latches. However, the more fearless amongst them patrolled on horseback the deserted streets of the city to gauge the atmosphere.

On 5 June 1857, almost at about 2 in the night, an English resident of 10, Middleton Row heard sounds of explosives from the direction of Alipur and promptly deduced that the mutineers had rescued prisoners from the jail and were now in a frenzied mood to attack the European population in the city. He went around waking up everyone in his locality. But, it was soon found that members of a wedding party were indulging in bursting crackers.[28]

Certain events that had taken place at the seat of supreme government were indeed responsible for creating this kind of situation. On 6 June 1857, Governor-General Lord Canning had passed an Act giving extraordinary powers to civil and military officers to carry out summary trials and punishment of all disturbers of the peace. Yet, the British populace believed that he had not cared to provide protection to Bengal and its capital.

'Loyal inhabitants of the city' pressed the Governor-General to form a volunteer corps and showed their readiness to serve in it. They felt that an entire regiment which was now responsible for the safety of the city could have been set free to act against mutineers. Some government officials too were in favour of a volunteer corps, and raised doubts about the strength of the loyal troops and the trustworthiness of the 'native' police. One of them was convinced that the effects of a mere street riot in Calcutta would be felt not only throughout Bengal, but in the very extremities of India. Canning rejected the offer of the Calcutta Volunteers and at the same time refused to disarm the sepoys at Barrackpur and Dinapur on the grounds that such a measure would exasperate the sepoys at other stations and that where there were no white soldiers to protect the Christians from the mutineers' vengeance; and also because he trusted the professions of loyalty which several of the regiments had been careful to make. At a later date, however, he could not but give consent to both demands.[29]

The Europeans from suburbs and neighbouring areas were not the only ones to flock to Calcutta. The last week of May 1857 saw an influx of Englishmen with their families from the north and north-west part of the country; so much so that the British population in the city rented a big house on Chowringhee to accommodate the refugees. The government granted permission to them to use a portion of Bishops College; the able-bodied among them were even inducted into the militia for a monthly salary. Reputed Bengali *babus* and aristocrats also extended their hand by opening a fund. Messrs Prasanna Kumar Tagore of Pathuriaghata, Ram Gopal Ghosh (a young Bengali and a leading member of British India Society), and Ramprasad Roy (one of the leading lawyers of the city) formed a committee to oversee aid to the European refugees. The weekly *Hindu Patriot* edited by Harish Chandra Mukherjee tried earnestly to convince the British authority that rebellion was nothing but the handiwork of superstitious sepoys and Indians were not at all sympathetic to the sepoys. In fact, their loyalty and allegiance to the British government remained undisturbed. Distinguished Bengalis expressed their loyalty and their intention to help the authorities by holding *sabhas* in different places of Calcutta. In these meetings they also condemned the treachery of the sepoys in Meerut, Delhi, and Kanpur. One such meeting presided over by Raja Radhakanta Deb was held on 22 May 1857 and involved Pratap Chandra Singha, zamindar of Paikpara, Jay Krishna Mukherjee of Uttar Para, Kaliprasanna Singha of Singhibagan, and other renowned intellectuals of the day.[30]

Calcutta was not the only place where such meetings were held. Reports of such meetings also came from district towns and the *mofussils*. One such report came from the district of Rajshahi, where the inhabitants met at the house of Raja Prosunnonath Rai Bahadur of Dighaputiah on 13 June 1857 to express their loyalty to the British government; they formed a committee and the members decided to undertake steps to quell the rebellion. The *sabha* passed the following resolution:

> That in case the members come to know that any mutineer or spies have taken shelter in the district, or are instigating others to join them in their armies, immediate measures must be taken to arrest such offenders, together with those who may be harbouring them and make them over to the nearest police, and give to the latter every necessary aid in securing their persons.[31]

An undercurrent of suspicion, fear, and apprehension prevailed among the 'native' especially the richer section of them, no matter what the outcome of the *sabhas* were. The editor of *Sambad Prabhakar* expresses such an apprehension when he wrote on 28 May 1857 that, even if the rebels was successful in attacking Calcutta, it would not be easy for them to carry out the atrocities they committed in Meerut. Since the 'cowardly Bengali' would not able to check the invasion of the mutineers, this task was best left to the Europeans who would give a fight to protect the city.[32] The editor gentleman was concerned over the fact that, in case the sepoys who were in charge of security of the fort, mint, and government treasury would rebel, the sowars of the Governor-General's bodyguard might join them, and then the situation would get out of hand.

An article titled 'Battle-dress and Preparation for War of Rich Calcuttans' came out in the *Sambad Bhaskar* on 18 June 1857. The rich Indians were busy making military preparations in accordance with their promises to the British government. A great deal of this indeed was the outcome of their fear and the panic created largely by rumours. Whatever may be the cause, Raja Pratap Chandra Singha and Raja Iswar Chandra Singha of Paikpara Raj family installed 2,000 armed men in front of the royal highway. About forty or fifty of them were Europeans bearing loaded guns, while the Indian guards were busy patrolling the surroundings with their shields, swords, and guns. A militia equipped with firearms stood inside the royal palaces of Shobhabazar. One could find the similar situation in the house of Rani Rashmani of Janbazar. And, other rich families like the Sen, Mitra, Basu, Tagore, Singha, Ghosh families from Kolutola to Bagbazar were also gripped by this fear. Those who were not so rich within their limited means employed *paiks* with shields, swords, and spears. Wealthy natives on horsesback or on foot patrolled the streets at night.[33] Holmes writes about the terrified condition of the 'natives' (mostly common people), who were crawling in their dwellings expecting every moment to be searched out and cut down by the rebellious sepoys and sowars whose coming they had heard.[34]

On 8 August 1857, Taracknath Sen, Additional Principal of Sudder Amin, 24 Parganas sent a letter to A.R. Young, Secretary to the Government of Bengal. Sen wrote that while collecting information on the mutineers he was proceeding along the lanes of Burabazar, the place of residence of the Hindustani *goondahs* and other bad characters. He found five or six men talking in a low voice about the present state of affairs. One of them asked how the mutineers dispatched letters from one camp to another. Others said that they hoodwinked the *mofussil* police by hiding the letter under the upper *sooktulla* or the leather in sole of the shoe. In fact, the police commissioner was thinking in terms of sending instructions to the magistrates on Grand Trunk Road (if approved by the Lieutenant-Governor of Bengal) to enquire about the authenticity of this information and the factors which induced these men to proceed to Calcutta.[35]

Meanwhile, reports were also coming from the magistrates, joint-magistrates, and commissioners of various divisions of Bengal to the judicial department regarding the state of affairs in the *mofussil* areas. The magistrate of Murshidabad, Dinajpur, Pubnah, the office of joint-magistrate, deputy-magistrate of Serajganj all were in favour of police patrolling in the districts. On 27 June 1857, the office of magistrate of Rangpur complained against the editor of a Bengali weekly newspaper (printed in Rangpur) for having inserted an article based entirely on a false report that the sepoys of Jalpaiguri had created a commotion. The magistrate of Dinajpur in a letter to the Secretary dated 25 July 1857 conceded the fact that a mutinous spirit had shown itself among the 'native' troops of Jalpaiguri.[36] Holmes, discussing about the situation in Bhagalpur Division (Eastern Bihar) during 14 August 1857, said that the headquarters of one of the detachments which had mutinied in Dacca were at the station of Jalpaiguri. Again, while reflecting about the exploits of Commissioner Yule and Dalrymple the Collector of Jalpaiguri, he said that on 29 November when Yule had left Bhagalpur for Jalpaiguri, two cavalry detachments at Madariganj and Jalpaiguri mutinied.[37]

The reports from Nadia and Khulna subdivisions showed that the people were well disposed to the government and no sympathy was shown to the mutinous sepoys who were considered belonging to an inferior race. In the subdivision of Magora, the people seemed almost ignorant of the Sepoy Mutiny and the only excitement appeared among persons possessed of property.[38] On Saturday morning (8 August 1857), W.C. Spencer forwarded a letter from the magistrate of Murshidabad to the secretary in which he reported that outwardly everything seemed quiet in the district, but he had come to know from a trusted source that the disarmed soldiers (who were Brahmins) had been making secret enquiries regarding the possibility of obtaining arms from the neighbouring bazars and the city. This was indeed the outcome of a rumour spreading everywhere that the government would forcibly interfere with the sepoys' religion. It had also been brought to Spencer's notice that the Dacca cotton boats which were constantly passing down the river towards Calcutta had large numbers of 'upcountry' men as guards on board. They were not actual servants of the *mahajans* dispatching the boats, but appeared to have been taken on board indiscriminately. Once they went to Calcutta, they never returned. So enquiries were sought about this.[39]

Hundreds of petitions from Calcutta and the suburbs were coming to the Home Department of the Government of India asking for protective measures. On 21 August 1857, C. William and 252 other inhabitants of Calcutta and its suburbs sent petitions. They apprehended that the disturbance might have extended over relatively quite areas of Bengal and even to Calcutta itself. The petitioners had no confidence in the 'Native Police' either of the *mofussil* or of Calcutta. They felt that executive civil authorities were not sufficiently powerful to quell a disturbance of any magnitude and that under such circumstances, martial law alone can afford protection. The government did not however entertain the idea of proclaiming martial law. It was of the opinion that under the circumstances volunteer guards and trained police forces would be adequate for the protection of the city and suburbs, and it was not possible to send additional troops for the purpose.[40]

In Howrah, a number of Europeans in conjunction with the police earnestly tried to preserve law and order in the district that was under the control of committee formed by them. The committee submitted a recommendation to the government that during the approaching Muslim festival, they should at least be allowed the use of arms from the arsenal. The committee suggested that should the government be pleased to sanction this application, the members would hold themselves responsible for the storage, and return of the arms, or compensate for any loss or damage that may occur.[41] Interestingly, if one goes through the pages of government documents of those times, it becomes clear that regular exchanges of letters took place between the various offices of district commissioners, magistrates, and the Bengal government secretariat. The panic situation rose to such levels that individual government establishments and private European and Indian companies were asking for arms and protection.

The directors of the Bengal Coal Company communicated their desire to A.R. Young, Secretary to the Government of Bengal on 7 August 1857, to take into their service a body of twenty to thirty Europeans accustomed to the use of arms for the purpose of protecting their property at Raniganj. They applied to be enrolled as volunteers for a limited service, and for a sergeant to command them who would be maintained at the expense of the Bengal Coal Company and also to supply them with arms which will be returned at the expiry of period of service. A letter from Gordon Stuart (Secretary, Bengal Coal Company) to A.R. Young on 7 August 1857 pointed out the immense importance of Raniganj in the situation when supplies of coal was urgently required for up-country steamers conveying troops. The directors wanted the government to spare European soldiers for the protection of Raniganj against mutineers from Hazaribagh.[42] Messrs Mackay Barry & Company of Sirajganj also thought it prudent to engage the services of an officer and European seamen, with six Europeans of their establishment to protect the cash in the factory as well as to protect the goods and arms worth between

Rs 50,000 and 60,000 which were carried between Dacca and Sirajganj at least two or three times every month to the government treasury. This company also begged the government for a supply of 15 stands of arms and two 3- or 4-pounder howitzers with 50 rounds of ammunitions.

Paranoia had already set into the psyche of the British rulers. They and their allies were so sucked into rumours that it became almost a necessity to introduce a control mechanism in the usage of firearms amongst the Indians. The EIC elite, in order to secure itself against future rebellion, intensified its intelligence network. Detectives now monitored every purchase of firearms. Dossiers was maintained on all dealers and every individual purchaser of arms: the background, economic situation, political bent.

It was during this time that the Calcutta Police was formally taking its shape under a commissioner. In order to safeguard the interests of the administration and those of the common man, the EIC brought in measures to curtail the enthusiasm of voluntary guards and patrols that had mushroomed in the city. These volunteers often took the law into their own hands, although they were liable to act only under the instructions and command of the police commissioner. A letter dated 24 June 1857 from the Commissioner of Calcutta, chose to inform the Secretary to the Government of Bengal that

> Bands of guards on horse backs were seen poking with their bayonets at the native commoners and yet these arms were supposedly from the state Arsenal! The natives of Calcutta as a consequence became extremely irritated and many left Calcutta for places where there was a lesser probability of being insulted by Europeans.[43]

The police commissioner appealed to the Bengal government that no one should be allowed to possess arms without prior government sanction. Those who were roaming the streets of Calcutta without authorization ought to be disarmed by the police and the volunteer guards (who were aiding the police) under the Military Act of XIII of 1856. In fact, the police commissioner was thinking in terms of issuing a notice to this effect, but he was hesitating as his apprehension was that such measures might bring the police in direct opposition with the armed Europeans. He strongly recommended calling in all the arms that had been distributed from the arsenals. Then only, he believed, would peace be restored in the city. The police commissioner sent a copy of the notice he was going to issue to the Bengal government. (In fact, he had the power to enforce all instructions given in the notice under the Provisions of Act XIII of 1856, Section 47 to Section 81, Clause 13.) The patrols of the Calcutta Volunteer Guards received similar instructions. All arms taken from persons in the street, after this notification, would be at the discretion of the commissioner of police and could be confiscated. Every person discharging firearms within the precincts of Calcutta was liable to a fine of Rs 20.[44]

A.R. Young, Secretary to the Government of Bengal, under instructions from the Lieutenant-Governor requested the officiating commissioner of police, Calcutta and the magistrate of the 24 Parganas to make an enquiry regarding the possession of arms within their jurisdiction, and check whether there had been any noticeable sale of firearms to the 'natives' under suspicious circumstances. The police commissioner informed that he had already made necessary enquiries regarding huge purchases of guns by 'natives'. It was a fact that a large number of firearms had been sold by various dealers of Calcutta, but these were mostly to European concerns and the majority of the buyers were Christians. If one were to make investigations in all the Christian households of the city, every such household would have at least one pistol or musket in its possession. Almost all the firearms purchased in Calcutta in the last few months were taken to *mofussil* areas and villages for use by indigo planters and zamindars who were living in great fear. One of the European importing organizations had sold 1,500 muskets to a 'native' dealer in arms a few days previously. Once the police commissioner came to know that the purchaser was one of the biggest arm dealers of Calcutta, an enquiry was ordered. The investigation found that he had actually placed the order of 1,500 different types of firearms one and half years before the date of enquiry. And of the ordered items all were not delivered on time. The dealer's account book revealed that during last three years 110 guns and muskets had been sold from his shop, and this number was not that huge. One had to keep in mind that these firearms, mostly imported from Europe, had to go through the Customs House before they were delivered to different buyers. However, only a few guns came from Mungher. In the present situation, the dealers were concerned that the government might confiscate their stock of firearms or seal their establishment. As a result they lost no time in selling their products. It was this unusually rapid sale of arms from the shops of the 'natives' that made the European residents of Calcutta anxious.[45]

According to the police commissioner, this was the perfect time for introducing an Act which would obligate the individual buyers to register their names. This would in turn help the magistrates of south Bengal to take strict measures to disarm suspicious elements. It was also probable that such a measure would enable the government to reduce the quantum of dacoities in Southern Bengal. A revision, especially extension of Section 70 and four following sections of Act XIII of 1856 was immediately called for. A similar act, argued the police commissioner, should also be enforced in other parts of India. In a nutshell, his suggestion was to have a comprehensive data regarding the possession of arms by the common man as well as the privileged 'natives' in order to ensure the monitoring of firearms in the country and to keep a check on any rebellious act in future.[46]

Wanchope, the Police Commissioner, also wrote to the authorities in Fort William stating the availability of several thousand muskets for sale in Moorgihatta, a street in which nearly all the 'native' gun makers of Calcutta resided. After making an enquiry to ascertain the actual number of the muskets on sale, he found that there were altogether 900 muskets for sale. He planned to bring all these arms to the police headquarters, keeping in mind the tension which had set in the psyche of the local European population. He thought of doing this in consultation with the arm dealers, issuing receipts to them. He hoped that the Governor-General would give his consent to this plan. In fact, while bringing such weapons to the police headquarters, a heavy cannon had to be literally dragged through the streets.[47] During his investigations Wanchope went to the shop of D.N. Biswas & Company. There, he ordered Dwarikanath Biswas to prepare a list of all his customers who had bought firearms in the past and those who had ordered the 45 muskets present in his shop. D.N. Biswas assured Wanchope that he would not sell any gun without prior permission.[48]

On 31 July 1857, Cecil Beadon, Secretary to the Government of India, wrote to A.R. Young, Secretary to the Lieutenant-

Governor of Bengal, informing him that the commissioner of police, Calcutta had actually managed to bring arms from the arms dealers to the police headquarters. Beadon's recommendation was that the arms would be in safer custody if they could be shifted to Fort William where they would remain under the charge of the fort major.[49] The Governor-General had no reservations regarding the matter. The letter also revealed that the dealers who surrendered their muskets had actually bought a major portion of the same from a businessman named Harish Chandra Bose. Enquires were made. The police found 6,000 old guns and barrels which the businessman claimed he had purchased as scrap metal from the government arsenal. Many of the barrels where neatly cut to size and recycled into pistols and smaller barrels. 'Native' craftsmen modified some of the old scrap into re-usable guns. Hence, the suggestion from the head of the police to the government was to direct the authorities in the arsenal to completely incapacitate the muskets, guns, and spring locks before throwing them away as scrap. The Bengal government supported Wanchope on this and appreciated his suggestion.[50]

A.R. Young in another letter to the district magistrate of 24 Parganas asked for his intervention in discouraging arm dealers to sell arms to 'suspicious characters'. Brigadier Grant, commanding officer at Barrackpur, expressed his intention to disarm villagers in the vicinity of Barrackpur for the security of the cantonment. In a letter to the joint magistrate of Barasat, Grant requested assistance and cooperation in his 'search for arms' operation. However, the office of commissioner of Nadia Division was not in favour of this and considered it 'inexpedient as well as illegal to resort to a measure of such extremity'.[51]

Going through all the letters written by the officer-in-command, Barrackpur, commissioner of police, the district magistrates, and the secretaries to both the Government of Bengal and Government of India, it became clear to me that the EIC authorities discouraged the sale of arms and possession of them by 'natives' as a preventive measure. The panic syndrome had taken root in the government as a fallout of the 1857 Uprising in the north and east of India. As a result, the authorities were seriously thinking in terms of introducing countrywide Arms Regulatory Laws.

Interestingly, foreign suppliers of arms also fell under the vigilant eyes of the commissioner of police. An example of this is indicated in the letter from the commissioner's desk to the secretary to the Government of Bengal dated 4 August 1857. A catalogue published on that day by Messrs Mackenzie Lyall & Company announced the auction of 20 lakh percussion caps. The police commissioner immediately assigned the deputy commissioner to stop the same which was promptly put into effect.[52] The collector of customs Calcutta detained 15 casks of musket (containing 300 muskets) imported by Mackenzie Lyall & Company under instructions of the government. Mackenzie Lyall & Company put forward charges against the custom officials for detainment and bad handling of the shipment and asked for compensation for the losses. On 17 August, a letter was sent from the office of collector of customs to Messrs Mackenzie Lyall & Company as regards the safe custody and good condition of the 15 casks of muskets which was valued at Rs 3,000. The letter emphasized that the custom officials were not answerable to the company. The letter which was a follow up to the charge labelled by Messrs Mackenzie Lyall & Company indicated that payment of the billed amount was completely out of question and that the arms had only been detained, not 'taken over', as indicated by the company.[53]

In another letter to the secretary to the Government of Bengal, the commissioner of police talked about an advertisement published by the Messrs Tulloh & Company for the selling of 3,75,000 gun caps. Necessary actions were taken to stop any kind of transaction. Messrs Tulloh & Company had expressed their extreme regret that the advertisement was inserted by a 'native' of their establishment entirely without their knowledge.[54] A.R. Young, secretary to the Government of Bengal wanted the police commissioner to make an enquiry regarding the disposition of large quantity of copper caps and some firearms which have been imported by a 'native merchant' in the ship named *Blondel* within the last few days. The police commissioner assured that these shipments would in no way be delivered to the 'native' importer, instead all the imported firearms, gun caps which were detained in custom house premises would be sent to the Arsenal of Fort William for safety. Instructions to this effect were forwarded to the office of the collector of customs.[55]

CONCLUSION

The gun dealers of 1857 Calcutta amassed huge fortunes by selling firearms to Europeans and Indian Christians as was pointed out by one of the leading intellectuals of the day, Shibnath Shastri in *Ramtanu Lahiri O Tatkalin Bangasamaj*. On the other hand, the colonial authority and its police department kept a vigilant eye on the everyday transactions of the 'native' dealers and the procurement of the arms by the 'natives'. Governor-General Canning did not pay any heed to the outcry of the threatened British residents when they demanded the authority to snatch away the arms and weapons of the 'natives' and to pass a strict Military Act against the possession of arms by them. On 31 July 1857, Canning drafted a Bill which was not sanctioned finally until 11 September 1857. This Bill, instead of giving solace to the European population, intensified their indignation because it would take away from the European and Eurasian population the right to carry arms without license.[56] It is probable that the government wanted to check the arms possessed by the 'natives' but at the same time was also aware of the fact that imposition of restrictions only on 'natives' of the city would cause strong opposition from them.

Samarendranath Daw talks about the '*Parwana* System', according to which the influential elite among the 'natives' could possess six to eight guns in accordance to their need and had to enter the names of their armed retainers for the official records. This system probably continued till 1878 when Lord Lytton came out with his great discriminatory Arms Act. Later, the princes of Jaipur, Jodhpur, Cooch Behar, and Tripura got a respite from the *Parwana* System. In 1868, Queen Victoria as a prize to their loyalty to the British government had given permission to Mahatab Chand of Burdwan and his successors to keep as many as arms and armed retainers as they needed. Lytton's Act for the first time introduced the system of obtaining license from district magistrate for possessing weapons and firearms throughout British India, but the Europeans were kept outside the binding of this Act. 'Native' buyers were permitted to possess only inferior quality firearms. As far as European gun dealers were concerned, they could continue to do well with their profitable business. The 'native' dealers however, did not face much hazards as 'native' elites, their most important clients from time to time got respite from this Act. Indian arms dealers, in order to carry on their day-to-day business in an unhindered manner, chose to show their mark of loyalty to the crown by flying the British flag atop their establishments. The impact of the 1857 Uprising went so deep into the psyche of the rulers that it lasted until the Partition of India into two nations. The nation's freedom struggle as a whole, and sporadic movements within it, were invariably dealt with a ruthless iron grip. Especially when the administration got a whiff of possession or movement of arms by revolutionary groups during the freedom movement, the fingers of suspicion were immediately pointed at Indian businessmen involved in the trade of firearms. With the passage of time, the families of the Calcutta arms dealers not only stuck to their calling but expanded the family business to other important cities like Allahabad, Kanpur, Ranchi, Patna, Bhagalpur and Gauhati.

ACKNOWLEDGEMENTS

I am indebted to Late Samarendra Daw of N.C. Daw & Co., and Mr. N. Roy, former Curator of the Police Museum, Kolkata.

NOTES

1. Interview with Sri Ananta Kumar Biswas, the owner of East India Arms Company at his residence on 10 June 2006.
2. 'Hawa Bandook', *Jugantar*, 31.10.1893.
3. Sarit Datta, 'Jorasankor Bandook Bybashayi Daw Paribar', an unpublished piece written between June 2002 and January 2004, at the request of Samarendra Daw primarily for private circulation; interview with Samarendranath Daw, present proprietor of N.C. Daw & Company and with Alok Kumar Daw of A.T. Daw & Company on 7 May 2006.
4. Gyanendra Nath Kumar (ed.), *Vamsa Parichay*, vol. 1 (Calcutta, Baishakh 1328), pp. 19–21.
5. Shekhar Bandopadhyay, *From Plassey to Partition: A History of Modern India* (New Delhi: Orient Longman, 2004), pp. 108, 115.
6. Commissioner Order Book, vol. 3, 25 February 1857, Kolkata Police Museum, North D.C. (H.Q), Kolkata.
7. Ibid.

8. Kumar (ed.), *Vamsa Parichay*, pp. 20–1.
9. Pradip Sinha, *Calcutta in Urban History* (Calcutta: Firma KLM Private Ltd., 1978), pp. 67–8.
10. Balai Chandra Barui, 'Laban Ekadhipatyar Biruddhe Pratirodh, Company Banam Sthaniya Zamindar (1772–1800)', *Sampratik Itihas Charcha*, 2005, p. 94.
11. Sinha, *Calcutta in Urban History*, p. 71.
12. John M. Mackenzie, *The Empire of Nature: Hunting, Conservation and British Imperialism* (Manchester: Manchester University Press, 1997), pp. 168–95.
13. Kumar (ed.), *Vamsa Parichay*, pp. 410–11, 435–6.
14. Sarit Dutta, 'Jorasankor Bandook Bybashayi, Daw Paribar', p. 9; Interview with Alok Kumar Daw on 7 May 2006.
15. The Maharaja of Cooch Behar, *Big Game Shooting in Eastern and North Eastern India* (New Delhi: Mittal Publishers, 1958), pp. 459–61.
16. Allister Macmillan, *Seaports of India & Ceylon: Historical and Descriptive, Commercial and Industrial, Facts, Figures and Resources* (FRGS, 1928), pp. 137–40.
17. All these guns are preserved in Ramnagar Royal Palace, Museum.
18. 'Gun-Runners of Esplanade', *Statesman*, 16.10.78.
19. Macmillan, *Seaports of India & Ceylon*, pp. 139–40.
20. *Bengal Harkaru and India Gazette*, vol. LX, no. 119, New Series, Calcutta, 20 May 1857, Front page, Column 1.
21. F.L. Halliday, *Annual Report of the Police Administration of Town of Calcutta and its Suburbs*, Appendix III, 'Statement of arms and ammunition imparted by sea during the year 1909 by each dealer of the town of Calcutta', p. 32.
22. W.H. Carey, *The Good Old Days of Honourable John Company: 1600–1858* (compiled from newspaper and other publications), vol. 1, ed. Nisith R. Ray (Calcutta: Riddhi, 1980), p. 209.
23. Board of Custom Salt and Opium (Custom), Enclosure no. 42, 9 May 1850, no. 68, 20 May 1850, no. 69, 23 May 1850.
24. W.K. Firminger, *Thackers Guide to Calcutta* (Calcutta: Thackers Spink & Co., 1906), pp. 159–60.
25. Kaushik Roy, 'Equipping Leviathan: Ordnance Factories of British India', *War in History*, vol. 10, no. 4 (2003), pp. 398–423.
26. T. Rice Holmes, *A History of the Indian Mutiny and of the Disturbances Which Accompanied it Among the Civil Population* (London: Macmillan & Co. Ltd., 1913), pp. 170–1.
27. Holmes, *A History of the Indian Mutiny*, p. 171.
28. Swapan Basu, 'Kolkata 1857', *Saradiya Bartaman*, 2004, p. 44.
29. Holmes, *A History of the Indian Mutiny*, pp. 163–4.
30. Shibnath Shastri, *Ramtanu Lahiri O Tatkalin Bangasamaj* (Kolkata, 1957), pp. 96, 196; Basu, 'Kolkata 1857', p. 44.

31. Judicial Proceeding, no. 38, 27 June 1857, WBSA, Calcutta.
32. Kaliprasanna Sinha, 'Mutiny', 'Hutompancher Naksa', Part I, in *Chirayata Shahitya Sangrara*, vol. 1, ed. Kanchan Basu, Calcutta, July 1991, p. 48.
33. Benoy Ghosh (ed.), *Samayik Patre Banglar Samay Chitra*, vol. 3, Calcutta, p. 390.
34. Holmes, *A History of the Indian Mutiny*, p. 460.
35. Judicial Proceedings, no. 188, 7 August 1857, no. 210, 8 August 1857.
36. Ibid., no. 93, 22 August 1857, no. 191, 27 June 1857, no. 227, 25 July 1857.
37. Holmes, *A History of the Indian Mutiny*, p. 469.
38. Judicial Proceedings, no. 93, 22 August 1857.
39. Ibid., no. 190, 8 August 1857.
40. Ibid., no. 159, 21 August 1857.
41. Ibid., no. 755, 29 July, 1857.
42. Ibid., no. 201, 7 August 1857.
43. Letter from the office of commissioner of police, Calcutta to the secretary to the Govt. of Bengal, Judicial Department, Judicial Proceedings, no. 430, 24 June 1857.
44. Judicial Proceedings, no. 31, 24 June 1857.
45. Letter from the office of commissioner of police, Calcutta, to the secy. to the Govt. of Bengal, Judicial Department, Fort William, Judicial Proceedings, no. 40, 23 July 1857.
46. Judicial Proceedings, no. 40, 23 July 1857.
47. Ibid., no. 42, 25 July 1857.
48. Ibid., no. 43, 25 July 1857.
49. Ibid., no. 45, 31 July 1857.
50. Ibid., no. 46, 27 July 1857.
51. Ibid., no. 42, 11 July 1857, no. 57, 16 July 1857.
52. Ibid., no. 252, 4 August 1857.
53. Collector of Custom Calcutta, Enclosure nos. 34–6, 17 August 1857, Enclosure no. 37, 18 August 1857.
54. Judicial Proceedings, no. 253, August 1857.
55. Ibid., no. 255, 15 August 1857.
56. Holmes, *A History of the Indian Mutiny*, p. 175

CHAPTER 6

1857 and the Bengali Imagination: The Role of Literature in Shaping Discourses on Nationhood

SWARUPA GUPTA

The revolt of 1857 continues to be a *cause celebre* because it acts as a pivotal site for redefining the relation between the Indian people and their past. Setting up a relation with the past provides the central, analytic entry-point for understanding and interpreting an iconic event such as the revolt. But as the revolt was a complex movement in which emotions played an important role,[1] a nuanced exploratory approach delving into multilayered mentalities may serve as an analytic tool for illuminating hitherto understated/unexplored aspects of 1857. Prevailing historiographies have stressed the localized nature of the revolt, and consider regions such as Bengal as 'loyalist' terrains offsetting a violent north-central India in flames. I wish to re-examine such oppositional portrayals and explore complex mentalities through the prism of literature to uncover the dynamics of what happened in Bengal (at the levels of processes and mentalities) during the years following 1857. By formulating this problem, I argue that patterns and trajectories of mentalities and responses in Bengal as expressed in literature went beyond simplistic 'loyalist'[2] frames, and fed into specific discourses on nationhood. Prioritizing literature as a freer ideological space for such expression, this essay explores representations of the revolt in various Bengali literary tracts such as novels, short stories, and plays that proliferated within about seventeen years of this 'event'. It situates such representations in a critical and comparative light *vis-à-vis* historical, first-person/on-the-spot/experiential and travel accounts of the Bengali literati, demonstrating that representations of the events and ideologies of 1857 in the fictive space of literature accentuated tones of veiled/overt criticism of the alien Raj, articulated anti-loyalist protest, and even rebellion. I engage with certain key themes: (1) representations of 'betrayed'/ 'unlucky' sepoys; (2) inscribing rebel leaders into a nationalist iconography; and (3) depictions of *swadesh* and dreams of its independence (even through armed help to the rebels) to show that nationalism and the novel intersected to produce a discourse on an empowered identity. This discourse was influenced by the events and ideologies of 1857, but conceptualized in subtly different ways, which contrasted the 'mentality of the mutiny' underlying event-oriented or actual rebellion in the storm-centres of north and central India.

THE CONTEXTS AND DYNAMICS OF LITERARY REPRESENTATIONS

The contexts and circumstances within which historical, first person/on-the-spot/travel accounts on the one hand, and the literary tracts on the other, were written differ on crucial points. When the rebellion raged in north and central India, the predicament of an empire in flames and the iron hand of British repression that followed made it difficult for a colonial intelligentsia to represent mentalities of dissent in overtly antagonistic ways. Moreover, their material interests were bound up with the colonial order, and Western education and intellectual currents moulded their thought-processes. Opposition and protest were naturally muted. Most of the contemporaneous and near-contemporaneous travel and first-person accounts were markedly loyalist[3] (in the sense of not engaging in overt opposition of the Raj or supporting armed rebellion). Nevertheless, some of these tracts reflect a redefinition of identity through expressions of discontent, veiled criticisms of alien rule, dreams about progress, and the gradual unfolding of the idea of India.[4] As circumstances changed, mentalities metamorphosed subtly. The aftermath of the revolt and the cumulative effect of the Black Acts (1849), the Vernacular Press Act (1879) and the Ilbert Bill Controversy (1883), underline the asymmetry between the ruler and the ruled. The change was evident in later historical accounts (which saw the revolt in retrospect) such as the multi-volume *Shipahi*

Juddher Itihas by Rajanikanta Gupta (1876). Literature sharpened the dormant oppositional mentalities by negotiating antagonisms in a fictive space through a skilful interplay of myth, fact, hearsay, and legend.[5]

As imagination and its articulation do not operate in a void, the historical circumstances and events (mentioned above) and the prevalent socio-cultural climate formed the ideological setting against which the portrayals of 1857 in Bengali literature need to be viewed. This essay sets the ideas of the literati within specific socio-cultural and historical contexts to explain the dynamics of authorial intentions, to probe internal shifts, and trace ideological convergence to uncover the nuances beneath the form and content of the literary productions. From the second half of the nineteenth century, mentalities transformed in the wake of colonial sociological exercises, and the Hindu *Mela* (1867), the first organized expression of cultural nationalism, influenced a quest for an empowered identity in Bengal. The literati awakened to the central significance of history in recreating a people. The search for a 'new' history in Bengal came to be pivoted around cultural markers.[6] A history of culture and attachment to the social collectivity (*samaj*)[7] as distinct from political history was deemed to provide an imaginative unity to the past. The centrality of literature springs from this primacy of imagination in a 'new' history that could bring the collective self into existence. History became a theatre of dreams and wish fulfilment, and a new genre of historical literature burgeoned. In 1862, Bhudeb Mukhopadhyay coined the term 'historical novel' (as a distinct genre).[8] The 'modern' novel in Bengal had emerged through an encounter between the European/Western and the indigenous literary traditions. The 'new' forms (though influenced by 'Western' types) continued to draw on earlier literary traditions, techniques and forms.[9] In this fusion of the old and the new, the re-fashioning of Bengali literature assumed a unique note, and the form and content of the literary productions became the site of adaptation, contestation and the underlining of differences. It became a terrain for redefining the self and thus fed into the wider discourse on identity pivoted around a history of culture and attachment. From the third quarter of the nineteenth century, a distinct genre of anti-colonial literature[10] had emerged, in which major historical events, movements, and phases in Bengali and

Indian history formed the chief subject matter. Fictional/imaginary history/the historical novel constituted a freer space for the expression of a meaningful relation with the community's past. The fuzziness of the community[11] (seen in the use of *jati* in multiple senses) implied the opening out of the boundaries of the community towards a greater 'we', and an appropriation of wider histories implied in interaction between Bengalis and other Indians was a common theme from the second half of the nineteenth century. Movements in other parts of India figured crucially in the Bengali historical imagination, and also became the subject of historical novels, plays, and short stories. Portrayals of the 1857 Revolt in Bengali literary productions reflected this trend.[12]

The representations of 1857 formed part of this wider genre of anti-colonial literature concerned with distinct heroic historical phases and events. Unlike colonial literary writing which created a new genre, the Mutiny novel,[13] in Bengali literature was part of a wider genre of anti-colonial fiction. Yet this location (within a wider genre) had a crucial significance. As literary representations of 1857 focused on an all-India theme (unlike the Indigo Rebellion in 1860), they set the 'national' element in sharper focus, and prompted the reworking of region and national interconnections. Fictional representations of 1857 did not follow any unilinear/uniform/monolithic trajectory. In many ways, the literary imagination was fragmented. The concern here is to segregate and highlight those ideas thrown up in portrayals of 1857 which had an impact on discourses on nationhood, and to show how these complemented, connected with, as well as contrasted historical, on-the spot and experiential representations of the revolt.

'LOYALISM' RECONSIDERED: DEPICTIONS OF SEPOY REBELS IN LITERATURE

The 'loyalist' Bengali continues to form an enduring motif in historiographies of the revolt, sharply contrasted with the 'rebel' sepoy. Perceptions within and beyond academia[14] perpetuate the stereotype of a 'loyalist' Bengali, where the Western-educated, mainly high caste, professional intelligentsia formed a counter-image of the 'uncivilized' and backward-looking sepoy mutineer.

As the Bengali intelligentsia's interests were bound up with the material order of the colonial authority, and Western intellectual currents moulded their thought processes, they remained aloof and critical toward what they perceived to be the polar opposite of the civilized norms of an 'aristocracy of culture': the 'savage' sepoys who convulsed and overturned an ordered world. The intense urge for social progress made the Bengali middle classes critical toward conservative, backward currents in Bengal and elsewhere. Benoy Ghosh has argued that the apathy of the intelligentsia toward the sepoy rebels was a facet of their anti-conservative attitude within Bengal, and their hostility toward reactionary organizations and groups.[15] Such contentions are valid only contextually, and need to be related to other strands of mentalities for a deeper understanding of the dynamics of Bengali 'loyalism'. Qualifying such positions, I argue that the 'loyalism' of the Bengali intelligentsia contained internal dilemmas, contradictions, and shifts, thus opening a space for moving beyond terminologies of 'loyalist'/'rebel'. Mentalities of dissent had a different complexion in Bengal, and though the idiom of expression of disaffection was very different from the means of resistance and combat adopted by the sepoy rebels, it stemmed from a common feeling of discontent. Oppositional mentalities, articulated in a form and rhetoric different from those of the sepoys/rebel leaders, nevertheless drew on certain aspects, events, and ideologies of the revolt, despite a (contextual) critical stance toward the rebels. The issue of Bengali 'loyalty' thus floundered on the voicing of discontent in specific forms.[16]

Loyalism in the form of condemnation of the sepoys did not constitute a uniform trajectory. Though some fictional works criticized the sepoys as the savage and barbaric 'other' of civilized and cultured Bengalis,[17] others sharply deviated from such unqualified denigration. Literature transmuted images of the 'sepoy traitor' in subtle as well as overt ways. The same work often contained contradictory and ambivalent strands. Kaliprasanna Sinha's portrayal of 'sepoy rage' (*shipahi khepechhe*)[18] intertwined and alternated with other strands. Despite professing loyalty to Queen Victoria, Kaliprasanna's was not a voice of unqualified praise. His critical eye satirized British connivance and mediation in the unleashing of sepoy rage on the Bengalis, and disparaged the unmitigated loot and plunder by the British in Lucknow. According to Kaliprasanna, colonial responsibility heightened the predicament of Bengalis. The British gave orders to grab all weapons from the Bengalis and denied them high posts in the administration. The only effective organ of liberty, the press, which made it possible for Hutom (the author/narrator) to express his candid opinion, was fettered during the Mutiny.[19] These undercurrents of criticism in a 'loyalist' work must be seen as qualifying constructions of 'sepoy *versus* Bengali'. Such contradictions in the same tract offer insights into intricacies of authorial intention. As the narrative voice is projected in the text, the narrator is not ontologically distant, but a character (a 'paper being' to use the words of Roland Barthes). Through this 'internal focalization', the text underlined and reflected the narrator's own reactions/thoughts.

In other fictional works anti-loyalism was more overt. Upendra Chandra Mitra's novel *Nana Saheb ba Bharater Sukhasapna* transmuted familiar images of uncivilized sepoy traitors into deeply 'patriotic' victims of a betrayal by fate:

> Like their leader Nana Saheb, the sepoys were also patriotic to the core. They opposed the British through armed violence because they were inspired by the love of the land. They lost out because of their own weaknesses. It was a betrayal by fate and by *loyalists* who wanted favours from the British.[20]

Here not only are the sepoys regarded as patriotic, but also the 'loyalists' are disparaged. This counterpoising of the 'patriotic' sepoys to 'loyalist traitors' in a Bengali fictional work muted the polarity of sepoy and Bengali loyalist.[21] The sepoys were seen as victims of cruel fate. The revolt was a golden opportunity, a momentous phase, a turning point, but doomed to failure. While history lamented this loss by describing what actually happened, literature reversed the reality by depicting what could have happened. Upendra Chandra Mitra describes a different course of events in a dream sequence. He referred to the Proclamation from Peshawar (6 July 1857),[22] reversing the reality of imperial glory and victory of arms. In his novel, the British were plunged into a serious predicament: 'The British were determined to destroy the religion of the Hindustanis. They sent soldiers to India, but the Turkish Sultan issued a *farman*, and the King of Egypt assembled soldiers at Alexandria and sank all British ships.'[23] Such a metamorphosis of events and the conviction about sepoy patriotism demonstrate how the fictive space of literature could articulate mentalities of dissent.

Such longings were closely related to a fundamental question: could alien rule be justified? Chandicharan Sen, condemned sepoy atrocities but justified their rebellion. He questioned the basic legitimacy of colonial rule in India. By saying that such a rebellion was necessary against the 'misrule' of the British, Chandicharan voiced his conviction that until the English adopted liberal principles in India, the fire of revolt would rage.[24] He lamented that the rebellion was doomed to failure, but was convinced that it was a necessary step in altering the degraded social and political situation in the country. He supported the idea of wider popular participation in the sepoys' struggle, hoping that it would bring progress and social improvement. The voice of Narayan Trimbak (father of the mistress of the King of Jhansi) in Chandicharan's novel eloquently expressed this conviction, underlining the necessity of rebellion:

> Unless the fire of revolt purifies the moral atmosphere of the country, unless the blood of countless men floods and nourishes the earth, unless the souls of the common people of the country are inspired by love for the commonality and the *samaj* [social collectivity], knowledge and righteousness will never burgeon in this land.[25]

The transmutation of the 'sepoy traitor' thus operated in a mould of *samajik* improvement and progress, which underlay the forging of an empowered identity. While factual/historical accounts steered clear of overt revolt, fiction underscored popular participation, and even inclusions of Bengalis in the rebellion. In some fiction Bengalis actually helped rebel leaders and participated in a common struggle against the British. Such counterfactuals operated at two levels: (1) armed struggle (of the sepoys) was justified by the basic illegitimacy of alien rule; and (2) Bengali rebels were drawn into the vortex of the revolt because of a grievance or injustice. This camouflaged the actual causes, and contextually masked acts of flagrant defiance. In some cases, Bengali participation took the form of protest in oblivion and anonymity. Chandicharan Sen did not mention the name of the Bengali youth who 'rebelled', leaving the reader to guess whether he was 'Abinash'. Girish Chandra Ghosh in *Chandra* was more direct. Somnath or Haran (the central character in the novel) was a disciple of the *sannyasi* who led the rebels.[26] Somnath joined Nana Saheb and Azimullah.[27] These portrayals formed a backdrop for comparing and integrating far more overt strands and depictions of anti-loyalism in fictional accounts of post-colonial India. Obviously, with the end of empire, contexts changed crucially, but earlier works did form a retrospective reference point for later accounts which idealized Bengali rebel youths such as Tarak Chandra Ray,[28] and denigrated and ridiculed 'loyalist', 'cowardly'[29] Bengalis in Kanpur.

These examples of dilemma reveal the internal contradictions and attitudinal ambivalences in Bengali mentalities. To highlight such dilemmas within loyalism is not to deliberately obliterate an 'unexcavated loyalist past' from collective memory[30] by the hegemonic sweep of a nationalist meta-narrative. Rather, it is to focus on the fact that contextual collaboration and loyalism need to be re-examined through an intertextual reading of fiction and factual/historical accounts, which transform monolithic constructions of loyalty, and stereotypes of loyalist/rebel.

INSCRIBING REBEL LEADERS INTO A NATIONALIST ICONOGRAPHY

The depiction of the revolt in fictional frames involved a retelling of the story of 1857, and the crucial location of Bengal and Bengalis *vis-à-vis* the actors in the drama; sepoys and their leaders. We have seen how the linkage operated with regard to the reconstruction of sepoy rebel and Bengali 'loyalist'. This section delves into how fictional heroes of 1857 became nationalists.

The transformation of 'reluctant rebels' to 'nationalist icons', the replacement of one nationalist icon by another, and the dynamics of rebel leaders' actions form the subject of ongoing controversies. These may be said to have lineages in earlier representations, such as in late nineteenth-century Bengali fictional accounts about the revolt. While there was no uniform trajectory of unqualified valourization,[31] the multiple portrayals in fiction of the Rani of Jhansi, Nana Saheb, and Tantia Tope, reflected the ways in which they were incorporated into a nationalist discourse on a heroic history of patriotism. Their characterization as 'nationalist' did not follow solely from the fact that they engaged in an anti-colonial struggle against the British. It had subtler inflections. In many cases, it was clearly admitted that some of these leaders were 'reluctant rebels', compelled by the force of events and situations beyond their control to join in a struggle against the British. Bengali novels often cited 'historic' sources to bolster the theory of reluctant leadership. Convictions about the 'reluctance' of leaders such as Nana Saheb continued well into twentieth-century literary works (such as in Pramathnath Bisi's short stories woven around the events of 1857). According to Bisi, Nana Saheb never dreamed that he would become the leader of the sepoys. He had many grievances against the British, but even after the mutiny at Meerut, he had sympathy for the East India Company. Even when thousands of sepoys came and laid arms at his feet, called him the 'Badshah' of Hindustan, and said they would uproot the Company Raj and establish Peshwa rule, he did not wish to jump into the flames. The Nana was almost a victim of sepoy conspiracy and of the machinations of his 'associates', Zubeidi and Azimullah.[32]

Like Nana Saheb, the Rani of Jhansi was also regarded as a reluctant rebel. The Rani of Jhansi has been 'rescued' from nationalist appropriations which absorbed her into a nationalist paradigm as a fiercely anti-British rebel. R.C. Majumdar and Tapti Roy[33] concur that she was a reluctant rebel. What is missed out in existing works is, however, the fact that reluctant leadership need not clash with alternative and subtler constructions of nationalist frames, and inclusion of the Rani within them.

Many elements of nationalism/nationhood embedded in Bengali literary representations surface despite convictions that the Rani was a reluctant rebel. Writing in 1903, Jyotirindranath Tagore portrayed her participation as non-voluntary. She was the victim of circumstance, caught up in the cataclysm of 1857. He quoted the correspondence of Damodar Rao (the Rani's adopted son) to show how the Rani's involuntary participation was a terrible misfortune that spelt doom for herself, her people, and her land:

> Rani Lakshmibai, cutting herself off from all company, having given up the dream of getting her realm back, reconciled to her ill fate, was spending her days in contemplating God. But before her earlier phase of ill fate passed, a tremendous blow befell her. It was a terrible misfortune ... what was impossible even in a dream became possible...

and she faced terrible trouble despite staying within the precincts of the palace. All hopes of her own happiness and that of ours were ruined, and finally after giving up her own life, she left us with no shelter in this forsaken land of oblivion.[34]

Jyotirindra strengthened the image of the 'reluctant' rebel by saying that the Rani gave shelter to Europeans, including women, and even to those who escaped the Jhansi massacre. Among the latter was an Englishman named Martin who, according to the author, was 'still alive' (in 1903), and whose private correspondence to the Rani's adopted son revealed that the Rani had no hand in the Jhansi massacre.[35] The final act of defiance against the British was the result of miscommunication and misunderstanding,[36] and the fear that Jhansi would be destroyed by the sepoys if she did not join the struggle. Writing in 1888, Chandicharan Sen had also considered the Rani a reluctant rebel. The crucial point is that the reluctance of the Rani as a rebel leader did not preclude or clash with valourization of her bravery, which was then fitted into nationalist narratives seeking to counter colonial 'misrepresentations' and denigrations of the Rani. One of the main objectives of Sen's work was the correction of 'colonial falsehood' and historical slander.[37] The aim was therefore a 'true' representation of the Rani, rescued from colonial calumny such as her supposed complicity in the massacre, and fitting those representations into a frame of glorification and memorialization. Kaliprasanna Datta too, in his novel *Bijoy* (1883) underlined the fact that the Rani had no hand in the carnage at Jhansi, and lamented that she had not been lauded and glorified adequately by her own countrymen.[38]

While the element of antagonism (between the ruler and the ruled) expressed in the sepoy–British combat provided one of the reference points for including these leaders into a nationalist iconography, what was of equal or greater significance is that the struggle of these leaders was emblematic of deep love of the land (the specific *rajya* or realm in most cases). The writers idealized the connection between the people and the land. The leaders were valourized more for rising in arms to protect their own realm than for espousing the sepoys' cause. Bengali fiction underscored the determination of the rebel leaders not to give up their realms. Jyotirindranath Tagore narrated how the proud Rani of Jhansi proclaimed: 'I shall not give up Jhansi' to Major

Ellis[39] just after its annexation under the Doctrine of Lapse. The latter obviously fed into the idiom of struggle during the rebellion (as it was considered to be a war for the protection of the *deen*/realm against the infidel English),[40] but it could also be segregated as a form of protest in its own right. The Rani's opposition to the British was part of her opposition to any enemy of Jhansi. She sent troops against Sadashib Rao who assumed the title 'Maharaja of Jhansi' and against Nathe Khan who threatened it.[41] In the Bengali literary imagination, the nationalization of the leaders was approached via a glossing over/qualification/contextualization of the anti-British element, prioritizing the strand of patriotism which redefined place, its history and the connection it had with the people.

This brand of patriotism was bound up with a way of life grounded in observance of ancient ideals of *dharma*. The Rani of Jhansi was deeply influenced by the religious philosophy of Ramdas Swami. After becoming a widow, she led an austere life of worship.[42] What was valourized in addition to her courage in the battlefield, were her devotion to God (especially to the deity, Mahalakshmi), her sense of duty, her wisdom, and her devotion to her subjects, not to speak of charity, hospitality, and generosity.[43] Interestingly, these very qualities were considered by eminent Bengali writers such as Rajnarain Basu, as necessary for the improvement and progress of the *samaj* (social collectivity) in Bengal. They were associated with the norms of cultural Aryanism implying adherence to the epics and Puranas, linguistic connections with Sanskrit, and belief in a supreme Godhead. The construction of the Rani as a heroic, and devout woman was central to such figurations of 'Aryan' values and conduct. The double deification implied in the construction of Jhansi as mother (an example of the notion of nation as mother) and the Rani as the mother of Jhansi, devoted to her subjects,[44] forged a connection between the land/realm and the role of the ruler of the land in glorifying, unifying and protecting the land through conduct.[45]

The ideals of *nyaya* (justice) and *dharma* essential to this grounding of patriotism were linked with actual physical valour and bravery on the battlefield. Most fictional accounts, even while proclaiming the Rani a 'reluctant rebel', agreed that once she was drawn into battle, she displayed extraordinary courage. Similarly, Chandicharan Sen was enamoured of the bravery of

Tantia Tope and Holkar. He glorified Tantia Tope as a brave warrior who wished above all, the independence of the *desh*.[46] Such portrayals fed into a broader discourse on heroic Aryan history of valour and courage. Fictional representations related the courage of the rebel leaders to the roles of past exemplars, weaving both strands together in a history of heroism. Actual physical courage was not enough. It had to be supplemented by a righteous life and commitment to the ideals of *dharma* and *nyaya*. Nana Saheb was therefore lauded only conditionally. He and the rebels under him were 'patriotic' but Nana was defeated, and his fate was sealed because of his own weaknesses and the flaws in his character.[47] Upendra Chandra Mitra believed that Nana Saheb was patriotic to the core. After India's imaginary independence (in the novel, *Nana Saheb ba Bharater Sukhasapna*), he was crowned king,[48] but the glory of independence was short-lived. The dream was dispelled because of internal weaknesses in the Nana's character and his betrayal by close associates. This was a definite shift from denigrations of Nana Saheb in historical texts which saw him as the perpetrator of the Kanpur (Sati Chaura Ghat) massacre. Interestingly, such attempts to rescue Nana Saheb from denigration formed a theme in Hindi fiction too, which went a step further than Mitra's work. Hari Krishna Premji, the author of *Sheesh Daan* (1907), was oblivious to the weakness in Nana's character. He depicted the Nana as a stickler for war rules, a humane non-violent ruler who was betrayed by his subordinates.

While there was no uniform eulogizing of all rebel leaders in Bengali fiction, the theme of Aryan courage and the elements of *nyaya* and *dharma* as constituting a specific type of patriotism were central in most works. The equation of 'Bengali' and 'Aryan' was central to this discourse. Bengalis were considered to be co-sharers of a glorious Aryan heritage and a heroic history of traditionally 'valiant' races such as the Marathas, Rajputs and the Sikhs. Pre-rebellion leaders, rebel leaders, and valiant Bengalis—who had displayed 'Aryan' courage and valour and upheld the ideals of *dharma*/righteous conduct—were linked together as the joint bearers of this heroic legacy. The grafting of the roles of the valiant rebels of 1857 on to a heroic history of Marathas, Rajputs, and Sikhs (of an earlier era) and of Bengali chieftains and kings of the late medieval period (such as Pratapaditya), reflected an interesting set of overlaps and juxtapositions—Orientalist legacies of an 'Aryan' golden age, configurations and linkages between the region (Bengal) and the nation (expressed as *Bharatbarsha*) through a common history, and connections forged between Bengalis and other Indians traditionally noted for their heroism in attempts to counter and erase the colonial slur of Bengali effeminacy. Sarala Devi returned from Maharashtra and started the Pratapaditya Utsab (festival) along the lines of the Shivaji festival in Maharashtra.[49] By the turn of the century, the rebel leaders of 1857 had been absorbed into a pantheon of 'national' heroes who were also heroes of Bengal (*Banglar jatiya bir*). This trend gathered momentum during the Swadeshi period. By this time, the emphasis on Hindu–Muslim unity led to the inclusion of Mir Kasim and Sirajuddaula along with traditional Bengali Hindu heroes such as Pratapaditya into a history of valour celebrated in literary genres such as drama[50] and novels, as well as in historical accounts.[51]

SWADESH AND ITS INDEPENDENCE

Portrayals of 'patriotic' sepoys and 'righteous' rebel leaders were associated with the uplift and protection of the land (*swadesh*). The *swadesh/desh* during this period was the major site around which discourses on nationhood in Bengal were woven. Since the middle of the nineteenth century, a turn to a history of culture and attachment woven around the social collectivity valourized and deified the land as a lived-in, emotive space, inhabited by the *jati* (the collective self). *Desh* became multi-connotative: signifying village, province, and country, apprehending the idea of India.[52] A living link between the land and the people, and the land and its history/histories thus became central to the nationalist imagination. 1857 in the Bengali literary imagination was a means of re-articulating and exploring this central link between the land and the people, via a reconsideration of the patriotic roles of the sepoys, their leaders, and their commitment to the land. How did such re-articulation differ from other familiar images and constructions of *swadesh* in historical tracts, travel accounts and memoirs of the late nineteenth and early twentieth century? How did fiction strengthen and move beyond images of an empowered homeland/country of birth inhabited by a *jati*, and memorialized through history? At a time when it was difficult for a colonial intelligentsia to nurture dreams of complete independence from alien rule, specific novels and plays written on the theme of the revolt gloried in fantasies of freedom, even through armed struggle. These tracts deified *swadesh* (implying both Bengal and India), which had to be freed through patriotism and sacrifice. What is remarkable is that this theme was present even in 'loyalist' fictional works such as Gobinda Chandra Ghosh's *Chittabinodini*. The hero of his novel, Charuchandra (who was a 'loyalist'), abhorred sepoy atrocities, but lamented the loss of independence of the motherland: 'O Mother India [*Bharatbhumi*/land of *Bharat*]! I cannot witness your torment and pain anymore. Mother, are we worthy enough to give you independence?'[53]

The equation of *swadesh* with Bharat/India was a common feature in fiction and resonated with the interrelation between *Bharatbarsha* and Bengali *samajs* (as seen in the works of Bhudeb Mukhopadhyay and Rabindranath Tagore) as part of a wider construction of a utopic social universe encompassing India. Upendra Chandra Mitra dreamed of the freedom of *Bharatbarsha* or India through selfless sacrifice and patriotism of all Indians:

> Listen, all sons of Bharat, having one heart and soul
> If you wish to bring back Bharat's pride and glory
> Lay down your lives
> All you people who live in Bharat.[54]

The *modus operandi* and goals of this counterfactual independence through struggle and sacrifice operated within twin ideational trajectories of righteousness (*dharma* as moral courage) as well as physical valour. The Bengali *sannyasi* youth (Haran/Somnath) in Girishchandra Ghosh's novel *Chandra* joined the rebels, and exhorted them to rise in arms to save the motherland and rescue the ideals of *dharma* and righteous life from the current degradation:

> O Awake, awake, awake
> Seize your swords
> Cannot you see that the motherland is dying?
> Fie on your useless lives

Gone is all meaning from life
With the departure of *dharma*
And of our pride and dignity
This pain is slashing my heart.[55]

Fiction led the way from darkness to light. Independence was not only a striven-for, distant ideal, but an attained goal in the arena of literature. Upendra Chandra Mitra's *Nana Saheb ba Bharater Sukhasapna* tried to capture the glory of this independence: an unforgettable moment:

Today, all Bharatbashis are delirious with delight
Look! The sun has risen in the sky
And is emanating golden rays of glory
Irradiating our world with happiness
I say with pride: 'Victory to Bharat'...
Let us all join in the celebration
And make the earth reverberate with our cries of victory.[56]

But, the dream was dispelled. Independence gained could not be retained. Upendra Chandra Mitra and Chandicharan Sen, lamenting the lost paradise, emphasized the reason: moral decline, degrading social customs, flaws in character (particularly of the rebel leaders such as Nana Saheb, and the sepoys) and conduct that failed to live up to the ideals of *dharma*. The brief elation turned to sombre self-reflection and an inner critique expressed by the crucial question: are we worthy of independence? Selfless sacrifice, courage and patriotism needed to be conjoined to correct conduct and observance of *dharma*. Both sepoy rebels and some of their leaders failed to live up to these ideals. Thus, 1857 was a moment of betrayal and failure. But, hope lay beyond. What was lost in 1857 could be gained in future if one overcame the reasons for the loss. If Indians (including Bengalis) adhered to correct codes of conduct and *dharma*, and then glory would return. Situating the means and the goal within a frame of the past-present-future, fictional representations resonated with the idea of moral and social (*samajik*) progress, a composite idea and movement made up of many links[57] as reflected in historical, biographical and social tracts in Bengal. The orientation was different from those of the sepoys in northern and central India, for it did not look back to a shattered past even if it sought to build a new future. As Upendra Chandra Mitra put it:

> Nowadays the hope of progress and improvement of the country [*desh*] flows in the veins of its people. [We are now asking], "What belittled or lowered us? What made us lose everything? What would give back our self-identity and all that we have lost?" This hope is a potent propelling factor, and to get back what we have lost is the aim of the modern, progressive society.[58]

The national element thus perceived in the social progress of the *swadesh* expressed a distinct regional dimension, which contrasted the mentality of the mutiny in an all India sense, even while being influenced by the events and ideologies of 1857.

CONCLUSION

This essay has focused critically on certain key themes and representations of 1857 as reflected in Bengali fiction during the late colonial period. It has argued that we need to look beyond existing historiographical frames which stereotype Bengal as 'loyalist'[59] on the ground that actual protest and armed rebellion was absent. By showing that fiction, intersecting with historical/travel/biographical accounts, formed a key site for rethinking 1857 (the sheer number of fictional works belonging to the genres of novel, short-story, and drama dealing with 1857[60] reflects interest rather than indifference), this essay has delineated specific ways in which constructions of identity in Bengal were woven around 1857 along trajectories different from the mentality of the mutiny in an all-India sense, could also be fitted into a nationalist paradigm. The three major themes investigated in this essay point toward (1) the existence of mentalities of dissent which had anti-colonial tones, though they co-existed with contextual loyalism; (2) an interrelationship between Bengal and India, and Bengalis and other Indians; and (3) constructions of the idea of India based on the primacy and need of a righteous social and moral order.

The regional representation of an iconic national event in Bengali fiction had a crucial function. It transcended the sense of failure and finality which the revolt meant to many minds. 1857 was a milestone in a journey toward a better future through social and moral reconstruction, which underpinned the idea of independent India. The need for moral and social transformation was underscored by an experiential journey and struggle (of the sepoys, their leaders and some Bengali individuals) in the fictive space, and the inherent limitations of that struggle. The genre of historical novels focusing on 1857 showed the social world not only as it was, but also suggested how, at times, it came close to being quite different, and how even after the loss of imaginary independence, it could indeed become different. In this margin of historical possibility, fictional consciousness had free play. The idea of social progress and future glory had resonances with historical, travel, and experiential accounts also, though the ways of articulation and the means of connecting it with the events and ideologies of 1857 were different. But this intersection shows that fiction can at times masquerade as fact, especially when the framework within which social and political parameters and contexts (as well as the future) are situated, is historical. Celebrating history as a realm of wish fulfilment and contingency, fictional accounts of 1857 became a means of articulating history's (and the revolt's) hidden and unfinished discourse. The trajectory of social progress underpinning constructions of *swadesh* and ideas about a *Bharatbarshiya* universe in fictional accounts thus transcended the limited, marginalized and localized nature of the revolt, and also constructed it as evocative of future nationalist hopes and aspirations.

NOTES

1. Rajat Kanta Ray has explored different layers of the mentality of the uprising. Race, religion, and protection of the realm were central concerns which fed into the complex emotional weave of this mentality. See Rajat Kanta Ray, *The Felt Community: Commonalty and Mentality before the Emergence of Indian Nationalism* (New Delhi: Oxford University Press, 2003), pp. 353–467. My essay explores patterns and shades of mentality in Bengal as expressed in literature/fiction. Representations of the revolt in Bengali fiction formed major strands of a mentality that differed from the mentality of the mutineers in an all-India sense, but which drew on the events, ideologies, and antagonisms of 1857 to produce a discourse on an empowered identity.
2. The problem of sharp, dichotomous terminologies and labels (loyalist/rebel) has been addressed by E.I. Brodkin. See E.I. Brodkin, 'The Struggle for Succession: Rebels and Loyalists in the Indian Mutiny of 1857', *MAS*, vol. 6, no. 3 (1972), p. 277. He points out that while in some instances such labels may help, in other contexts they merely confuse. I have

shown elsewhere that Bengali attitudes to the revolt cannot be cast in any simple 'loyalist' mould just because actual protest and armed opposition was muted in Bengal. See Swarupa Gupta, '1857 and Ideas about Nationhood in Bengal: Nuances and Themes', Special Issue of *Economic and Political Weekly* (12–18 May 2007) reprinted in *1857: Essays from Economic and Political Weekly* (Hyderabad: Orient Longman, 2008), pp. 279–302.

3. See, for instance, Durgadas Bandyopadhyay, *Bidrohe Bangali ba Amar Jibancharit*, printed in *Janmabhoomi*, 1889–91.
4. Jadunath Sarbadhikary, *Tirthabhraman* (*1853–1857*), ed. Nagendranath Basu (Calcutta, 1915).
5. Though literary productions drew on 'real' and 'historical' sources, including colonial records, imagination was crucial in the interplay of fiction and fact. Jyotirindranath Tagore's *Jhansir Rani* (1903) was based on a translation of a biographical account of Lakshmibai by a Maratha writer, and drew on 'historical' sources such as works written by Englishmen, on colonial and government documents, and on first-person accounts of those who actually accompanied the Rani to the battlefield as well as of her nearest relatives. The use of 'real' and 'historical' sources was supposed to make the work unbiased according to Jyotirindranath Tagore. Uma Chakravarty has underlined that popular histories such as Rajanikanta Gupta's five volume *Shipahi Juddher Itihas* (Calcutta, 1876) formed the basis of novels. See Uma Chakravarty, 'Whatever Happened to the Vedic Dasi? Orientalism, Nationalism and a Script for the Past', in K. Sangari and S. Vaid (eds.), *Recasting Women: Essays in Colonial History* (New Delhi: Tulika, 1989). However, this viewpoint misses the ways in which the 'imaginary' element in literature reflected facets of a complex mentality influenced by formative factors other than popular histories.
6. The quest for a 'new' history lay at the heart of a composite movement for an empowered identity in which literature (fictional works), and historical, travel, biographical, and autobiographical works formed interactive genres. Especially significant here are the specific modes of interaction between the genres/currents. The mid-nineteenth century formed a significant period in this respect, when these various currents began to confluence, reflecting the complex ways in which constructions of selfhood were situated *vis-à-vis* the notion of a nation. Theatre was one significant mode of representation and dissemination of such ideas. From the 1850s an organized mode of theatrical representation crystallized. In 1872, the birth of the 'National Theatre' symbolized the proclamation of the self albeit the fact that elements of emulation (of Western models) persisted. See Sudipto Chatterjee, *The Colonial Staged: Theatre in Colonial Calcutta* (Calcutta, 2008).

7. For details about notions of nationhood woven around, and historically rooted in, the evolution of *samaj*, see Swarupa Gupta, 'Notions of Nationhood in Bengal: Perspectives on *Samaj*, 1867–1905', *MAS*, vol. 40, no. 2 (2006), pp. 273–302.
8. Meenakshi Mukherjee has underlined the significance of the emergence of the novel, a genre generated and sustained by the middle class, and incorporating the values of this class against the feudal values of the epic and romance. In late colonial fiction dealing with the revolt, these genres and distinctions were blurred: in many of the historical novels the hero's fate was linked to the destiny of the community and a chivalric/heroic code (transmuted through the principles of cultural Aryanism implying acceptance of the epics, connections with Sanskrit and belief in a supreme Godhead) was a major theme in most works. Meenakshi Mukherjee, *Realism and Reality: The Novel and Literature in Colonial Society* (Delhi, 1985), p. 4.
9. For details, see Meenakshi Mukherjee, *Realism and Reality*, p. 3.
10. Modern forms of narration and performance e la Western types (such as the novel or the sonnet) were adapted into the form of Bengali literary productions. Chandicharan Sen's *Jhansir Rani* was, as stated on the title page, 'A Historical Romance'. It contained a blend of supernatural events and fact, real and imaginary characters. At the same time, as Bengali literature drew on Western types/forms, there was a drive to mirror a disenchanted, scientific world-view in the contents. But this did not mean a total dissociation from the past indigenous literary traditions. The interfusion of the old and the new was a distinct feature of anti-colonial literature. By the turn of the century, the functions and significance of this brand of literature were widely recognized. Surendranath Banerjee commented: 'Both from the dramatic and literary points of view, *Sirajuddaula* (by Girish Chandra Ghosh) is destined to occupy a high and an enduring place in our national literature.' This comment was printed in *Bengalee*, 3 February 1906.
11. Sudipta Kaviraj, *The Unhappy Consciousness: Bankimchandra Chattopadhyay and the Formation of Nationalist Discourse in India* (New Delhi, 1995), p. 113.
12. It is difficult to agree with Gopal Haldar that the events, ideologies and spirit of the Revolt could not captivate the Bengali literary imagination. See Haldar, 'Bengali Literature Before, and After 1857', in P.C. Joshi (ed.), *Rebellion 1857: A Symposium* (Calcutta, 1957, rpt.: Calcutta: K.P. Bagchi, 1986), p. 269. Haldar's point that in the changed socio-cultural/political climate of the 1870s, the revolt had only an oblique and indirect effect in the works of Bankimchandra Chattopadhyay and Hemchandra Bandyopadhyay eludes the fact that 1857 formed the backdrop of so many plays, novels and short stories from 1874 onwards (as has been

observed by Bijitkumar Datta in *Banglasahitye Aitihasik Upanyash*, Calcutta, 1995), and constituted a significant theme in a literature of patriotism that burgeoned during the late 1850s and continued well into the twentieth century. Nor does Haldar's perspective take note of the ways in which the events, ideologies, and spirit of 1857 were configured in the fictive space of literature (through subtle metamorphosis of the idioms, rhetoric, and mentality of rebellion in north and central India), which shaped discourses on nationhood.

13. Hilda Gregg in an article entitled 'The Indian Mutiny in Fiction' printed in *Blackwood's Edinburgh Magazine* in 1897, observed: 'Of all the great events of this century, as they are reflected in fiction, the Indian Mutiny has taken the firmest hold on the popular imagination.' See Gautam Chakravarty, *The Indian Mutiny and the British Imagination* (Cambridge: Cambridge University Press, 2005), p. 1.
14. See, for instance, Kamala Sarkar, '1857 and the Bengali Mind', *The Statesman*, 27 May 2007. The stereotype of a loyalist Bengal whose intelligentsia was strongly opposed to the sepoy rebel was underlined in the works of Benoy Ghosh and Gopal Haldar. See, for instance, Haldar, 'Bengali Literature Before and After 1857', in P.C. Joshi (ed.), *Rebellion, 1857: A Symposium*, p. 259.
15. Benoy Ghosh, 'The Bengali Intelligentsia and the Revolt', in Joshi (ed.), *Rebellion: 1857: A Symposium*, pp. 103–17.
16. The very principle of social progress stemming from the literati's liberal bourgeois ideology, which was seen by Benoy Ghosh and Gopal Haldar as a stumbling block to supporting the sepoy cause in the revolt, became a means and an idiom/rhetoric for articulating the Bengali nationalist imagination. An understanding of 1857 was derived via the conceptual category of *samaj*, and 1857 was viewed as a vital link in a chain of social transformation. This showed how the idiom for expressing mentalities of dissent in Bengal was not religious/racial, but social/*samajik*. The perspective reconsidered and contextualized the polarity between colonial modernity (symbolized by the intelligentsia's urge for social progress) and the backward looking feudal elements ingrained in the mentality of the mutiny, and fitted 1857 into the framework of modernity/social progress.
17. The first historical novel written against the backdrop of the revolt, Gobinda Chandra Ghosh's *Chittabinodini* (Calcutta, 1874), sharply contrasted the uncivilized and superstitious sepoys with the progressive and loyal Bengalis. This work was markedly loyalist in character.
18. A relatively recent newspaper article has contended that the revolt meant nothing but an outburst of sepoy rage to most Bengali writers and the Bengali mind was indifferent to the revolt. See Kamala Sarkar, '1857 and the Bengali Mind', *The Statesman*, 27 May 2007. The article misses the nuances embedded in works such as Kaliprasanna Sinha's

Hutom Pyanchar Naksha, and bases its conclusions on a decontextualized reading of limited sources.

19. Kaliprasanna Sinha, *Hutom Pyanchar Naksha*, ed. Brajendranath Bandyopadhyay and Sajanikanta Das (Calcutta, 1948), p. 54.
20. Upendra Chandra Mitra, *Nana Saheb ba Bharater Sukhasapna* (Calcutta, 1879, rpt. 1883), mentioned in Sukumar Mitra, *Atharasha Satanna O Bangla Desh* (Calcutta, 1960), p. 43. Emphasis mine.
21. Uniform denigration of sepoys was also absent in travel accounts such as Jadunath Sarbadhikary's *Tirthabhraman*. Jadunath disparaged those zamindars who helped the British (ascribing to them the derogatory epithet of 'Khoyer Khan') and praised the valour of the Kshatriya sepoys in Kashi/Varanasi. He quoted the words of the rebel Guman Singh to underline the patriotism of the sepoys, valourizing *dharma* as an essential element in their idea of a new order based on righteousness and ethical rule (*shu shashan*). See *Tirthabhraman*, pp. 475, 498–9, 505.
22. Upendra Chandra Mitra referred to Rajanikanta Gupta's historical account of the revolt as a source. The details of the Proclamation are to be found in Rajanikanta Gupta, *Shipahi Juddher Itihas* (Calcutta, 1877), vol. III.
23. Upendra Chandra Mitra, *Nana Saheb ba Bharater Sukhasapna*, mentioned in Sukumar Mitra, *Atharasha Satanna O Bangla Desh*, p. 91.
24. Chandicharan Sen, *Jhansir Rani* (Calcutta, 1888), pp. 151–2.
25. Ibid., p. 113.
26. Girish Chandra Ghosh, *Chandra*, serialized in *Kusum Mela* from 1884 onwards, mentioned in Sukumar Mitra, *Atharasha Satanna O Bangla Desh*, pp. 51–3. The image of the *sannyasi* leader and armed rebellion reflects the idea of a particular brand/cult of revolt, which found expression in other Bengali works, and fed into anti-colonial mentalities in Bengal. One of the most poignant expressions of this strand was Bankimchandra Chattopadhyay's *Anandamath* (Calcutta, 1881).
27. Girish Chandra Ghosh, *Chandra*, mentioned in Sukumar Mitra, *Atharasha Satanna O Bangla Desh*, p. 53.
28. Pramathnath Bisi, 'Chhinna Dalil', in *Chapati O Padma* (Calcutta: 1955), pp. 55-60.
29. This reflects an interesting connection with earlier mentalities, manifested even in 'loyalist' works such as Kaliprasanna Sinha's *Hutom Pyanchar Naksha*. Kaliprasanna also thought that Bengalis remained 'loyal' because of their intrinsic cowardice. In a self-critical and scathingly satirical vein he wrote,

    [During the Mutiny], thrust into a corner after realizing their predicament, the Bengalis assembled in the house of Gopal Mallick. They tried to convince the British that "though a hundred years have passed since the establishment of British rule, they were still the unlucky, spineless Bengalis. Even after years of contact with the British, after receiving western-education, and having learnt and adopted British customs and manners... many of the well known *babus* do not take a boat ride on the Ganga for fear of a storm... these people are scared of their own shadows. That they will fight is absolutely impossible". As for British manners and customs, 'the Bengalis can return them (like worn and used clothes) if the government so orders'.

See Kaliprasanna Sinha, *Hutom Pyanchar Naksha*, ed. Brajendranath Bandyopadhyay and Sajanikanta Das, pp. 54–5.

30. Swapan Dasgupta has recently argued that post-Independence histories have perpetuated the trend of obliterating India's loyalist past from the collective memory. See Swapan Dasgupta, 'Plassey versus the Mutiny in Indian History: The Neglected Battle', *The Telegraph*, Calcutta, 15 June 2007.
31. Though most works lauded the heroism of the leaders, inscribing them into a nationalist history of patriotism, some works denigrated the leaders of 1857. Iswar Gupta and Gobinda Chandra Ghosh strongly criticized the Rani of Jhansi and Nana Saheb respectively. See Gobinda Chandra Ghosh, *Chittabinodini.*
32. Pramathnath Bisi, 'Nana Saheb', in *Chapati O Padma* (Calcutta, 1955), pp. 131–2.
33. R.C. Majumdar, *The Sepoy Mutiny and the Revolt of 1857* (Calcutta, 1963), p. 427, and Tapti Roy, mentioned by Indrani Sen, 'Inscribing the Rani of Jhansi in Colonial Mutiny Fiction', in *1857: Essays from Economic and Political Weekly*, pp. 255–6.
34. Jyotirindranath Tagore, *Jhansir Rani* (Calcutta, 1903), p. 23.
35. Ibid., p. 28.
36. Ibid., pp. 43–4.
37. See Chandicharan Sen, *Jhansir Rani.*
38. Kaliprasanna Datta, *Bijoy* (Calcutta, 1883), mentioned in Sukumar Mitra, *Atharasha Satanna O Bangla Desh*, p. 57.
39. Jyotirindranath Tagore, *Jhansir Rani*, p. 19.
40. Rajat Kanta Ray, *The Felt Community*, p. 358.
41. Jyotirindranath Tagore, *Jhansir Rani*, pp. 31–3.
42. Ibid.
43. Ibid., pp. 35, 38, 39.
44. Ibid., p. 40.
45. Where there was a fall from such virtues and standards of moral conduct, valourization was conditional and qualified, and glory won could well be lost by such lapses.
46. Chandicharan Sen, *Jhansir Rani*, p. 58.
47. Nana Saheb was the subject of controversy and conflicting representations of him abounded in literature. While his patriotism was lauded by

Upendra Chandra Mitra, and his defeat was attributed to conspiracy and his own weaknesses and flaws, other writers such as Chandicharan Sen and 'loyalist' works such as Gobinda Chandra Ghosh's *Chittabinodini* adopted a tone of unqualified denigration. See Gobinda Chandra Ghosh, *Chittabinodini*, and Upendra Chandra Mitra, *Nana Saheb ba Bharater Sukhasapna* for contrasting images of Nana Saheb. In much later works such as in the short stories of Pramathnath Bisi, there were echoes of earlier representations, as well as the recasting of Nana as an enigmatic figure forever eluding discovery (he fled to Nepal and died there in 1860 according to hearsay). The portrayals included humorous and satirical sketches in short stories such as 'Nana Saheb'. A sympathetic tone was also evident in convictions about Nana being the victim of a conspiracy, the humanization of an elusive enigma through a final denouement when the Nana is 'discovered' and collapses at the feet of his long-lost wife. See Pramathnath Bisi, *Nana Saheb*, in *Chapati O Padma: A Collection of Short Stories Relating to the Revolt of 1857.*

48. Upendra Chandra Mitra, *Nana Saheb*, referred to in Sukumar Mitra, *Atharasha Satanna O Bangla Desh*, p. 46.
49. This was also mentioned in Jyotirindra Tagore's *Purbikram* (1874).
50. Girish Chandra Ghosh, *Sirajuddaula*, printed in Rathindranath Ray and Debipada Bhattacharya (eds.), *Girish Chandra: Samagra Rachanabali* (Calcutta, 1969), pp. 561–2.
51. Akshoykumar Moitreya, *Sirajuddaula*, *Sekaler Sukhdukhha*, *Gourer Katha* (rpt. Calcutta, 1984).
52. For details, see Swarupa Gupta, '*Samaj*, *Jati* and *Desh*: Reflections on Nationhood in Late Colonial Bengal', *Studies in History*, vol. 23, no. 2 (2007), pp. 177–203.
53. Gobinda Chandra Ghosh, *Chittabinodini*, quoted in Sukumar Mitra, *Atharasha Satanna O Bangla Desh*, p. 36.
54. Upendra Chandra Mitra, *Nana Saheb*, mentioned in Sukumar Mitra, *Atharasha Satanna*, p. 47.
55. Girish Chandra Ghosh, *Chandra*, mentioned in ibid., p. 52.
56. Ibid., p. 46.
57. Shibnath Shastri, *Ramtanu Lahiri O Tatkalin Bangasamaj* (Calcutta, 1904), p. 202.
58. Upendra Chandra Mitra, *Nana Saheb* (2nd edn., Calcutta, 1883), Introduction.
59. Gopal Haldar, Benoy Ghosh and Sajanikanta Das agreed on the point that Bengal remained indifferent/loyalist during 1857. Sajanikanta Das underlined the tremendous hostility of Bengali writers to the revolt, but could not mention the name of any major literary figure to support his claim except that of Iswar Gupta (whose works reflected mockeries of Rani of Jhansi and Nana Saheb). See Sukumar Mitra, *Atharasha Satanna O Bangla Desh*, p. 2.

60. Though these literary works did not have monolithic strands, areas of congruence could be mapped. Further, it is possible to trace the connection between fiction and public opinion by comparing the relative popularity which one work had over another. For instance, unlike Gobinda Chandra Ghosh's anglophile and loyalist novel *Chittabinodini*, Upendra Chandra Mitra's *Nana Saheb ba Bharater Sukhasapna* (celebrating India's brief independence, with a hopeful and progressive streak) had wider popular appeal. Its second edition was printed and dedicated to Rajendra Narayan Ray Bahadur, patron of Dacca Bangiya Sahitya Samaj and benefactor of Bangiya Sahitya. See Sukumar Mitra, *Atharasha Satanna O Bangla Desh*, p. 42. Similarly, Girish Chandra Ghosh's *Chandra* published in the periodical *Kusum Mala* from 1884, three years after the publication of Bankimchandra Chattopadhyay's *Anandamath*, reflected how dreams of the independence of *swadesh* and struggle for it (present in *Chandra* and *Anandamath*) almost simultaneously engrossed two well-known writers, and awakened and stirred public imagination and interest.

CHAPTER 7

Writing Fiction and Constructing History: A Case Study of the Literature on 1857

SATYAKI KANJILAL

In contemporary critical discourse, 'narrative' has been a site for discursive contention. Historians are preoccupied with the idea of 'truth', as though it had an objective existence. It is amazing that historians like Jerzy Topolski believe that history is indeed a 'truthful' presentation of past. It appears from Topolski's essay that 'truth' has an 'objective' and 'ethereal' value which can be synthesized and represented.[1] In the post-Nietzschean world, however, one is critical of truth's objectivity. Does it have an epistemological and an ontological value? Can there only be versions of 'truth', not of 'the truth'? This dilemma problematizes the purpose of writing history.

C. Behan McCullagh addresses this dilemma and suggests a solution:

> The personal value which directs their [historians'] construction of a narrative is precisely the desire to represent its subject fairly. As for preconceptions, yes, the historian always has a general idea of the nature of his central subject, of its kinds of properties and relations, which guides his search for facts about it.... [S]uch preconceptions need not misrepresent reality. If the historian's evidence does not fit them, then they have to be abandoned.[2]

McCullagh apparently believes that through careful selection of evidence, a 'fair' representation of a past reality is possible. The historian would be able to present a narrative without value judgement. David Canandine has shown that historians are interested in the past for issues that concern their present.[3] Accepting Canandine's argument, McCullagh suggests that the idea of the past may itself change. But what if we are presented with two contradictory narratives of the same incident? Which will be the one to be 'abandoned'? Even though McCullagh does not address this problem, he implies that one of those narratives must be 'fair' representation, without being explicit as to whose narrative is to be accepted as such a representation.

John Passmore has made a noteworthy contribution to the debate on history and fiction. He is of the opinion that we are born in a world of stories and a historian can criticize and rectify the writings of other historians which, again, are based on existing stories, myths, and legends. Identifying 'events' as belonging to the ontological mode and 'narratives' as belonging to the linguistic mode, he suggests that in history we deal not with 'events' but with 'event-description'. Thus, history switches from the ontological mode to the linguistic mode and becomes a linguistic practice. 'Events', being pluralistic in nature are interconnected in a complex network of causality. History is concerned with 'events' in an evaluative sense, i.e. 'events' which have a 'particular place in particular courses of events'. History thus becomes 'utilitarian' in its objective, is narrated as 'particular courses of events' that are 'of interest to somebody'. Explaining history in utilitarian terms serves a dual purpose. It helps us answer the basic purpose of writing history as well as contemporary practices of writing 'popular history'.[4] Passmore's approval of the commonplace of narrativism, by accepting the argument that some historical works have the general structure of novels and myths, blurs the distinction between history and other narratives.

The affinity that history shares with fiction cannot be ignored. The past, mainly in fragments, seems to be accessible through texts that survive in archives. A historian weaves a plot out of these fragments by stringing them together in a common thread and thereby attempts to form a whole. Whether this is capable of reflecting 'historical reality' has been a subject of critical debate.[5] History, as Passmore has rightly suggested, is concerned with 'event-description' and 'events' belong to the ontological mode. However, he seems to have missed the point that when one describes an event, one mediates as well as translates from the ontological mode to the linguistic mode. Writing history, thus, involves both mediation and translation, and it is the 'historian' who acts as mediator and translator. A historian selects from the evidence he has at his disposal. In the process of this selection, his ideology guides him. This process of selection robs history of its claim to objective 'neutrality' and makes it analogous to writing fiction, since a writer of fiction is also guided by his ideology.

Hayden White stresses this process of selection of materials by an historian. He suggests that history is not just about 'events', but also about a possible set of relationships that can emerge out of these and the relationships between these disparate 'events' exist only in the mind of the historian.[6] White seems more interested in what a historian makes of the evidence or the sources at his/her disposal than in the sources themselves. Not so much evidence, as the person using it, is what becomes important to White. It seems that White is suspicious of the expression of knowledge of the past outside the modes of expression that a historian has at his/her disposal; the modes being tragedy, comedy, romance, and satire. This shows that White is concerned with the communicative function of historical discourse. He explains:

> According to this view of history as communication, a history is conceived to be a "message" about a "referent" (the past, historical events, and so on) the content of which is both "information" (the "facts") and an "explanation" (the "narrative" account). Both the facts in their particularity and the narrative account in its generality must meet a correspondence, as well as coherence, criterion of truth value.[7]

Defining discourse from this communicative perspective as 'an apparatus for the production of meaning' and not just 'a vehicle for the transmission of information about an external referent',[8] White continues:

> In historical discourse, the narrative serves to transform into story a list of historical events that would otherwise be only a chronicle. In order to effect this transformation, the events, agents, and agencies represented in the chronicle must be encoded as story elements; that is, they must be characterized as the kinds of events, agents, agencies, and so on, that can be apprehended as elements of specific story types.[9]

White distinguishes between 'historical' and 'fictional' stories based on their content by arguing that, the content of the former being events that really happened, while that of the latter being 'imaginary events, events invented by the narrator'.[10] However, he also points out the similarity between the two:

> Like literature, history progresses by the production of classics, the nature of which is such that they cannot be disconfirmed or negated, in the way that the principal conceptual schemata of the sciences are. And it is their nondisconfirmability that testifies to the essentially literary nature of historical classics.[11]

There have been criticisms of White's views. Mary Fulbrook in *Historical Theory* accuses him of making an 'unfounded and circular assertion'.[12] She criticizes White's assertion that the relationship between different 'events' in the past exists only in a historian's mind. This runs counter to human existence and behaviour. She tries to prove her argument with the example of Holocaust. If one accepts White's argument, then one has to accept that there is no relation between Hitler's appointment as Chancellor in 1933 and the Holocaust of 1941–5 and provides a counter argument that historians work within certain paradigms, 'certain collective traditions of enquiry'.[13] Fulbrook is of the opinion that historiography is about 'emplotment' and 'puzzle solving' from the evidence at disposal and not about weaving a plot or story out of the blue. She agrees that: '. . . it is certainly the case that, within any particular historical discourse or paradigm, particular accounts, interpretations or explanations are potentially "disconfirmable" (to use Hayden White's term).'[14] In Fulbrook's opinion, it is the duty of a historian to test or challenge these 'received interpretations'.

Incidentally, William Dalrymple's *The Last Mughal*[15] has instigated a critical debate among India's historians. Any narrative belongs to the mimetic mode. However, history is concerned with how certain events happened in the past. In narrative history, a historian attempts to bring the past and the present together. In doing so, the historian communicates through a plot and shows how certain acts were 'enacted' in the past. Unlike a narrative, a play belongs to the diegetic mode. The empirical existence of past events cannot be ignored. In epistemological terms however, they can be accessed through texts. Though narratives concerning the past can be constructed, these events were lived through only by certain people. In retrospect, the past seems like a play enacted by those present in the cast. Dalrymple in his *The Last Mughal* seems to be aware of this and perhaps for this reason provides us with a *dramatis personae*. His using of *dramatis personae* places *The Last Mughal* at the crossroads of diegetic and mimetic mode. No wonder that Sushil Chaudhury has applauded it as 'popular history'.[16] Even though it is not quite clear as to what Chaudhury regards as 'popular history', it seems that he is referring to a method of writing history which is interesting to the reader and engrossing at the same time. Perhaps he is referring to a mode of writing which shares affinity with fiction. In European critical tradition, history and poetry (literature) have been strictly identified as two different modes of writing since antiquity. India, a former British colony, inherited that tradition. In spite of post-modern insistence on more resemblance than difference between these two modes, this dogma appears to cast a heavy weight on the minds of Indian historians. Critical responses to Dalrymple's *The Last Mughal* have pointed out that among Indian historians the distinction between history and other genres, especially fiction, exists, just as it used to in the early decades of the last century. It has also brought into light the debate revolving around history and narrative.

It would not be irrelevant here to refer to Flora Annie Steel's *On the Face of the Waters*,[17] an account of an English woman in Delhi during the Great Rebellion. It is interesting that Steel professes that the major events in the novel 'really happened'. In her 'Author's Note' she mentions:

> As the writer, I have only to point out where my history ends, my story starts. Briefly then I have not allowed the fiction to interfere with fact in the slightest degree. The reader may rest assured that every incident in the remotest degree on the Indian Mutiny, or on the part which real men took in it, is scrupulously exact, even to the date, the hour, the very weather. Nor have I allowed the actual actors in the great tragedy to say a word regarding it which is not to be allowed in the accounts of eyewitnesses, or in their own writings.[18]

In making these admissions Steel is assuming that there was an actual course of events and this could be communicated effectively to readers. She is insistent in her assertion that she has not digressed from the actual course of events.

As suggested earlier, fiction writing and historiography are analogous, as both are constructed under the guiding influence of their creator's ideology. The 1857 Uprising, which initially started as a mutiny, escalated in scale and intensity to pose as a stiff challenge to the EIC. British historians, publicists, and policy-makers were at a loss for a rubric that would describe this event.[19] This rubric was also to serve as a validation for the atrocities and violence that followed the counter-insurgency operations, hence the institutionalization of Victorian 'womanhood' and myths of their violation. British women were projected as helpless, and sensational stories of their rape and mutilation were given great importance. Medieval chivalry and masculine heroism were sought to be revived in these narratives. Often a native threatened a woman[20] with abduction and rape and it was by the virtue of gallantry of a British gentleman that she was saved. Steel's *On the Face of the Waters* is both a critique of this objectification of Victorian womanhood to justify the British violence that followed the Rebellion, as well as an appropriation of this trope.

Victorian society was essentially patriarchal. It is no wonder that the presence of British women was suggested as one of a possible reason for the deterioration of the relationship between the British and the Indians and severe repercussions that followed the Rebellion. Perhaps it would be just to refer to a passage from Wilfred Scawen Blunt's *Ideas About India* (1885):

> It is a fact that the Englishwoman in India during the last thirty years has been the cause of half the bitter feelings there between race and race. It was her presence at Cawnpore and Lucknow that pointed the sword of revenge after the Mutiny, and it is her constantly increasing influence now that widens the gulf of ill-feeling and makes amalgamation daily more impossible.[21]

Indeed, in the early years of the EIC, the relationship between the British and the Indians was not as formal as it became in the nineteenth century. There were people like David Ochterlony, Fraser, Gardner, and James Skinner who were more 'native' than British in their habits and had a number of Indian wives. The relationship started changing with the expansionist policy of the British in the post-1818 period. After 1818, a large number of British women arrived in India; both upper class and middle class. Blunt suggests that had women not come to India, there would have been no massacres of women and hence no severe atrocities inflicted on Indians. Steel's fiction, working within a tradition, critiques the basic assumptions of this tradition.

Initially, it would appear that Steel's fiction is working within the tradition of a code of masculine chivalry encouraged British to fashion their reaction to the 1857 Rebellion. Her attitude is essentially imperialist and colonial. Throughout the novel, the idea of white man's burden seems to dominate. The fiction also suffers from typification of characters. Bahadur Shah Zafar is presented as an effeminate, feeble, and an inefficient old man, Abu Bakr as a sensualist and debauch, Tara as a fanatic. Like a taunting whore in Meerut,[22] Zinat Mahal instigates the sepoys into a frenzy. According to the verdict of history, Zinat Mahal belonged to the pro-British faction during the 1857 Rebellion and was constantly working to get her son Mirza Jawan Bhakt recognized by the British as the successor of Bahadur Shah Zafar. Steel's portrayal of Zinat Mahal as an instigator of violence belongs to the tradition of Mutiny novels where Indian women are shown as debased, sensuous, and cruel, instigating men to violence. This ideology transformed Rani Lakshmi Bai into an icon of Oriental beauty; sensuous, cruel and responsible for the murder of British women and children. The medieval notions of despotism, tyranny, and wealth that were associated with Islamic East were reworked in order to create a discourse of savagery associated with decadence of civilization.[23] Steel's Zinat Mahal belongs to this mode of linking Oriental characters with barbarism. Her obsession with the accuracy of events has been documented elsewhere.

Flora Annie Steel was the wife of a civil servant and she had access to a box of confidential papers.[24] This brings us to an interesting issue—why, as a conservative historian would say, did Steel deviate from 'historic truth' in the case of Zinat Mahal? This may lead one to assume that the writer is acknowledging the objective existence of 'truth', thereby also segregating the construct of 'truth' into 'historical truth' and 'non-historical truth'. 'Truth' does not have any objective existence; it is a construct, usually textual. It is beyond doubt that Steel was working within an established tradition of imperialist, masculine, and racist ideology which required her to demonize certain Indian characters. However, this also prompts one to ask if there was any document in the concealed box which proved to Steel that Zinat Mahal was pro-active as a rebel. If there was, it is now lost for good.[25]

Though Steel uses the tropes of the Mutiny novel, *On the Face of the Waters*, like most of other Mutiny novels is not a British propaganda of valour, male prowess, or white man's invincibility. Kate Erlton who was trapped hopelessly in an unhappy marriage, saw the 1857 Rebellion as an opportunity to liberate herself from the bonds of her marriage and find happiness with Jim Douglas. Kate Erlton is not depicted as essentially helpless like Jean Atherton or Isobel Hannay (thereby conforming to the Victorian cult of the veneration of women). She saved herself a number of times through her own ingenuity and sometimes with the help of Tara, an Indian widow. The novel is essentially critical of British atrocities and crimes in the wake of the 1857 Rebellion, which were justified as vengeance seeking acts for the murder of British women and children. Steel reprimands Nicholson and Henry Hodson, both notorious for impulsive decisions. Douglas says, 'We exaggerated the position from the first; we exaggerate the dangers of it now.'[26] Steel's critique becomes clear in the question that Douglas asks Major Hodson: 'Is the crisis so desperate that we need levy the ladies?'[27] Later, when Douglas takes seriously Nicholson's orders to 'Save that poor lady—or—kill somebody! It's all we are doing',[28] the narrator informs us, 'Kate, however, had already been found, or rather she had never been lost'.[29] Major Hodson was responsible for the cold-blooded murder of three Mughal princes, Mirza Moghul, Mirza Abu Bakr, and Mirza Khizr Sultan.[30] An eyewitness praise for vengeance in the same place where 'Englishwomen had been outraged and murdered',[31] is immediately countered by a judgement passed by the narrator: 'A strange perversion of truth responsible, perhaps, not only for the praise, but the very deed itself.'[32] Finally, the novel ends with a note on Brigadier General Nicholson: 'So, in a way, John Nicholson stands symbol of the many lives lost uselessly in the vain attempt to go forward too fast.'[33]

Dalrymple's *The Last Mughal* highlights the post-modern blurring of identities as the narrative mode follows a pattern in which 'fictions' are written. It opens with an account of the marriage of Mirza Jawan Bhakt, which seems initially irrelevant to the narrative. Gradually, he explains the politics that were involved in the arrangement of such elegant marriage processions. In his introduction, he criticizes the school of 'Subaltern Studies' for their obscurity.[34] Identifying two parallel schools of historiography on the 1857 Rebellion, he claims to unite them for the first time, in the following words:

> The British histories, as well as a surprising number of those written in English in post-colonial India, tended to use only English-language sources, padding out the gaps, in the case of more recent work, with a thick cladding of post-Saidian theory and jargon. The Urdu histories written by contemporary Muslim scholars in India and Pakistan, on the other hand, tend to make use of an entirely separate and often very rich seam of Urdu primary sources. Moreover, in the case of Delhi there exist some wonderful works of secondary scholarship, such as Aslam Parvez's fine Urdu biography of Zafar, which remain unknown to English-speaking readers. One of the principal aims of this book is to bring the voluminous Persian and Urdu primary and secondary sources on Delhi in 1857 before an English language readership for the first time.[35]

Dalrymple's ideological objective becomes clear: to construct a narrative about Delhi during the Great Rebellion, which would be easy to read and would be a bridge between the two historiographical schools, for his English-speaking readers. By using multilingual sources, he attempts a narrative that would incorporate both points-of-view, British and Indian, 'colonial' and 'rebel'. Indeed, *The Last Mughal* seems to be a collage of fragmented narratives. On the one hand we have Sir Thomas Metcalfe's personal life, his relationship with his daughter Georgiana and his son Theophilus Metcalfe, Georgiana's love affair with Edward Campbell, the death of Theophilus Metcalfe's wife, the eccentric characters of the Delhi British community, etc. On the other we have rivalry between Zauq and Mirza Ghalib, Ghalib's participation in *mushairas*, Zafar's harem and concubines, etc.[36] Besides providing us with accounts of Bahadur Shah Zafar, Dalrymple presents us with accounts of Zahir Dehlavi, Sarvar ul-Mulk, Mufti Sadruddin Khan 'Azurda', Bakht Khan, Sudhari Singh, Gauri Shankar Shukul, and others. Although Dalrymple describes the plight of the common people, he cannot provide us with accounts of common people or soldiers in as great detail as he does with the Delhi elite or the leaders of the rebel force. This is a drawback from which historiography suffers—only fragments of a past can be inferred from circumstantial evidence.

It is interesting that although Harris's diary and Pearce's novel share the same subject—the Siege of Lucknow, which commenced from 30 June 1857 and continued approximately for four and half months—their treatment of the Siege and Rebellion differs considerably. As Gautam Chakravarty has rightly pointed out, the first person accounts provide a bank of topoi which are selectively reinscribed into the texture of the novels.[37] Whereas Harris notes in her diary the struggle, anguish, and perils of the besieged in Lucknow, for Pearce the perils of the besieged becomes a subject of romance. The Siege thus becomes the subject of a narrative that would define colonial superiority, and about the masculine adventurism of the British in India. For Harris, one of the survivors of the Siege, it was a nightmare. It was also a crisis which helped to redefine British national identity. Passmore quite rightly suggests that turning from one narrative to another for verification of the narration is naïve and there cannot be any 'correct description of an event'.[38]

Though later proved otherwise, it was initially suggested that the 1857 Rebellion was started by rumours. These were 'native' accounts of British conspiracy of mass conversion of Indians to Christianity. Whereas these indigenous oral accounts were written off by colonial administration as rumours, the British oral accounts of the Rebellion that found their way into the archival texts, especially the first-person narratives, were regarded as 'facts'. More often than not, these oral narratives were nothing more than rumour from unconfirmed and fictitious sources. Thus the information encrypted in some of the archival texts from which Mutiny novels drew were fictitious in origin. It is interesting to note that although the diary is supposed to be on the Siege of Lucknow, Harris' diary begins on 15 May 1857 with an account of insurrection and the gruesome murder of British resident of Delhi. The murder of the British in Delhi serves as a prologue to the perils of the besieged. Of the 120 pages of *A Lady's Diary on the Seige of Lucknow*,[39] only eighty-eight are devoted to the Siege. The rest of the text acts as an auxiliary to the narrative. The interplay of 'facts' and 'fictions' in Rebellion narratives pave the way for the growth of 'mutiny myths'.

Flora Annie Steel's *On the Face of the Waters* is an interesting example. Jim Douglas in the guise of a Pathan sowar rescues Mrs. Elton in Delhi from mutinous sepoys and they spend three months in rebel-held Delhi, disguised as a Pathan couple. Their spending three months in enemy territory is quite incredible.[40]

This is an appropriation of the myth of Miss Wheeler of Kanpur, youngest daughter of General Wheeler, rightly identified as 'Judith of Cawnpore' by Jenny Sharpe.[41] Miss Wheeler, it was initially believed, avenged her abduction by a Muslim sowar by killing five of the rebels including her abductor and then killed herself. Later investigation into the matter revealed this as a figment of fiction. Miss Wheeler had actually converted to Islam and was living in peace with her abductor. In Steel's novel, we have an appropriation of this myth. Mrs. Elton is abducted and spends more than two months with a Pathan in Delhi. (The appropriation being that this Pathan is Jim Douglas in disguise.) Harris' *Diary* can also be located in this site of myth construction and propagation. It mentions a certain Miss Jackson who was assumed kidnapped by a sowar and then given to a raja, thereby reenacting the trope of Oriental depravity and sensuality.

Harris's opening account of the Delhi massacre is based on a vague and unconfirmed telegraphic message. It is supplemented by further telegraphic accounts that reached Lucknow via Agra. She promptly scribbles those vague and unreliable accounts in her diary. There are two clear instances of these accounts contradicting, negating, and violating each other—entries made about Monstuart Jackson and his sisters and about the reoccupation of Delhi. The entries of 13 June, 16 June and 25 November contradict each other as one asserts their death while the other expresses the hope of them being alive. These are based on different rumours revolving around the fate of the Jacksons as well as their fellow prisoners. Another entry is made on 24 June about Delhi being retaken by British forces.[42] Despite warning by John Kaye regarding the unreliability of these first person narratives, contemporary historians like Charles Ball and Nolan often drew upon these personal narratives in order to describe the events of a particular region, during the 1857 Rebellion.

Often first person narratives of 'native' atrocities on British subjects fall back on hints and implications rather than explicit description. Describing the massacre at Sitapur, Harris mentions: 'The bare idea of the fate of the unhappy ladies at Sitapur is too horrible; there was no indignity that was not afflicted on all the women the wretches got hold of.'[43] Harris, like other women diarists of the 1857 Rebellion, does not explain what she means by 'no indignity'. Since Mrs. Harris was a clergyman's wife, the fate would have been despicable and also sacrilegious. It is left to the reader of the story to imagine what happened. Such implicit statements construe linguistic slips and these linguistic slips create a spatial void that appeal to a reader's imagination and are duly filled up by the latter. This is often noticed in contemporary histories of 1857, as well as in some contemporary newspaper reports.

In Charles Ball's *History of the Indian Mutiny* there are pictorial illustrations of the event. It is interesting to note that three of them, 'Massacre in the Boats of Cawnpore', 'Massacre of English Officers and their Wives at Jhansi' and 'Miss Wheeler Defending Herself Against the Sepoys at Cawnpore' share one common feature—the murder of innocent babies and humiliation of women. 'Massacre of English Officers and Their Wives at Jhansi' is almost pornographic in its details. As suggested earlier, Ball and historians like him often used first person narrative as evidence. These histories had immense influence on the imagination of contemporary writers. It would be interesting to refer to the newspaper article of a clergyman, published in the *Times* on 25 August 1857:

> They took 48 females, most of them girls of [*sic*] from 10 to 14, many delicately nurtured ladies,—violated them and kept for the base purposes of the heads of the insurrection for a whole week. At the end of that time they made them strip themselves, and gave them up to the lowest of the people to abuse in broad daylight in the street of Delhi. They then commenced the work of torturing them to death, cutting off their breasts, fingers, and noses, and leaving them to die. One lady was three days dying.[44]

This incident is worth noting as the writer of the letter was stationed in Bangalore, thousands of miles from the scene of action. The letter subsequently found its way into several newspapers and seemed to have been a major influence on James Grant's *First Love and Last Love,* where it is cited as an account of native eyewitness.[45] With 'Miss Wheeler Defending Herself Against the Sepoys at Cawnpore', as the cover illustration for Jenny Sharpe's *Allegories of Empire* and 'Massacre of English Officers and Their Wives at Jhansi' as the cover illustration for Nancy L. Paxton's *Writing Under the Raj,*[46] one wonders whether myths of the Rebellion have even infected modern American writers!

It is interesting to read Pearce's *Love Besieged*[47] along with Harris's *Diary* as both of them treat the siege of Lucknow. While the former's treatment is romantic the latter's is realistic. Quite surprisingly, though Pearce was trying to knit a romance out of a historical event and Harris was living that event, there are pieces of information in *Love Besieged* which Harris misses. For example, Harris does not make any mention of the Abyssinian slave of the deposed Nawab Wazid Ali Shah of Awadh. Posted in Johannes's House, this crack shot was a terror to the British and was nicknamed 'Bob the Nailer' or 'Jim the Rifle' for his expertise with the double-barreled rifle.[48] He was shot dead when a sortie was carried out on 7 July 1857 at Johannes' house. This rebel sniper is also mentioned in Henty's *In the Time of Peril* as 'a black scoundrel, a negro, in the service of the king of Oude'.[49] Pearce also provides us with a catalogue of the loss that the British suffered at Chinhut and of ammunition during the transfer of the garrison of Machhi Bhavan to the Residency.[50] Harris just makes a passing reference to these events. Besides, Pearce's work is also noteworthy as it records the rumours that were buzzing in the British camp. It is quite amazing that Pearce attributes the rebel victory at Chinhut to three factors—the British being outnumbered by the enemy, the treachery of the 'native' soldiers, and, most important of all, the rebel 'natives' being led by a European, suspected to be a Russian. Even the accurate artillery fire of the 'rebels' is attributed to the skillful leadership of the 'European leader'.[51] Harris' diary does not make any mention of Russian involvement in the Siege of Lucknow. L.E. Rees refers to an European officer commanding the 'rebel' artillery in his *A Personal Narrative of the Siege of Lucknow*.[52] Rees identifies this officer as Captain Roulton, 'an Englishman in service of the ex-king of Awadh, who had adopted native ways'. Pearce's modification of this piece of information is worth noting. This identification of the European artillery officer as a Russian is reflective of the working of the partisan feeling and the colonial anxiety of a European becoming the 'other' in Pearce.

Ania Loomba traces this colonial anxiety haunting the British imagination to the seventeenth century, generated on account of the possibility of Christians 'turning Turk'.[53] This same colonial anxiety is responsible for the suppression of the counter narrative of Miss Wheeler's conversion to Islam and cohabitation with her abductor. As I have suggested above, British discursive responses to the 1857 Rebellion had institutionalized the idea of the 'English lady' and the narratives of her violation through rape and dissemination were meant to justify the violence of the counter-insurgency operations. The image of the mild and imbecile 'Hindoo', was propagated in pre-Rebellion colonial discourses intermittently to explain the Indian's repeated subjection to foreign invasions. In response to the 1857 Rebellion, the British wanted to coin a linguistic sign that would represent a Hindu in all his treachery and savagery. Although later 'savage Hindoo' was coined, 'blood-thirsty Mussulman' was still regarded as the perpetrator of the most heinous of crimes. C.E. Pearce too introduces the character of Azimullah Khan, trusted lieutenant of Nana Sahib, as the treacherous ex-*khidmatgar* of Jack Hawke.

Pearce's presentation of Azimullah Khan in *Love Besieged* shows the unabashed working of a colonial ideology. Azimullah Khan was the secretary and adviser of Nana Sahib, sent by Nana Sahib as his emissary to plead his case in London. Katherine Frank in her *Lucie Duff Gordon* describes Azimullah's stay in England.[54] Lucie, wife of Alexander Duff Gordon, elder than Azimullah by almost ten years took him as her protégé and introduced him to her Whig peer Lord Lansdowne and her other friends. Young, charming, and intelligent, with a handsome physique, Azimullah was rumoured to have had affairs with unmarried and married women and also to have secretly become engaged to one of them. Lucie in one of his letters had described Azimullah as a 'Musselman Maharajah'. She may have got this fanciful idea from Azimullah's surname 'Khan' which means 'king'. As Lucie's husband took a reactionist view of the 1857 Rebellion, she poured her outrage on behalf of the Indians. She wrote to Lansdowne, and Laynard. 'The real truth of the whole outbreak, I believe we shall never know—I mean the native side of the question.'[55]

P.J.O. Taylor notes in *A Companion to Indian Mutiny of 1857* that Frederick Roberts wrote to his sister that, in Nana Sahib's palace at Bithur they had found numerous letters of Azimullah written by various English women, many of which were assumed to have been from Lucie Duff Gordon. Frank also refers to this discovery of letters by English soldiers.[56] There are varied opinions on Azimullah's death. Taylor notes that he probably died from the fever of Terai at Bhutwal in October 1859. Taylor also refers to A. Busteed, who has written at the back of the India Office Library's copy of Mowbray Thompson's *The Story of Cawnpore* that Azimullah was supposed to have died of small pox while trying to make his way into Calcutta to ask a native banker about Nana Sahib's property. Pearce's *Love Besieged* opens with the chapter 'Azimoolah Khan'. In Pearce's fiction, Azimullah is introduced as a 'prince', who meets Jean Atherton in London and is smitten by her beauty. General Patterson recognizes him and denounces him. To win Azimullah's favours, Lady Constance Harwood tries to help him in his dubious and unscrupulous intentions, which he harbours against her ward Jean. In *Love Besieged*, it is Lady Harwood, an inveterate gambler, who introduced Azimullah in the English circles. The character of Lady Constance Harwood seems to have been drawn on that of Lucie Duff Gordon. The incident of discovery of Azimullah's letters by English soldiers is used by Pearce in his fiction. To retain Azimullah's favours, Lady Harwood writes him a letter in which she mentions that Jean Atherton likes him. Mrs. Ross later uses this letter to brew up a scandal in the besieged Lucknow Residency to disgrace Jean. Later, following the established tropes of the Mutiny novels, Jack Hawke kills Azimullah in a single combat. A person who was sympathetic to the 'natives', becomes an inveterate gambler. Her letter is used by a Eurasian to denigrate English women. Last but not the least, Azimullah becomes a scheming imposter.

Pearce's narrative in some parts varies considerably with that of Mrs. Harris. Following the practice of Anglo–Indian Mutiny fictions, Pearce presents Henry Lawrence as almost a saint facing death with calm fortitude.[57] Harris's entry shows that Lawrence was an ordinary mortal who screamed in agony prior to his death.[58] Harris's journal records the hardships and the humiliations that the British had to endure during the Siege. There were frequent outbreaks of epidemics, along with suicide and murder, among the besieged. In the entry made on 20 July 1857 one finds Mr. Harris subjected to the utmost indignity: he had to crawl out in 'a state of nature' from his bath to save himself. Though the fictions on the Siege mention the perils of the besieged, they do so to define the racial superiority of the British who survived hardship. However, seldom do we find in this genre/type of fiction accounts of suicide and murder committed by the British. Seldom do we find more than passing reference to hospitals and the unhygienic atmosphere of the churchyard in the Mutiny novels, to which J.G. Farrell does justice in his *Siege of Krishnapur*.[59]

The objective of this paper has been to show that in the construction of narratives, ideology plays a prominent part. Harris's *Diary*, Pearce's *Love Besieged*, Steel's *On the Face of the Waters*, and Dalrymple's *The Last Mughal* all take distinct positions on the 1857 Rebellion. Often, first-person narratives were selectively used as sources. This material was often condensed, and narrative segments were displaced, which led to modification or elision of the original. Pearce's showing Henry Lawrence as a saint and Steel's showing Zinat Mahal[60] as an instigator of violence, exemplify this. As suggested earlier, in none of the novels on the 1857 Rebellion do we have murder or suicide committed by British men. Harris' *Diary* is an exception. Mrs. Harris notes in her diary that on 15 June 1857, a Sergeant-Major of 7th Cavalry had murdered the riding master of the same regiment. She also mentions the suicide of Mr. Grahams on 5 September 1857 and suspected suicide of Captain Fullerton on 15 September 1857.[61] It can be well understood that if such incidents had been incorporated in the novel, the position of the English as a conquering race would have been put to test. Though Harris and Pearce differ in selection of the events, they share the same ideology—the imperialist and colonialist. Their narratives confirm contemporary racial prejudice and depict Indians as insolent and cowardly.

Among the narratives on the 1857 Rebellion, the Mutiny novels are important for an understanding of the British reactions to the Rebellion in 1857. Mutiny novels can be broadly classified into two distinct types—those written by writers like G.A. Henty and C.E. Pearce, whose fictions are seldom more than a narrative of conquest, and those written by writers like P.M. Taylor and F.A. Steel who use the tropes of the Mutiny novel for an ulterior purpose. Henty uses Rujub and Ralph Bathurst in his *Rujub the Juggler*[62] to vindicate the imperial discourse and locates his novel near Kanpur, the site from where many of the myths of rape originated.[63] Bathurst is presented as a workaholic devoted to the mission of white man's burden. His first meeting with Rujub is interesting. A tiger was about to maul Rujub's daughter when Bathurst scared it away with a horsewhip. This incident is important as contemporary illustrations show the tiger as the symbol of Indian rebels. The message is clear: Rujub's powers may confound English minds, but he has to offer his service to Bathurst and thereby betray his employer Nana Sahib, to survive the Rebellion. Among the novels is Philip Meadows Taylor's *Seeta*, more a novel on Indo–British relationships, than that of the 1857 Rebellion. Though the notion of white man's burden seems to be scattered throughout *Seeta*, it seems to be the least racist of novels on the 1857 Rebellion. Besides, *Seeta* is the only Victorian novel in which a woman dresses in a 'simple boy's dress'[64] and rides with her husband to share her husband's duty of maintaining law and order.[65] However, in reproducing the older script of an Englishman 'saving brown women from brown men' and making Brandon marry Seeta, Taylor creates a narrative problem for himself. He designs a plot that requires Seeta to sacrifice herself to save Philip who would later marry Grace Mostyn. As for *On the Face of the Waters*, I have suggested above that Steel's objective seems to critique the imperial discourse that used women to validate violence.[66] Also, by making Jim Douglas stay in a rebel city for over two months to gather information, Steel creates a fantasy of counter-insurgency, which Gautam Chakravarty identifies as 'a significant literary development'.[67]

However, much these novels may vary in their objective, almost all of them have two features in common. First, 1857 is presented as providing erring characters to redeem themselves. Ralph Bathurst is cured of his psychological inability to tolerate gunfire, Alice Gissing dies protecting the infant Sonny Seymour,[68] and Edith Ross receives a mortal wound protecting Jack Hawke.[69] Second these novels share in common the element of counter-insurgency. Ralph Bathurst, Jim Douglas, and Jack Hawke are excellent linguists and easily disguise themselves among the 'natives'.

In conclusion, one can well reflect on the relationship between the past and the present. Linda Hutcheon is of the opinion: 'Historians are aware that they establish a relationship between the past they write about and the present in which they write.'[70] In a world threatened by Islamic fundamentalism and Western imperialism, Dalrymple correlates 1857 with today in the following words:

The histories of Islamic fundamentalism and European imperialism have very often been, closely and dangerously, intertwined. In a curious but very concrete way, the fundamentalists of both faiths have needed each other to reinforce each other's prejudices and hatreds. The venom of one provides the lifeblood of the other.[71]

NOTES

1. Jerzy Topolski, 'Historical Narrative: Towards a Coherent Structure', *History and Theory*, vol. 26 (1987), pp. 75–86.
2. C. Behan McCullagh, 'The Truth of Historical Narratives', *History and Theory*, vol. 26 (1987), p. 42.
3. David Canandine, 'The Present and the Past in the English Industrial Revolution: 1880–1980', *Past and Present*, no. 103 (1984), pp. 131–72.
4. John Passmore, 'Narratives and Events', *History and Theory*, vol. 26 (1987), pp. 68–74.
5. For further discussion on this issue refer to McCullagh, 'The Truth of Historical Narratives', pp. 30–1.
6. Hayden White, 'The Historical Text as Literary Artifact', in Hayden White, *Tropics of Discourse* (1978, rpt., Baltimore, Maryland/London: John Hopkins University Press, 1985), p. 94.
7. Hayden White, 'The Question of Narrative in Contemporary Historical Theory', in Hayden White, *The Content of the Form* (1987, rpt., Baltimore, Maryland/London: John Hopkins University Press, 1990), p. 40.
8. Ibid.
9. Ibid., p. 43.
10. Ibid., p. 27.
11. White, 'Historical Text', in White, *Tropics of Discourse,* p. 89.
12. Mary Fulbrook, *Historical Theory* (London: Routledge, 2002), p. 54.
13. Ibid., p. 66.
14. Ibid., p. 68.
15. William Dalrymple, *The Last Mughal: The Fall of a Dynasty, Delhi 1857* (New Delhi: Penguin Books, 2006).
16. *The Statesman*, 10 December 2006, p. 17.
17. Saros Cowasjee (ed.), *A Raj Collection* (New Delhi: Oxford University Press, 2005).
18. Ibid., p. 9.
19. Gautam Chakravarty, *The Indian Mutiny and the British Imagination* (New Delhi: Cambridge University Press, 2006), p. 23.

20. The class hierarchy of Victorian England is prominent in these narratives on Rebellion. The women threatened with rape were invariably 'ladies', of the middle class or upper middle class. The men who saved them were 'gentlemen', either commissioned army officers or civil administrative officers, and most of them seem to have been rewarded with the lady's hand in marriage if not with peerage and a Victoria Cross. Perhaps Hume Nishbet's *The Queen's Desire: A Romance of the Indian Mutiny* (1893) is the only exception, with Sergeant George Jackson and Sergeant Sammy Tompkins as prime characters.
21. Quoted in Jenny Sharpe, *Allegories of Empire: The Figure of Woman in the Colonial Text* (Minneapolis: Minnesota University Press, 1993), p. 91.
22. It appears that the idea of whores tempting sepoys into mutiny has even influenced the Indian idea of the Rebellion. In the Bollywood film, *Mangal Pandey* (2005), we have a scene where a whore mocks Mangal Pandey for selling his soul to the British. Cowasjee (ed.), *A Raj Collection*, pp. 161, 181.
23. Ania Loomba, *Colonialism/Postcolonialism* (1998, rpt., New York: Routledge, 2001), p. 109.
24. Sharpe, *Allegories of Empire*, p. 87.
25. Since Steel does not cite sources in her text, many would dismiss this as chimera.
26. Cowasjee (ed.), *A Raj Collection*, p. 323.
27. Ibid.
28. Ibid., p. 326.
29. Ibid.
30. G.A. Henty justifies the deed in his *In the Times of Peril*, p. 129 in the following words: 'These men in the carriage,' said he (Hodson) in loud tones, 'have not only rebelled against the government, but have ordered and witnessed the massacre and shameful treatment of women and children. Thus, therefore, the government punishes such traitors and murderers!' Then drawing his revolver, before the crowd could move or lift a hand he shot the three prisoners through the head. The crowd, awed and astonished, fell back, and the carriage with the dead bodies passed into the city. Project Gutenberg. December, 2004 http://www.gutenberg.org/dirs/etext04/8perl10.txt
31. Cowasjee (ed.), *A Raj Collection*, p. 375.
32. Ibid.
33. Ibid., p. 382.
34. Dalrymple, *The Last Mughal*, p. 13.
35. Ibid., p. 15.
36. Ibid., pp. 40–5, 50–6, 105, 111–12, 117. As suggested earlier in this section, the empirical existence of the 'facts' cannot be ignored. However, people like Zauq, Ghalib, Zahir Dehlavi, Edward Campbell,

and Theophilus Metcalfe had lived through the multitude of events of the Rebellion. Metaphorically, they seem to be the cast of a play or characters of a fiction.

37. Chakravarty, *The Indian Mutiny and the British Imagination*, p. 128.
38. Passmore, 'Narratives and Events', p. 71.
39. G. Harris, *A Lady's Diary of the Siege of Lucknow* (1858, rpt., New Delhi: Asian Educational Services, 1997). Henceforth *Diary*.
40. Steel seems to have guessed the improbability of the situation and attempts to convince her readers by claiming: 'Regarding my fiction, an Englishwoman was concealed in Delhi, in the house of an Afghan, and succeeded in escaping to the Ridge just before the siege. I have imagined another; that's all. I mention this because it may possibly be said that the incident is incredible.' Later in the novel Steel takes care to point it out that Kate was not the only woman in Delhi concealed in an Afghan's house. The quotation is from p. 9. Cowasjee (ed.), *A Raj Collection*, pp. 9, 318.
41. Sharpe, *Allegories of Empire*, p. 71.
42. Harris, *Diary*, pp. 44–6, 67–8, 173.
43. Ibid., pp. 37–8.
44. Quoted in Steel. See Cowasjee (ed.), *A Raj Collection*, p. 66.
45. Sharpe, *Allegories of Empire*, pp. 85–6.
46. Nancy L. Paxton, *Writing Under Raj: Gender, Race and Rape in the British Colonial Imagination 1830–1947* (New Jersey: Rutgers University Press, 1999).
47. Charles E. Pearce, *Love Besieged: A Romance on the Defence of Lucknow*, ed. Ralph Crane (New Delhi: Oxford University Press, 2003).
48. Ibid., pp. 127–34.
49. G.A. Henty, *In the Times of the Peril*, Project Gutenberg. December 2004, p. 140. <http://www.gutenberg.org/dirs/etext04/8perl10.txt>
50. Pearce, *Love Besieged*, pp. 95, 110.
51. Ibid., p. 117.
52. Quoted in ibid., p. 227.
53. Loomba, *Colonialism/Postcolonialism*, pp. 106, 114.
54. Katherine Frank, *Lucie Duff Gordon: A Passage to Egypt* (London: Tauris Parke Paperbacks, 2007), pp. 177–80.
55. Ibid., p. 192.
56. P.J.O. Taylor (ed.), *A Companion to Indian Mutiny of 1857* (New Delhi: Oxford University Press, 1996), pp. 29–30, 190.
57. Pearce, *Love Besieged*, pp. 114–15.
58. Harris, *Diary*, p. 77.
59. James Gordon Farrell, *The Siege of Krishnapur* (1973, rpt., Introduction by Pankaj Mishra, New York: New York Review of Books, 2004).
60. As long as one has a document to prove Steel's portrayal of Zinat Mahal, it cannot but be considered an act of elision.

61. Harris, *Diary*, pp. 51, 108, 112.
62. G.A. Henty, *Rujub the Juggler*, Project Gutenberg, January, 2005. <http://www.gutenberg.org/dirs/etext05/rujub10h.htm>
63. Paxton, *Writing Under Raj*, p. 129.
64. Philip Meadows Taylor, *Seeta* (1881, rpt., Delhi: Asian Educational Services, 1989), p. 286.
65. Ibid., p. 318.
66. Paxton is of the opinion that though Steel starts by criticizing imperial propaganda, she ultimately ends up validating it. For further discussion, see *Writing Under Raj*, pp. 133–6.
67. Chakravarty, *The Indian Mutiny and the British Imagination*, p. 156.
68. Cowasjee (ed.), *A Raj Collection*, p. 194.
69. Pearce, *Love Besieged*, p. 214.
70. Linda Hutcheon, *Politics of Postmodernism* (1989, rpt., London/New York: Routledge, 2003), p. 67.
71. Dalrymple, *The Last Mughal*, p. 84.

CHAPTER 8

Looking Back at the Killing Fields: Reminiscences of a Soldier: 1857–1859: William Forbes Mitchell

UTTARA CHAKRABORTY

No one has asked me to write my recollections of the past and my impressions of the present. I do so to please myself, because on re-visiting the scenes of the Mutiny I have been forcibly impressed with the fact that, like so many memories, the soldiers and civilians who were personal actors in the great uprising are fast passing away... I feel tempted to put on record the recollections of the past and the impressions which my recent return to those scenes has revived.... In writing of the past I shall be careful to discriminate between what I saw myself and what I heard from other witnesses, whether native or European.... I intend to...more particularly notice the action of individual soldiers, and other incidents which came under my own notice, which have not, to my knowledge, been recorded by any historian or author of the numerous narratives, personal or other, which have been written about the Indian Mutiny.[1]

In 1893, Macmillan of London published, in its Colonial Library Series, a book called the *Reminiscences of the Great Mutiny 1857-59*, with the sub-title, *Including the Relief, Siege, and Capture of Lucknow, and the Campaigns in Rohilcund and Oude.* The book was written by William Forbes Mitchell, Late Sergeant, 93rd Sutherland Highlanders.

There was nothing apparently exceptional about the book, as there had been a plethora of contemporary writings on this particular event of the Great Mutiny. The book was published quite late too. By that time John Kaye's *The History of the Sepoy War* in three volumes (published respectively in 1864, 1874, 1876) had hit the stalls. Kaye had preferred to call it a war and not a mutiny. Though George Bruce Malleson, who commenced to write from the end of second volume of John Kaye's book retitled it as the *History of the Indian Mutiny.* Several other volumes had come out in the years immediately following the suppression of the revolt. Of these mention must be made of *India under Dalhousie and Canning* by the Duke of Argylle and published from Longmans in 1865. Several notable eyewitness accounts also were published. *The Mutiny in India: Essays on the Mutiny,* by John Holloway was dedicated to Lady Inglis, wife of Sir John Inglis who was killed fighting in the thick of the Revolt. Holloway's wife was killed at Kanpur, and his was an eyewitness account published in 1864. And there was Henry George Keene's *Some Account of the Administration of Indian Districts during the Revolt,* brought out in 1883, which narrated differently the causes of the Revolt as felt by an officer posted in the districts. There is also Justin McCarthy's redoubtable *History of Our Own Times* in which he hailed the Great Indian Revolt of 1857 as a revolution similar to the French Revolution.

Yet Mitchell's account was different. It is this difference that makes his *Reminiscences* stands out. It was a participant's account, the narrative of a soldier who found himself in a strange land, amidst killings and cruelty in inhuman proportions. Mitchell told his tales as he remembered them, recollecting many an anecdote and incident which found no mention in any other contemporary stories of the 1857 Revolt. One may doubt the veracity of his descriptions, but the sincerity and earnestness of the author is easy to discern. Above all, his many anecdotes have indeed lifted his *Reminiscences* above the ordinary and made his narrative singularly distinctive.

IN ALLIANCE AND ACCEPTANCE: THE HIGHLANDER SENTIMENT

William Forbes Mitchell was a soldier participant who fought with an unknown people in an unfamiliar land often facing death. He spent days in hunger without food and resources, marched miles and miles in the biting cold of the northern Indian plains, was burnt and scorched by the unfamiliar terrible heat of the tropical sun—such experiences were indeed real and he described his situation aptly. With him, the reader of his account visualizes the ravaged towns and cities and feels the cold and the heat of a country the author had never known before. Yet at the end of it all, Mitchell the Scot soldier left his homeland of green hills and misty lakes, to settle down eventually in this strange, menacing country, no longer threatening at all, but made familiar and closer by experience and understanding. And what an experience, this young soldier had! It was an experience of going through fire and hell. Coming out of it, Mitchell was a different man. No more a stranger but endeared to the native people by long familiarity. The 'other' was no longer the 'other' but his known neighbour in this country he adopted as his own new home.

Mitchell published his book in Calcutta where he had settled after his fighting days were over. His *Reminiscences* begin with a flashback as he revisits the fields of battle. He starts at the point when he first arrived in India (21 September 1857) the day of his first contact with this country. At the time he wrote his account, he lived in 46 Garden Reach, a house upon which his eyes fell because of its magnificent white grandeur, when he first entered Calcutta through the mouth of the river Ganga. The bonding began from then as the steamer carried him and his fellow Highlanders along the river towards Prinsep's Ghat. Mitchell particularly mentions the strange coincidence of how he came to possess that house and lived in it.[2]

The exhilaration of a young soldier is easy to gauge. Mitchell begins his *Reminiscences* at the point of his arrival in an 'old wooden ship *Belleisle* [that] was tugged along the river, watching the crowd on the riverside waving at them and feeling proud in his full Scottish Highlander kilt' and 'pipers playing on their poop'. He writes: 'The arrival of the Ninety-third caused quite a sensation in Calcutta, where but few Highland regiments had ever been seen before.'[3]

Contemporary vernacular newspapers commented upon the arrival of the Highlanders in Calcutta. There were a few sarcastic remarks about the unfamiliar dress of the Highlanders, like the one about the 'Queen had sent women in skirts to fight since there was a dearth of men in England in those critical times'. A contemporary Bengali satirist, who was also a distinguished 'native' notable of Calcutta, wrote:

White soldiers with hats on, have come from England
The ground trembles at their footfall
They live in the Highlands
Tantia Topi's pride will be reduced to dust
Delhi shall be recovered, and
Nana shall be caught.*

On 16 March 1858, a Bengali daily heaped praise on the Highlanders for their courageous efforts in vanquishing the enemy and once again making the banks of the Bhagirathi safe and secure.**

A question that emerges from Mitchell's memoir is the issue of his national identity. Is Mitchell pointing out his specific nationality (Scottish) with a purpose—perhaps to denote his 'difference ness' from the English? Is he trying to establish his own identity and that of the 93rd in contrast? Is it an attempt to set right, at the start, that there was no homogeneous, wholesome English nation as was claimed? Mitchell of course never discoursed on that, but now and again in expressing abounding sympathy for the fighting enemy (in contrast to the heartless cruelty of the white soldiers) he was pointing out to a gap, to a different kind of 'otherization'.

TIME PAST AND TIME PRESENT

There were two kinds of time present in Mitchell's *Reminiscences.* His own present time, when he revisited the places where he once fought and recalled the scenes and then came back and sat down to put down all that came back to him, in a rush, it seemed. There was also the time of his past, when as a young man fought with death facing him squarely on the face. Mitchell does not mention how old he was at the time of action, but he does mention a gap of thirty-six years and staying at Number 46 Garden Reach after thirty-two years. He refrained from writing anything more about himself: 'I took possession of No. 46, where I have established the Bon Accord Rope Works. But enough of this: I am not writing my autobiography.'[4]

*Arun Nag (ed.), *Hutom Pyanchar Naksha*, actually written by Kaliprasanna Sinha.

***Sambad Prabhakar*, ed. Iswar Chandra Vidyasagar, 16 March 1858. Translation by the author.

It is the task of the reader to construct the individuality and the mentality of this young Scottish soldier from various aspects of his account and also the discourses projected by him. The discourses took unified shape as he proceeded through his battles. The young Scotsman seemed to mature as he moved from one battlefield to another and as he watched men being killed and wounded on his own side and on the combating 'other'.

The 93rd Sutherland Highlander Regiment had returned to England after the end of the Crimean War and was quartered in Dover. In April 1857 the regiment was detailed for an expedition to China under Lord Elgin. Mitchell tells us that ten service companies were recruited with volunteers from the other Highland Regiments, each giving a certain number of men, bringing the 93rd up to a corps of 1,100 bayonets. On 20 May, the 93rd reached Portsmouth, where they were reviewed by the Queen accompanied by the Sir Colin Campbell. On 3 June, three companies embarked upon *Belleisle* an 84-gun two-decker for the China Expedition. The detachment of the 93rd was commanded by Colonel Adrian Hope and the Captains of the other companies were Cornwall, Dawson and Williams. His company was under Captain E.S. F.G. Dawson an officer of great experience, wrote Mitchell. The *Belleisle* reached Simon's Bay, passing Cape Verde on the afternoon of 9 August, when, writes Mitchell, they first heard the news of the Indian Mutiny and the destination was changed from China to Calcutta.[5] It was indeed a fateful change of destination for young Mitchell.

AT THE WARFRONT

Mitchell's experiences in this country are described in the *Reminiscences* in fifteen chapters. Sailing day and night the *Belleisle* arrived and reached the pilot station at the Sandheads on 19 September. As the ship and its crew and the regiment reached Calcutta, they got the news of the Siege of Delhi and Lucknow and the 'horrible massacre' at Kanpur. On 25 September the whole of 93rd met together at Chinsura, then moved in parts towards Lucknow from Raniganj. The Highlanders marched an average of 25 to 30 miles a day. They stopped at midday and resumed in the evening, marching the whole night. They reached Benares and from there moved towards Allahabad. At Allahabad there was a gathering of all the Highlanders. The only complete regiment on the British side was the 93rd Highlanders, over a thousand men, in splendid condition. Here, Mitchell met some 'native' Christians, who knew Dr. Alexander Duff (the Scottish Missionary who had arrived in Calcutta a few years earlier and set up the General Assemblies School, now known as Scottish Church College and Collegiate School) and were happy to see 'Dr. Duff's countrymen' as they called the Highlanders.

From Fatehpur, the 93rd marched to Kanpur, residing at the dak-bunglow. At the time of his revisit thirty years later, he found this converted into the Victoria Hotel. In Kanpur, the men of the 93rd visited the scenes of the massacre committed by Nana Sahib as was believed. He found the rooms still strewn with women's and children's clothes, broken toys, torn pictures, books, and pieces of music. Mitchell found a copy of the New Testament lying about. He felt that the Testament must have belonged to some Scotch Highlander in the garrison. He kept it and at the time of writing still possessed it. He had often thought of sending it home to the Highland Society as a relic of the Mutiny. The Satichaura Ghat and the Bibighar where the massacre of English women and children took place were next visited by the Highlanders. Most of the European women had been barbarously murdered, but they were not 'dishonoured', Mitchell emphasizes. These are the opinions that Mitchell formed in October 1857, three months after the massacre, and nothing which he had since learnt during his thirty-five years residence in India led him to alter them.

From this juncture of his *Reminiscences*, Mitchell makes a departure from the usual contemporary English writings. The signs of diabolical torture that the prisoners suffered had been graphically described by him. At the same time the method of vengeful punishment that was meted out as ordered by General Neill were not acceptable to the young Scottish soldier. Young Mitchell tried to reason out the outrage and the extreme feeling of revenge that Neill felt when confronted with the scenes of massacre and also tried to fathom his mental state when he saw those inhuman signs of killing. Yet, Mitchell felt that the tortured punishment inflicted in revenge upon people who were in no way connected with the incident, could not in any way be condoned. Mitchell mentions in the most categorical manner that there was no writing on the wall in charcoal or in pencil at the time of his visit to these places, and firmly believed that these were put up later, on purpose, to arouse the revengeful anger of the English soldiers.[6] While reminiscing all these the older Forbes Mitchell seemed to be remembering those days and also recalling the same feelings he had, thirty-two years earlier. There was no imposing of an older reminiscing mind on his younger self. Indeed, there was no imagined self created in this recollection—a trend that memory often tricks us into believing.

As his regiment marched towards Lucknow, Mitchell saw many deserted villages. The people, it seemed, had all fled on the first advance of Havelock; it was felt that as they had not returned, it was clear that the whole population was against the British. As the soldiers marched, they had few rations to sustain them. There could be no cooked food as the cooks had gone, with their utensils. So, probably, the soldiers took food from the unwilling villagers. Mitchell mentions that the 'natives' were scared of the counter-atrocities of General Havelock and Neill.

THE PROUD HIGHLANDER

More often than not Mitchell mentions the endurance of the Highlander as against the others, hastening to add that the Crimean War had toughened them. It seems therefore that his sense of 'other' included the English, separating the Scottish Highlander from the rest of the Britons. Always thinking of special Scottish treats, Mitchell mentioned how they had a soup of green tobacco leaves, which they had never seen and not grown in their misty rolling greens; it was mistaken for 'Scotch curly kail', a curly variety of cabbage—a favourite among the Scots.

As Mitchell remembers, he refers to the fidelity and bravery of the *bhistis* who were never known to forsake the army they accompanied. While he discussed the long and weary march on foot to Lucknow, he discoursed on the nature of the mutiny, describing it as *guerre a la mort* and the ruthlessness and cruelty shown on either side. The massacre at Kanpur was matched by the killing of the prisoners by the English. In November, the 93rd along with other troopers reached the vicinity of Lucknow. The 93rd was led by Captain Adrian Hope. A vivid description of the Highlanders is found in the *Reminiscences*, many of them wearing their medals from the Crimean War and standing at the extreme end as Colin Campbell took the guard of each regiment. The 93rd was in full Highland costume, with feather bonnets and dark waving plumes, a solid mass of brawny men. And they cheered Sir Colin as an old and long time beloved leader. To Mitchell's recollection, this was indeed the most magnificent regiment.[7]

Mitchell was proud to belong to it and eloquent about its magnificence. That he was not exaggerating is corroborated by other writers as well. Colonel George Bruce Malleson picked up the threads of John Kaye's *The History of the Sepoy War*, and continuing with further additions to the narrative in four more volumes, described the same event in the fourth volume:

> Sir Colin Campbell took guard of the 9th Lancers, the Sikh Cavalry, and the 4th Punjab Infantry. Last stood many in numbers in tall and serried ranks the 93rd Highlanders. A waving sea of plumes and tartans they looked, as, with loud and rapturous cheers which rolled over the field, they welcomed their veteran commander, the chief of their choice. It was curious to mark the difference between the old Indian troops and the Highlanders in their reception of Sir Colin, anxious and fixed with the gaze of the former as he rode down their ranks-men evidently trying to measure the leader who had been sent to them, from so far. Enthusiastic beyond expression was his reception by the latter.[8]

Malleson, who was part of the British army, an officer at the commissariat, seemed to be echoing what Mitchell had written in his memoirs.

The relief of Lucknow has been described by Mitchell at length. The attack was planned from the side of the Dilkhusa Palace and Gardens. Mitchell saw deer, both black buck and spotted deer, in the Garden and then along the Martiniere College. He remembered the striking up of the Highland Charge by Pipe-Major John McLeod to inspire them with the 'national music'—*On wi' the Tartan*. In every detailed description of the Battle at Lucknow, taking of Secunderbagh, narrating the strange incident of James Wallace who joined the 93rd to see a hated man called Hope, die in describing the 93rd as the most Scottish of all the Highlander regiments, having a military parish, minister, and elders, complete with regular service of the Communion plate, in describing so often their feather bonnets, redcoats and heavy kilts, Mitchell was actually expressing his own roots and the difference he felt not so much with the enemy as with the English.[9]

Mitchell also narrated a strange incident at Secunderbagh. A woman 'dressed in a tight-fitting red jacket and tight-fitting rose-coloured silk trousers' was killed. She was shooting down upon the soldiers of the 93rd and the 53rd from the top of a large *pipul* tree in the 'inner court' of Secunderbagh. It was only when she was shot and fell to the ground, that it was discovered that she was a woman.[10] This small incident mentioned only by Mitchell gives a rare and different dimension to the history of the Great Revolt from the Indian and also from the gender perspective. Apart from women like Lakshmibai or Hazrat Mahal Begum of Awadh who was on the first rank of rebel leadership, we hardly come across any information on how women participated.

Mitchell gives a detailed account of the Battle at Secunderbagh and the taking of Shah Najaf, a small hamlet with a mosque and a tomb named after a town in Baghdad, and a place of pilgrimage for the Muslims. He refers to the use of bows and arrows by the rebels. Sergeant Daniel White's comment when he was struck by an arrow on his feather bonnet (as quoted by Forbes Mitchell) is worth quoting: 'My conscience! Bows and arrows! Bows and arrows! Have we got Robin Hood and Little John back again.... Ah! That Daniel White should be able to tell in the Saut Market of Glasgow that he had seen men fight with bows and arrows in the days of Enfield Rifles!'[11]

Mitchell however mentions that man after man fell to the arrows shot by the 'Jack Pandeys' (All sepoys were uniformly called Pandeys by the English soldiers as they arrived in India to fight the suppression of the Revolt of 1857 not knowing that Pandey actually was a high caste surname. The prefix Jack was to denote the jackal or fox-like 'cunning' of the sepoy) in those days of 'Enfield Rifles'. He narrated a strange night's experience: discovering, lamp in hand, a room full of gunpowder in the mosque at Shah Najaf where he and his fellow soldiers rested. He could have been blown off by a chance spark of the lamp! That a soldier who faced death so many times earlier in the day could be so alarmed at the possible accidental death was a thought which kept him awake the rest of the night of that 16 November 1857.

Mitchell describes the day-to-day battle scenes at Secunderbagh and Shah Najaf for the relief of Lucknow, focusing on the bravery and courage of the Highlanders, and would often express his sentiments in Scottish rhymes or verses by Walter Scott making his Scottish exclusiveness prominently standing out against the rest of the Britons. Yet, occasionally he narrates incidents which expose his profound sympathy for the enemy and as he remembers the battles he fought and the fighting days, his sympathies deepen. Towards the end of his reminiscences he seems to discourse on the validity of the war and the justice of it all. A feeling of consideration for the soldier on the other side as a fellow soldier, is to be found quite frequently in his narrative.

There is an anecdote about a Bengali clerk, 'an amusing incident' according to Mitchell. Hiralal Chatterjee, 'a young *babu*', a boy of seventeen or eighteen years of age and belonging to the Commissariat Department was put in charge of a broken-down cart laden with biscuits. The young Highlanders ripped open the biscuit bags and started filling their haversacks. Just then, an officer of the 9th Lancer passed by and Hiralall ran to him and complained 'My lord, you are my father and my mother! What shall I tell you! These wild Highlanders will not hear me, but are stealing commissariat biscuits.' That was Sir Colin Campbell to whom he complained. 'What can a poor *babu* do with such wild Highlanders?' Hiralal continued. Sir Colin gave a voucher to Hiralal so that he would not be held responsible for all the looting of biscuits.[12] What is worth noting is that Mitchell remembers this Bengali *babu* long after he himself left the army and had settled down in Calcutta. At the time of writing the Reminiscences, Mitchell mentions Hiralal holding the post of cashier in the offices of Messrs M. Neil and Company, on Clive Ghat Street. Amusing also is to read about a small pill of opium given by a 'native' servant called Hyder refreshing him after his tired march of the day. Forbes Mitchell refers to the 'sacred Ganges' and the 'sacred water of mother Ganges' more than once, not at all in sarcasm, but with simple adoration. The acculturation of the Scot and his slow but inevitable immersing in the local culture occurred gradually.

THE SYMPATHETIC SOLDIER IN THE WEB OF THE 'GORGEOUS EAST'

In describing the way the treasures of Nana was taken as loot in the name of the government, Mitchell recalls the incident of

Ajodhya Prasad, a contract supplier to the Commissariat of the Government, whose payment was due as for supplies and carriages of the army during the Second Sikh War. And at the time of the settlement of the accounts Ajodhya Prasad claimed three and a half crore of rupees. The Commissariat Department backed by the Government of India, not only repudiated the claim, but put Ajodhya Prasad on trial for falsification of accounts and attempting to defraud the government. Mitchell then describes how Mr. Lang became a familiar figure appearing before the Commission in his gown and wig. On the day of the judgement he opened his address by saying that he was placing the dead carcass of this shameful case before the judge in all its naked deformity. Lang concluded that the whole case against his client was a disgrace to the Government of India and to the Honourable EIC, who not only sanctioned this trial but also put every obstacle in his way to prevent him from coming to defend his client.[14] Ajodhya Prasad was acquitted and decreed to be entitled to all his claims.

Apparently this incident happened a few years before 1857, but, in narrating the tale of fraud and deception against a 'native' merchant, Forbes was perhaps trying to bring out the nature and enormous amount of injustice, discrimination, and ill-treatment that was being carried out by the EIC's government. Perhaps by this time as he fought, he was gradually considering the causes of the great rebellion, to quell which he had been sent out. It was no ordinary war as he had fought in Crimea. Here in India, he and his fellowmen were fighting not a regular army but batches of surging rebels who seemed to be fighting for a cause with whatever arms and weapons they get hold of. He was pondering over the immensity of the rising and also trying to gauge the enormity of the accumulated hatred of the 'natives' against the white rulers.

On the morning of 6 January 1858, Mitchell's regiment reached Fatehgarh which was under the rule of the Nawab of Farukhabad who had joined the rebels. The fort of Fatehgarh was found abandoned. It was here that the Nawab of Farukhabad was brought in bound and humiliated by the smearing of pig's fat, he was then flogged and hanged. Mitchell who had earlier raised the question of the charcoal writings on the walls of Bibighar and thought that these were later additions to rouse vengeance, did not however question the cries like 'Cawnpur avenged' or 'Remember Cawnpur'. But, as months passed by a sort of *ennui* overcame him and we find him questioning such inhuman acts as the one meted out to the Nawab of Farukhabad. Mitchell notes that both Colin Campbell and William Peel were said to have protested against such barbarity, but about this he is not certain.[15]

As they marched for the Second Relief of Kanpur and Lucknow, the soldiers of the 93rd reached Palamau. Here Mitchell witnessed a terrible scene. About 130 imprisoned rebels were hanged within the span of an evening and the subsequent morning. There was not a single branch left of that old *pipul* tree from which bodies were not hanging. It was on this occasion that his mate Jack Brian was promised a reward if he acted as the hangman; Jack's proud reply was that a Highlander's task was to fight an armed enemy and not kill the unarmed, not 'for all the loot in India'. On that same occasion, Mitchell witnessed a different Hodson of 'Hodson's Horses', notorious for his cruelty and acts of senseless and unnecessary violence. Hodson was suffering from anguish due to his past barbaric executions of the Indians. Even George Bruce Malleson, commenting on the murder of the sons of the Mughal *Padshah* had said about Hodson: 'In him human suffering awoke no feeling, shedding of blood caused him no pang, the taking of life brought him no remorse. He was a ... freelance of the Middle Ages.'[16]

Many instances recalled by Mitchell in the later pages of his *Reminiscences* reveal the change in mentality he underwent. Also his emotional responses to the turmoil and the brutal war were taking a different channel. He seemed to be realizing the significance of this Uprising. Henceforth, Mitchell was overcome by a sense of weariness and angst at what he thought ceaseless, merciless, and mindless killing. Two incidents occurred when his regiment was stationed near Lucknow. One is the episode of his meeting with Muhammad Ali Khan and the other of witnessing European officers on the side of the rebels. He had heard from some people the existence of white men among the sepoys fighting against their own race. He refers to a publication titled *The Siege of Delhi, by an Officer Who Served There.* The author's name is undisclosed. This was brought out by Adam and Charles Black Publishers, Edinburgh in 1861. He tells about a European deserter from Meerut had been struck down fighting in the sepoy ranks and was recognized by his former comrades. The author specifically stated that a young officer in the full uniform of a European was seen more than once with the rebel sepoys, guiding them and often in command. This was during the Battle of Badli-Ki-Serai. Usually as it had happened that the Europeans had a general contempt for the enemy's artillery. However, according to the anonymous author of *The Siege of Delhi*, the tone of conversation suddenly changed and from being an object of contempt, their skill became one of wonder and admiration, perhaps too great. Some British artillery officers asserted that the 'rebel' artillery fire was better than their own. Many believed that the 'natives' were firing under the superintendence of Europeans. Two men with solar helmets could be seen with the help of the best glasses in their batteries. Yet, writes the author, no one who knew how much of the work in India was really done by the 'natives', wondered at the practical skill they now showed. In corroboration of the anonymous author who wrote in 1861 one can cite the comments made by another English writer, James Routledge, who in his *English Rule and Native Opinion in India* (1878), states that the native of India is essentially a capable man, but is often badly used.

The same attitude is echoed in the writings of John Holloway, who was like Mitchell an army man and a non-commissioned officer in Her Majesty's 32nd Light Infantry. He wrote appreciatively about courage and endurance in the fighting in defence of the Lucknow Residency. Holloway also had praise for capable and efficient handling of artillery by the rebels. The artillery of the rebels proved an efficient arm indeed and convincing proof of the accuracy of aiming in the ruinous condition of mostly all the buildings of the Residency that had been assaulted by gunfire. When shells began to fail them, the rebels attempted to manufacture them for themselves, using as materials with brass, glass, and stone. Holloway said he heard the sepoys singing 'God Save the King' as they fought. His last comment was that during the progress of the Indian Mutiny, disciplined forces confronted disciplined forces.[17]

Mitchell for his part mentions that he heard the strange tale from one Mr. Rees of one of his own kin fighting on the enemy side during the Battle of Chinhut in Lucknow. Much later he heard from a jemadar that there were a few Englishmen on the enemy side. One was known as Brigadier Sibbald who was raised to a position next to Bakht Khan by the *Padshah* himself. The other two were one Adjutant Tucker and a Sergeant-Major.[18] These were not isolated incidents of sympathetic European soldiers who decided to take the side of Indian rebels.

THE TRANSFORMED MENTALITY: FORBES MITCHELL AND MUHAMMAD ALI KHAN

The story of Muhammad Ali had hitherto not been narrated by any British participant. Muhammad Ali was an associate of Azimullah Khan and joined the rebellion at the latter's instance. During the Second Siege of Kanpur and the taking of Lucknow, Mitchell came to know a cake seller called Jamie Green, who seemed to be a Eurasian. He was handsome and Mitchell was struck by the 'purity and easy flow of English' he spoke, rare among the Eurasians. More interestingly, this man as he sat down waiting for his payment would enquire about many things. He wanted to see the newspapers and seemed anxious to know what the English press said about the Mutiny, and to talk of all subjects connected with the strength of the army, the preparations made for the Siege of Lucknow, and how the newly-arrived regiments were likely to stand the hot weather. When asked about his superior quality and the fluency of English, he said he learnt it from the sahibs as his father was a mess-*khansama* of a European regiment and was brought up in close quarters of the English soldiers. Some time later this same man was arrested as a spy and brought to the camp to be executed the following day. The soldiers wanted to feed him pork forcefully, for, it was found out that he was no Christian but a Muslim. Such ways of humiliating and insulting the condemned had become a ritual in the army. But, Mitchell, who was in charge that night, sternly forbade such actions on pain of punishment. The grateful Muhammad Ali Khan, for that was his name, told his life's story to an unknown young Scot soldier on that last night of his life.

Like Azimullah Khan, Muhammad Ali Khan was an engineering graduate. He belonged to an aristocratic Muslim family in Rohilkhand, and studied in Bareilly College standing first amongst all students and in all subjects. From there he went to the

Government Engineering College at Roorki. He then joined the EIC at a very low post. The Englishman who was his senior was a man of little or no education and inferior in every way except, perhaps, in brute strength. So Muhammad Ali Khan left the job and went to work for Maharaja Jang Bahadur of Nepal; he went to England twice. During the second visit, he met Azimullah Khan who had gone to England as an emissary of Nana Sahib to plea for a raise in the latter's pension. Azimullah made him aware of the European political situation and how this could be brought to the advantage of Hindustan. There was a plan to take the help of the Russians against the English, for they were the common enemy. Thus, Muhammad Ali Khan who already had been firmly convinced of the ill treatment, gross injustice, and above all the loss of freedom at the hands of the British, joined this rising. The aim was to bring back the past glory, honour, and independence from *Ferangi* rule.

That was a strange night when the narrator was disclosing his life story and objectives to the enemy. Once again we find relationships overlapping and the line that divided the one from the other did not seem to have followed the normative notions of 'otherization'. Mitchell easily empathized with the 'enemy'. Although we have failed to wrest, said Muhammad Ali, the country from the English, I hope we have done some good, and that our lives will not be sacrificed in vain as I have read French History as well as English. Later in the day Mitchell saw the corpse of the proud and handsome Muhammad Ali hanging from a tree. What unnecessary and cruel death hurled upon this talented man more educated than any Englishman, just because he fought for his freedom, writes Mitchell. Ali gave him a ring and Mitchell kept that as a memento for his children.[19]

The same saddened and shocked emotion reappeared when Mitchell witnessed the loot of Lucknow. William Howard Russell, the *Times* correspondent, described the British atrocities and plunder of Lucknow.* W.H Fichet notes in his *The Tale of the Great Mutiny:* 'It is curious to note how all the swiftly changing events and passions of the mutiny are reflected in such of the diaries and journals of the period have been published and

*W.H. Russell, *My Diaries in India in the Year 1858–59* (London: George Routledge and Sons, 1859), pp. 189–96.

frequently a view of the actors in the great drama and of their actions such as grave historians, much to the loss of their readers, never give us.'[20]

A truism which is best applicable to William Forbes Mitchell's *Reminiscences*. The soldier Mitchell began writing about his warrior days from the time of his arrival in this country. But as he proceeded he seemed to be withdrawing from the actual scenes of battles and was watching, observing, and also contemplating. As there are two kinds of time in the *Reminiscences*, there are two Mitchells as well. The older Mitchell recalled the days of the younger and as he drew near the end of his recollections, his older self was superimposed on the younger. The 'time past' and the 'time present' of Mitchell were both present in the 'time future' as one would perhaps feel as one reads the postscript. Mitchell stayed back in India, in Calcutta, married an Indian, and lived in his beloved Number 46 Garden Reach where he died in the year 1905.

NOTES

1. William Forbes Mitchell, *Reminiscences of the Great Mutiny 1857–59* (London: Macmillan and Co., 1893), pp. 1, 2.
2. Ibid., pp. 7–8.
3. Ibid., p. 8.
4. Ibid.
5. Ibid., pp. 24–5.
6. Ibid., pp. 9–15.
7. Ibid., pp. 31–2.
8. Kaye's and Malleson's, *History of the Indian Mutiny of 1857–58*, ed. Col. Malleson (1897–8, rpt., Connecticut: Greenwood Press Publishers, 1971), vol. 4, p. 118.
9. Mitchell, *Reminiscences*, pp. 54–7.
10. Ibid., p. 58.
11. Ibid., p. 77.
12. Ibid., p. 121.
14. Ibid., pp. 155–8.
15. Ibid., pp. 168–9.
16. Kaye's and Malleson's, *History of the Indian Mutiny of 1857–8*, vol. 4, p. 52; Mitchell, *Reminiscences*, p. 170.
17. Mitchell, *Reminiscences*, Appendix B, pp. 278–83; John Holloway, *Essays on the Indian Mutiny*, pp. 165, 168, 217, 345. Publisher not

mentioned. The book has been 'Dedicated to the Hon'ble Lady Inglis, Widow of the Late Major-General Sir John Inglis K.C.B.'. Holloway's wife was killed in Kanpur—a victim of Bibighar. The book was probably brought out in 1864.

18. Mitchell, *Reminiscences*, pp. 278–83.
19. Ibid., pp. 173–93.
20. W.H. Fichet, *Tales of the Great Mutiny* (London: Smith, Elder & Co. 1902), pp. 237–8.

PART II

1857 UPRISING AND GLOBAL HISTORY

CHAPTER 9

The Taiping Rebellion in China: 1851–1868

MADHAVI THAMPI

Around the same time that the 1857 Uprising took place in India, a great rebellion known as the Taiping Rebellion was raging in China. In extent and duration, the Taiping Rebellion was much bigger than the 1857 Uprising in India. It lasted a full thirteen years, and it was seventeen years before the last remnants of the rebel forces were snuffed out. It covered a huge territory in the richest regions of central and southern China, and is estimated to have cost a staggering twenty million lives. Unlike the rebels of 1857, the Taiping rebels managed to set up an alternative power structure with their headquarters at Nanjing, which for about a decade governed vast areas under the name of 'Taiping Tianguo' (Heavenly Kingdom of Great Peace), even though it was constantly at war. Most significant of all, the Taiping Rebellion envisioned a socio-economic order that was a distinct alternative and challenge to the traditional social and economic order of China, and was driven by a new, uniquely Chinese, form of messianic Christian ideology.

There is a basis for comparing the Taiping with the 1857 Uprising in India apart from contemporaneity. Both rebellions can be said to have dealt nearly mortal blows to the ruling powers of the time—the British in the case of India, and the Manchu (Qing) rulers in the case of China. Both may be characterized as proto-nationalist movements that attracted the support of diverse social strata and groups over a very wide area. In both cases, the impact was so large that, looking back, it can be said that each represented in its own way a watershed in the modern history of the country. It will thus be instructive to consider the Taiping Rebellion in conjunction with the 1857 Rebellion in India, to see if the more-or-less simultaneous occurrence of two uprisings of such major proportions was just a coincidence, or whether certain common factors and forces were at play in both countries.

REBELLIONS IN CHINESE HISTORY

The Taiping Rebellion was the largest, if not the most successful, in a long line of peasant rebellions in China, records of which go back to at least the third century BCE. Peasant rebellions in Chinese history ranged from fairly localized affairs in just one or two districts to huge armies on the move that swept through several provinces. Two features of traditional Chinese peasant rebellion are of particular interest. The first of these was the phenomenon of secret societies. Secret societies were proscribed networks of organization widely prevalent at the base of Chinese society. Akin to simple mutual aid groups or 'brotherhoods' in normal times, they provided a readymade structure for rebellious groups in times of crisis and widespread discontent. Thus, when peasants of a certain area rose in revolt, they did not have to create their organizations from scratch: they already had their cells, hiding places, secret codes, informers, and supply and communication lines in place. This gave them greater staying power, particularly in the early stages, in the face of efforts by the authorities to suppress them. Apart from organizational structure, the secret societies also lent the movements a cohesive ideology or faith, usually of a messianic Buddhist or Daoist variety. These ideologies, which often posited visions of a new, more egalitarian society or of salvation for true believers, could be a powerful motivating force, inspiring followers to risk everything for the cause. It is not surprising that some of the most prominent rebellions in Chinese history are known by the name of the secret societies that led them, such as the rebellions of the Yellow Turbans, the Red Eyebrows, the White Lotus, and so on.

The other significant feature of Chinese peasant rebellions was their political impact. Here we are talking in the main of only the largest of the peasant rebellions. Peasant rebellions in China, even the more localized ones, were directed against the state as the main source of oppression, and not just against individual landlords. What we consider to be 'peasant rebel' usually included some discontented members of the local gentry also. Often, the first step in the outbreak of a revolt was an attack on the district official headquarters known as the *yamen*. It follows that when a revolt grew to a certain size, the focus of attack would go beyond the *yamen* to the ruling dynasty itself. The inability of a dynasty to crush a rebellion before it grew to huge proportions was in turn, perceived as a sign that the dynasty had lost its mandate to rule and that its end was in sight. This further weakened its legitimacy and power, and often provided the final 'push' to its collapse. Usually a military commander or powerful family would take advantage of the resulting chaos to seize power and restore 'order', which meant putting down the rebellion that had facilitated their rise to power in the first place. But on at least two occasions, at the founding of the great Han dynasty and the Ming dynasty, the founder of the new ruling dynasty was himself a peasant leader. Thus, in China peasant rebellions could and did in key instances go beyond a form of 'protest' to become the mechanism by which a new political authority was established. Once established, however, the new political authority invariably continued to rule on traditional lines. The 'Mandate of Heaven' was transferred to a new ruler, but the political system remained in place.

CHINA'S MID-NINETEENTH-CENTURY CRISIS

In the middle of the nineteenth century, China was ruled by an ethnically distinct group, the Manchu, who had established their dynasty, the Qing, two centuries earlier. Initially the Manchus, who hailed from a region to the north-east of China, had met with considerable resistance from the Chinese, particularly in the southern part of the empire. Within the first three decades, however, all active resistance was wiped out, and the Manchus, through a careful and judicious policy, succeeded in winning the cooperation of the Chinese elite and in establishing a stable and relatively prosperous rule. In fact, virtually the whole of the eighteenth century was marked by an absence of significant rebellions or external threat to the Chinese Empire.

By the nineteenth century, however, there is evidence of growing problems and unrest. Acute pressure on the land, caused in part by a doubling of the population and the 'filling up' of available arable land, led to rising social distress. Administrative decline, military weakness, fluctuating currency rates, the proliferation of banditry, as well as the sprouting of numerous rebellions, all contributed to the growing malaise. To these problems of a mainly domestic nature was added the challenge posed by the Western maritime powers, especially Britain. For two centuries, these powers had peacefully engaged in trade with China, mainly at the southern port of Canton. From the later eighteenth century the growth of smuggling, especially in the prohibited drug opium, had gradually contributed to undermining Qing administrative and financial authority in the southern coastal regions. In retaliation for Qing efforts to crack down on this trade, Britain, which had the greatest interest in the opium trade, launched a military offensive. This ended with the defeat of China in 1842 and the imposition of treaty terms distinctly unfavourable to China. The Opium War did not in itself threaten Qing rule, but it nevertheless contributed to its problems and also exposed its vulnerability. Overall, in the middle of the nineteenth century, all the dimensions of a major crisis were unfolding. This was reflected in a series of major and minor rebellions that erupted in different parts of the empire.

ORIGINS AND EARLY DEVELOPMENT OF THE TAIPING REBELLION

The Taiping Rebellion, the greatest of the uprisings that unfolded in mid-nineteenth-century China, arose in the remote south-western province of Guangxi. Guangxi was a poor and neglected frontier region, where the writ of the Qing administration did not run very deep, and where consequently banditry and various forms of outlawed activities were widely prevalent. Tensions were rife between the original inhabitants of the region and the more recent arrivals from other parts of the empire. These migrants were mainly from the Hakka community, who had a different cultural and ethnic make-up from the original settlers. Violent armed clashes between the two sides were frequent, and accounted for the high level of militarization of local society.

Despite its remoteness, Guangxi was also the neighbouring province and hinterland of the coastal province of Guangdong in which was situated the flourishing port of Canton. The dislocation to the trade of Canton caused by the Opium War and by the subsequent shift of much of the foreign trade northwards to Shanghai, had its impact on Guangxi. It was not just the boatmen, smugglers, and porters who lost their livelihood and went back to Guangxi and stirred up things there. A vigorous pirate-suppression campaign launched by the British in the coastal waters also drove a number of these pirates upriver into Guangxi, where they continued their banditry.

It was in this unsettled region that a heterodox sect calling itself the Society of God-Worshippers took root among the Hakka through the efforts of a maverick leader named Hong Xiuquan and his band of followers. Hong Xiuquan was a Hakka originally from Guangxi, who had spent some time in Canton and Hong Kong, where he was exposed to Christianity. Frustrated by failure at repeated attempts to pass the civil service examination, Hong apparently suffered a nervous breakdown. It was during his illness that he had visions which convinced him that he was the younger brother of Jesus Christ and instilled in him the mission to spread the faith. For a few years, Hong and his early converts were no more than an expanding sect of fanatic believers confined to Guangxi. The administration, however, viewed all such heterodox societies as subversive and dangerous. The early attempts at suppression on the part of the local forces were beaten back by the God-Worshippers.

Buoyed with confidence after their initial victories, the members of the sect in 1851 took the decisive step of leaving their homes and coming together as an armed force. Openly unfurling the banner of revolt against the 'foreign' Qing rulers, and proclaiming the birth of the 'Heavenly Kingdom of Great Peace', they stormed out of Guangxi province and headed towards the rich regions of central China. Attracted by their egalitarian programme and their calls to oust the 'foreign' dynasty that was increasingly perceived as the source of all their problems, thousands from among the poor sections of rural society rose in support and joined the movement. The Taiping forces were well organized, and among their military commanders were some brilliant tacticians. The core of the Taiping forces, too, believed that they were fighting for a cause, and were inspired and disciplined fighters. The demoralized forces of the Qing dynasty were no match for them, and yielded town after town to the advancing Taiping forces. In a very short time, the Taiping forces had reached the Yangzi River in central China and also managed to acquire a naval force along the way. By 1854, they had seized the great city of Nanjing on the lower Yangzi. This was a victory of great symbolism since Nanjing had been the capital of the Chinese Ming dynasty that had been overthrown by the Manchus. While different Taiping commanders were sent in various directions to move the military campaign against the Qing forces, Nanjing was declared the new capital of the 'Heavenly Kingdom of Great Peace' and the main Taiping forces established their headquarters there.

THE TAIPING IDEOLOGY AND PROGRAMME

From just a sect professing a new and heterodox religion, the Taiping had evolved into a proto-nationalist movement when they first raised the banner of revolt against the Qing as a 'foreign' dynasty in occupation of China. Hong Xiuquan is supposed to have said:

> God has divided the kingdoms of the world and made the Ocean to be a boundary for them, just as a father divides his estates among his sons; every one of whom ought to reverence the will of his father, and quietly manage his own property. Why should now these Manchus forcibly enter China, and rob their brothers of their estate?[1]

Inveterate hatred for the Manchus was a prominent feature of the Taiping ethos, as it was of many other rebellious movements in China in this period.

However, for all their raising of nationalist slogans, the Taiping did not consider the Western powers a significant foreign threat, despite the humiliating defeat they had inflicted on China during the Opium War. It was the Manchus who were held responsible for the defeat. There is evidence that the Taiping actually looked upon the Westerners in a favourable light, as fellow Christians, even if many of the Western representatives in China at that time did not reciprocate that sentiment. Moreover, the Taiping leadership on several occasions made it clear that they desired to expand foreign trade and made overtures to the foreign representatives in Shanghai in this connection. Thomas Taylor Meadows, who had the opportunity to visit the Taiping territories in the capacity of interpreter for the British representative Bonham, recorded receiving a favourable response to their request that the trade at Shanghai be spared from attack. The letter from the powerful 'Eastern King' Yang Xiuqing declared:

> We therefore issue this special decree, permitting you the English chief, with the brethren under your superintendence, constant ingress and egress in full accordance with your own inclination and wish, whether to aid us in the extermination of the demons [Manchus] or to pursue as usual your commercial vocations.[2]

This single-minded hostility to the alien Manchu rulers, coupled with a fairly benign attitude towards the Western powers—whether born out of pragmatism or otherwise—was to characterize also the republican revolutionary movement led by Sun Yat-Sen half a century later.

Unlike earlier anti-Qing movements the Taiping did not limit their aims to overthrowing the dynasty and restoring an earlier, Chinese rule. On the contrary, they proclaimed a new egalitarian social and economic order that challenged the prevailing system in a most radical way. The key document of the Taiping in fact was entitled 'The Land System of the Heavenly Dynasty', which outlined not just the distribution of land but also the basic civil and military administration as well as religious organization of the rebel kingdom.

The Taiping envisioned a system in which all land belonged to the state, but would be distributed in equal portions to all men and, very significantly, all women over 16 years of age; children below that age were entitled to one half a share. A complicated formula was drawn up to ensure equitable distribution of lands of varying quality. A family was to keep enough of the produce to meet its own needs and submit the rest to a public granary. In the famous words of the 'Land System of the Heavenly Dynasty', the Taiping declared that 'land shall be farmed by all; rice, eaten by all; clothes, worn by all; money, spent by all. There shall be no inequality, and no person shall be without food or fuel.'[3] Nothing else demonstrated so powerfully the egalitarianism, and the message of sharing, that lay at the heart of the Taiping ideology.

In organizational terms the Taiping sought to impose a new pattern that combined administrative, military, and religious functions. The population as a whole was, according to this scheme, to be organized in identical units consisting of twenty-five families headed by a sergeant. These basic units in turn were combined to make larger units in a pyramidal structure, at the apex of which stood Hong Xiuquan himself, the Heavenly King, and his closest allies, also given the title of kings. Thus, in theory at least, the same type of organization that characterized the sect of God Worshippers was to be extended, with only some modification, to society at large.

With a zeal that perhaps derived from Christian inspiration, the Taiping sought to stamp out what they considered to be decadent social practices such as opium-smoking, gambling, drinking, the foot binding of women, prostitution, and so on. Their most radical departure from prevailing social practice was their attitude towards women. Women in general were treated on par with men. They could sit for the civil service examinations, take part in military activities, and in general move about freely. The Taiping went to the extreme of imposing complete segregation of sexes in some areas, even within families, although this was justified as a temporary expedient necessitated by conditions of war. Perhaps no other aspect of Taiping life impressed contemporary foreign observers more than the relative freedom and equality of women. 'The much higher social position of the Tiping ladies over that of their unfortunate sisters included with the Manchu domestic regime,' wrote Augustus Lindley, a contemporary eyewitness who spent considerable time among the Taiping, 'has long been one of the brightest ornaments of their government.'[4]

Obviously, since they were continuously at war and even the capital Nanjing was under prolonged siege particularly in the later years, the ambitious programme of the Taiping remained to a great extent an ideal. Historians have pointed out that in large areas under their control, the Taiping maintained existing land relations and even opposed non-payment of rent by tenant farmers to their landlords, in their drive to stabilize the economy and augment their revenues by whatever means. Even the regulations pertaining to social practices were notoriously not applied to the Taiping leaders themselves. However, as pointed out by Kathryn Bernhardt, on balance it would seem that Taiping rule did lead to some amelioration of the burdens on the poorer sections of the peasantry.[5] This was reflected in the folklore and oral traditions of the affected regions which, even generations after the suppression of the Taiping, regarded the movement as a liberation from the tyranny of landlords and corrupt officials. One such poem, still current a century later, goes:

> Bitterly, bitterly,
> The years creep slowly past.
> But when the Taipings come,
> Life will be good at last.
> The land will be divided,
> And contracts strewn on the roads.
> All people will be equal.
> There will be no rich households.[6]

Despite borrowing many elements from earlier heterodox and Confucian traditions in their programme and ideology, the Taiping clearly represented an unprecedented and unique phenomenon. How did a movement from a remote frontier region that launched a head-on assault on not just the ruling dynasty, but also on existing political institutions, social structure, and beliefs and values, assume such gigantic proportions and hold out for so long? The weakness and complacency of the Qing forces was undoubtedly a factor. The fighting qualities of the core of the Taiping forces, as well as their high morale and organization in the early stages, were other factors. But the extent and duration of the Taiping Rebellion, especially when seen in conjunction with the proliferation of many other revolts and rebellions in the same period, can only be explained by the deep and pervasive crisis that had emerged in China by the mid-nineteenth century. The Taiping could not have lasted as long as they did without considerable support from the disenfranchised members of rural society, to whom they held out some promise of freedom, howsoever this was understood, and for whom revolt against the Qing and the social order was their only hope.

DOWNFALL

The year 1856 was the high watermark of the Taiping power, with significant victories over the Qing forces. But, in that year, the tide began to turn. Acute infighting among the top leadership led to the loss of three of the top kings, part of the talented and experienced original core of Hong Xiuquan's supporters, together with their forces, in bloody internecine warfare. Thereafter,

Taiping power began to wane, but it was by no means finished, as the revival of fortunes under new leaders such as Hong's cousin Hong Ren'gan and Li Xiucheng in the period from 1858–60 showed. However, the Taiping were essentially on the defensive from that time on, and after 1861, they were increasingly hard pressed by the reviving loyalist forces. In 1864, Nanjing, finally fell to the imperial troops. As with the British suppression of the 1857 uprising in India, the vengeance of the Chinese imperial forces was ruthless and extremely bloody. The 'Heavenly Capital' was put to the torch and its inhabitants slaughtered, as were other towns and cities that were retaken, and the surviving rebel forces were hunted down and exterminated virtually to the last man.

The reasons for the Taiping failure were many. Whether due to faulty military strategy or not, the triumphant Taiping forces that swept their way into Nanjing failed to press home their advantage and finish off the Qing government, whose headquarters at Beijing was never seriously threatened. The different military expeditions that were sent off from Nanjing in different directions were not well coordinated and hence did not achieve lasting success. As a result the Taiping were constantly at war, and apart from the region immediately around Nanjing, their bases were never secure for any length of time. In the long run, the resulting dislocation as well as diversion of their energies from reform to warfare was to cost them popular support. The leadership crisis, including the catastrophic infighting of 1856, Hong's own withdrawal thereafter from active leadership into a world of his own delusions, as well as a loss of some of the leaders' original idealism, also affected morale.

Even more significant, perhaps, was the unexpected revival of the Qing resistance, just when all had seemed to be lost. This revival was based, not on the traditional military forces of the dynasty, but on a new collaboration between the beleaguered Manchu rulers and the Chinese elite to crush a rebellion that threatened not only dynastic power but an entire social system. The old balance of power which had been carefully constructed by the Qing, in which the Manchus had the controlling power, began to unravel under the pressure of rebellion. The initiative was taken by a combination of the local elite and top Chinese officials to create new, highly motivated and disciplined regional armies under their own command, which proved more than capable of taking on the rebel forces. The Qing had no alternative but to acquiesce in this devolution of power from their hands to their Chinese officials, and from the centre to the regions. More than the Taiping Rebellion itself, this shift of power, and the rise of new regional armies, was to have long-term implications for China's history in the twentieth century.

Another weakness of the Taiping was their inability to forge lasting alliances with other rebel movements. The Qing was confronted with not just one, but several rebellions simultaneously, including the Nian rebellion in the northern heartland and the Muslim rebellions in the north-west and south-west. This was a potentially deadly situation for them, but the Taiping, apart from occasional coordinated manoeuvres with the Nian, did not or could not take the initiative to form a joint front of all these forces. Perhaps their own unique ideology and programme and sense of mission prevented them from drawing closer to these other movements. As a result, it was the Manchu and Chinese elites who managed to form a joint front that first stamped out the Taiping, and then successfully took on the other rebellions one by one.

THE FOREIGN FACTOR

As pointed out earlier, the Taiping Rebellion showed some impact of the Western presence in China in its origins and in its Christian ideology. The Western influence was also manifest in the programme developed by Hong Ren'gan who wielded influence at Nanjing for a few years after his arrival in the city in 1856. Although never really implemented, Hong's proposals included encouragement to foreign trade, construction of railways, the setting up of modern banking and adoption of some elements of Western technology.

Their arrival in the lower Yangzi region and the establishment of their headquarters at Nanjing brought the Taiping within striking distance of the rapidly developing port of foreign trade at Shanghai. The Western traders, keen to ensure no disruption to their lucrative trade, initially followed a policy of neutrality in the civil war in China. They sent out feelers to the Taiping leadership, through representatives who visited Taiping-held areas. Initially, based on the reports of these representatives and other Western visitors, the Western community was inclined to look positively on these unusual Chinese insurgents who professed a form of Christianity. The high morale, clean living, high status accorded to women, and other features of Taiping life that they witnessed also had a favourable impact.

This situation began to change after 1860. The Taiping intolerance of opium, and their inability to stabilize their rule and ensure peaceful conditions, both were perceived as unfavourable for Western trade. Taiping Christianity, which had initially impressed the Westerners, was now instead seen to be blasphemous, particularly Hong Xiuquan's assumption of the position of the younger brother of Jesus Christ. Most significant of all was the new equation that developed between the Qing and the Western imperial powers after 1860. Defeated in the Second Opium War, the Qing was forced to make many more concessions to the Western powers, including the legalization of the opium trade. The Qing court also began to adopt a more conciliatory tone towards the Western powers, and charged the diplomatic younger brother of the Emperor, Prince Gong, with dealing directly with the Western envoys at Beijing. It was this group of envoys, and particularly the influential British envoy Frederick Bruce, who began to see in a revived and cooperative Qing dynasty their best option in China. The recently-suppressed uprising in India would undoubtedly have weighed heavily on British thinking at this time, probably influencing them to discreetly support the existing power in China rather than to use the crisis there to get more directly involved.

From a policy of 'armed neutrality', the Western powers therefore turned to a policy of 'limited intervention' in the civil war on the side of the Qing dynasty. This included supplying armaments and training to the imperial forces, permitting the involvement of Western mercenaries on the Qing side, and very limited direct use of Western troops against the Taiping forces, mainly in the region around Shanghai itself. While this help was very welcome to the Qing, and did make a difference to their campaign against the rebels, it is hard to say that it was decisive. Far more important was the role of the new regional armies under the command of Chinese officials like Zeng Guofan, Li Hongzhang and Zuo Zongtang. Even while cooperating with the Westerners, these Chinese officials were very determined not to let them take control of the campaign against the Taiping, even in Shanghai.[7] Thus, both the British and other Western powers' reluctance to get more directly involved, as well as the Chinese government's determination not to surrender the initiative to the Western allies, ensured that the deep crisis in China in the middle of the nineteenth century did not become the vehicle for the establishment of direct Western political or military power in China.

THE INDIAN CONNECTION

Interesting evidence has come down to us of an 'Indian connection' with the Taiping Rebellion. In the late 1850s, not satisfied with the concessions they had obtained in China after the First Opium War, the British began to prepare a renewed military offensive. Because of the outbreak of the 1857 Uprising in India, the bulk of troops dispatched from Britain for China under Lord Elgin were diverted to India instead. However, because of the insistent demands made by British authorities in Hong Kong, some detachments of Indian sepoys who were not 'infected' by the rebellious spirit were despatched to China. These included soldiers from the 47th, 65th and 70th Bengal Native Infantry, and the 38th Madras Native Infantry. A total of about 4,000 Indian soldiers were sent to China.[8]

After the conclusion of military operations in China in 1860, since the 1857 Uprising in India had also been suppressed, the bulk of the Indian troops from China were sent home. However, a smaller force which by this time included a regiment from Ludhiana, the 11th and 19th Punjab Infantry, the 5th Bombay Light Infantry and a portion of the Madras Artillery, was retained in China and sent to the region around Shanghai to take part in the operations against the Taiping rebels. It was in the course of these operations, some Indian soldiers deserted from their ranks and went over to the Taiping side. The Chinese general Zeng Guofan himself recorded: 'I have heard that in laying siege to Yushan country [in Jiangxi province] the rebel Prince Liu Xiucheng had a number of dark-skinned foreigners among his ranks.' Similarly, the other famous military commander Li Hongzhang noted that about '50 or 60 dark-skinned foreigners' were seen atop a wall of a city defending the Taiping, and that they in fact shot dead the French officer Tardif de Moidrey. Augustus Lindley also observed that Indian soldiers, including some from a 'Baluchi' regiment, were being systematically recruited to defect and fight for the Taipings. Lindley, who was himself a sympathizer with the Taiping, once found himself a co-passenger in a sampan of a 'swarthy, bearded East Indian' who, like him, was going secretly upriver from Shanghai to join the Taiping forces.[9]

These several instances of Indian soldiers joining the Chinese rebels are too numerous to dismiss as a one-time episode.[10] Rather, it perhaps shows that these soldiers too, like their brethren in India at that time, had been 'infected' by a spirit of rebellion that transcended national boundaries. Overcoming the hurdles of a different language and culture, as well as defying certain death if recaptured by the British or the Qing forces, they were, almost incredibly, drawn to the side of the Taiping movement in China. What did they see in the Taiping that inspired them to take such risks? We have no clear answers. But, if even hardened Western observers could be favourably impressed by the Taiping, then it is not hard to imagine that Indian soldiers harbouring discontent and resentment against their British rulers would be motivated to break ranks and join a movement that held out the promise of equality and brotherhood and perhaps a life of dignity.

CONCLUSION

Much more than the 1857 Rebellion in India, it would appear that the Taiping Rebellion was an essentially traditional response to an indigenous crisis. Large peasant rebellions driven by the political objective of overthrowing a ruling dynasty were not an uncommon occurrence in China's long history. The crisis that gripped China in the middle of the nineteenth century arose out of domestic problems such as a scarcity of land, administrative decline, the exacerbation of social tensions, and so on. It is true that the Taiping Rebellion was directed against alien rulers who took care to maintain their distinct Manchu ethnic identity even while adopting Chinese institutions. It is hard to say, however, that the fight to expel the foreign occupiers of China was the main element in the Taiping campaign. This element was only later emphasized, by leaders of the Revolution of 1911 that overthrew the Manchus, who saw themselves as heirs of the 'heroic' Taiping legacy. Yet it would seem that the socio-economic aspects of the Taiping programme, as well as their religious inspiration to create a new 'Heavenly Kingdom' on this earth, were at least as important as their anti-Manchu nationalism if not more. And as for the Taiping attitude towards the Western powers who had humiliated China and wrested privileges from her by force of arms, it was generally not unfavourable, and their opposition was limited to their dislike of the trade in opium.

Nevertheless, the size and scope of both the Taiping Rebellion and the 1857 Uprising set them apart not just from other revolts of the same period but from other rebellions in the histories of China and India. What makes both so fascinating is also the attempt in both to articulate some elements of a larger vision, of a new order, in their proclamations. The Taiping's ringing declaration that 'all shall have food to eat, clothes to wear', as well as the 1857 fighters' emphasis on the unity of people of different strata and religions, sound surprisingly modern and have a resonance even today. Certainly, both rebellions straddled two eras, and in their attitudes and objectives represented a unique melange of traditional and modern elements. Although both were completely extirpated, neither could be rooted out of public memory.

NOTES

1. Cited in Vincent Y.C. Shih, *The Taiping Ideology: Its Sources, Interpretations and Influences* (Seattle/London: University of Washington Press, 1967), p. 87.
2. Thomas Taylor Meadows, *The Chinese and their Rebellions* (London: Smith, Elder & Co., 1856), pp. 270–1.
3. Cited in Jean Chesneaux, *Peasant Revolts in China: 1840–1949* (London: W.W. Norton, 1973), p. 28.
4. A.F. Lindley, *Ti-ping Tien-Kwoh* (New York: Praeger Publishers, 1970), p. 301.
5. Kathryn Bernhardt, 'Elite and Peasant during the Taiping Occupation of the Jiangnan, 1860–64', *Modern China*, vol. 13, no. 4 (October 1987), pp. 406–7.

6. Cited in Bernhardt, 'Elite and Peasant during the Taiping Occupation of the Jiangnan', p. 379.
7. Philip A. Kuhn, 'The Taiping Rebellion', in John K. Fairbank (ed.), *The Cambridge History of China*, vol. 10, *Late Ch'ing, 1800–1911*, Part 1 (Cambridge: Cambridge University Press, 1978), pp. 308–10.
8. Madhavi Thampi, *Indians in China: 1800–1949* (New Delhi: Manohar, 2005), p. 152.
9. Ibid., pp. 151–4.
10. See also B.R. Deepak, 'The 1857 Rebellion and Indian Involvement in the Taiping Uprising in China', in Madhavi Thampi (ed.), *India and China in the Colonial World* (New Delhi: Social Science Press, 2005); and Yu Sheng-wu and Chang Chen-kun, 'China and India in the Mid-Nineteenth Century', in P.C. Joshi (ed.), *Rebellion 1857: A Symposium* (Calcutta: K.P. Bagchi & Co., 1986), pp. 337–52.

CHAPTER 10

1857 Uprising: Colonial War or Small War or Total War?

KAUSHIK ROY

Between 1857 and 1859, South Asia witnessed intense combat. What started as a mutiny of the Bengal Army gradually developed into a popular agrarian uprising in certain regions of north India. In late 1859, the British were able to re-establish their military domination over the subcontinent. Even while the 'Mutiny' was raging, British officers tried to analyse the nature of combat. In recent times, some historians have attempted to recreate the military drama of 1857.[1] However, a theoretical analysis of the nature of warfare in mid-nineteenth-century South Asia is still awaited. This paper is an attempt to construct a theoretical paradigm for understanding the logic and dynamics of warfare in India between 1857 and 1859. Various models of warfare as developed by scholars will be applied to understand the military scenario of the mid-1850s and then an attempt will be made to come up with a new framework. For understanding the uniqueness (or lack of it) of warfare in 1857 India, cross-cultural comparative analysis is necessary.

A theory of warfare not only tries to understand a particular war but also aims to study it as part of warfare throughout history and as a constant of history. A model of warfare instead of focusing on the specifics of a particular war tries to generalize and also identifies the permanent elements in war. The function of a model is to integrate the universal with the historical particulars. A model should not be used for the sake of simplifications, generalizations and predictions. After all, warfare is mostly a non-linear phenomenon. Alan Beyerchen says that non-linear systems are those that disobey proportionality or additivity. Such systems exhibit erratic behaviour through disproportionately large or disproportionately small outputs or they may involve synergistic interactions of the various constituting elements in which the whole is not equal to the sum of the parts. A non-linear system is characterized by structural instability. Such a system is characterized by chaos. Immeasurably small differences in input can produce entirely different results for the system, yielding different behaviour routes causing randomness. In such a system, chaos and predictable order could coexist.[2] In fact, the character of war can be said to be influenced by the 'butterfly effect'.[3] A micro cause can produce macro effect in warfare.[4] Now, let us shift the focus to the various models of warfare.

1857 MUTINY AS A SMALL WAR

In his masterpiece *On War* (1832) Carl Von Clausewitz, the Prussian philosopher (1780–1831) emphasizes conventional warfare within the European context. Clausewitz is famous (infamous according to commentators like Basil Liddell Hart and John Keegan) for philosophizing how conventional warfare could become absolute war. Liddell Hart and Keegan imply that Clausewitz's thinking about absolute war was indirectly responsible for the two world wars. However, *On War* also discusses in bits and pieces *Kleine Krieg* (Small War), conducted by the light infantry of regular armies. Small War involves, in Clausewitz's paradigm, patrols, raids, reconnaissance, and ambush. As we shall see, these were elements of colonial warfare also. Clausewitz's concept of small war was influenced by the anti-French uprising in Spain and Russia.[5]

The true father of the Small War paradigm dealing with colonial warfare is the British officer Charles E. Callwell (1859–1928), who may be described as the Colonial Clausewitz. Callwell's *Small Wars* was published in 1896 and reprinted several times. Callwell theorized on the nature of war between the Europeans (especially the British) and non-European people whom he considered uncivilized and belonging to the lower races.[6] It must be noted in Callwell's time the Victorian intellectual climate was tinged with quasi-scientific race theories. The race theorists constructed a hierarchy in which the Europeans were at the top and Asians and Africans were situated low in the scale.[7]

Callwell writes that all campaigns other than those where both sides consist of regular troops can be categorized as Small Wars. Since irregular armies are not willing to meet the regular armies in set-piece battles, decisive battles are absent in Small Wars.[8] He writes:

> Small wars include the partisan warfare which usually arises when trained soldiers are employed in the quelling of sedition and of insurrections in civilized countries; they include campaigns of conquest when a Great Power adds the territory of barbarous races to its possessions; and they include punitive expeditions against tribes bordering upon distant colonies.... Whenever a regular army finds itself engaged upon hostilities against irregular forces, or forces which in their armament, their organization, and their discipline are palpably inferior to it, the conditions of the campaign become distinct from the conditions of modern regular warfare.[9]

As regards tactical aspects, Callwell says: 'And the great principle which regular troops must always act upon in small wars—that of overawing the enemy by bold initiative and by resolute action whether on the battlefield or as part of the general plan of campaign.'[10] In other words, the tactical doctrine for the European armies in Small Wars was that offence is the best defence. Small Wars comprised ambushes, surprise attacks, murdering stragglers and stern reprisals.[11] However, at times, Small Wars become protracted wars of attrition. Callwell emphasizes:

> Insurrections and revolts in districts difficult of access where communications are bad and information cannot readily be obtained involve most troublesome military operations.... As a general rule the quelling of rebellion in distant colonies means protracted, thankless, invertebrate war.[12]

The very nature of the operational objectives of Small Wars makes them brutal. Calwell writes:

> [W]hen there is no king to conquer, no capital to seize, no organized army to overthrow, and when there are no celebrated strongholds to capture, and no great centres of population to occupy, the objectives are not so easy to select. It is then that the regular troops are forced to resort to cattle lifting and village burning and that the war assumes an aspect which may shock the humanitarian.[13]

The presence of stateless marginal groups generated different ethics of war. Callwell continues:

> The main points of difference between Small Wars and regular campaigns in this respect are that, in the former, the beating of the hostile armies is not necessarily the main object even if such armies exist, that moral effects are often far more important than material success, and that the operations are sometimes limited to committing havoc which the laws of regular warfare do not sanction.[14]

Callwell especially emphasizes the importance of logistics and human intelligence in Small Wars.[15] Callwell is aware of the unique features of the different Small Wars that occurred in different regions at different times.[16]

In the 1857 Uprising, besides skirmishes there were decisive battles and sieges. On 8 June 1857, the rebel soldiers moved out of Delhi and after marching for 4 to 5 miles entrenched themselves at Badli-Ki-Serai on the Grand Trunk Road. General Barnard's troops attacked them. Barnard decided on a frontal attack with a cavalry diversion on the rebels' left flank. The battle started at daybreak with an artillery duel. While the 1st Infantry Brigade took the rebel battery at the front centre of the rebel line, the 2nd Infantry Brigade charged the right. Simultaneously, Hope Grant appeared with his cavalry and guns at the left rear of the rebels. The rebels withdrew to the Delhi Ridge after losing 26 guns and 500 men; Wilson's troops had lost 51 killed and 130 wounded.[17] In June 1857, the siege train which the British concentrated for taking Delhi comprised of eight 18-pounders, four 8-inch howitzers, and twelve 5.5-inch mortars.[18] On 30 June 1857, at Chinhut, the rebel troops (whose numbers varied between 20,000 to 25,000) with 20 guns confronted the British force which marched out of Lucknow.[19] Defeated, the British force retreated into Lucknow and the Lucknow Residency was besieged by the victorious rebel soldiery. The rebels concentrated 10 regiments and two 9-pounder batteries against the Lucknow Residency held by Henry Lawrence and his troops.[20] Clearly, this had not been a Small War.

1857 UPRISING: A COLONIAL WAR?

In 1989, the Dutch scholar H.L. Wesseling developed a model of Colonial War in order to accommodate most of the wars conducted by European maritime states in Afro–Asia between the seventeenth and the twentieth centuries. The Colonial War model is a modified version of Callwell's Small War model. One of the characteristics of colonial warfare is the unlimited war aims of the belligerents. While in Europe, writes Wesseling, the aims were limited, in the colonies the aims of the European powers were unlimited and absolute. Colonial War was waged against two types of adversaries: those with a high level of state apparatus and stateless groups. The former were easy meat to the European armies in set-piece battles, but stateless marginal groups proved troublesome as they took to guerrilla warfare and ran rings around the slow European armies.[21]

It seems that unlimited warfare resulting in the complete destruction of the enemy forces, which is a characteristic of Total War, developed only between 1911 and 1945 in Europe. Yet, from 1841 onwards the French waged an economic war against the Muslims in Algeria by devastating their fields, orchards, and villages.[22] Again, in North America, writes Douglas Porch, Amerindian society was in a state of permanent mobilization which was equivalent to a perpetual *levee en masse.*[23] Porch asserts: 'Amerindian combat increased in desperation as both muskets and friction with colonists transformed indigenous warfare from a largely ritualistic demonstration in personal courage into something close to total war.'[24]

The People's War/Total War model has been developed by German and American historians in recent times in order to explain the rise of Germany and the USA since 1850. However, the roots of the Total War concept can be traced back earlier. The German General Erich Ludendorff used the phrase Total War in his book titled *Der Totale Krieg* published in 1935.[25] One of the characteristics of Total War is universal conscription.[26] In August 1793, the French Revolutionary government issued the *levee en masse* by which all single men between 18 and 25 were to register for military service. Between 1800 and 1811, Napoleon raised 1.3 million conscripts and one million between 1812–13.[27] Besides conscription, another characteristic of Total War is the deliberate targeting of the civilian population.[28] People's War (i.e. the American Civil War) first emerged in the Western world in the nineteenth century and was transformed into Total War in the first half of the twentieth century.[29] In the People's War, war was fought by an armed militia rather than professional armed forces of the state. In such conflicts, people's interests converge with the interest of the state. Hence, the people took up arms spontaneously and simultaneously they were also organized from above.[30] Propaganda played an important role in the People's War. Propaganda dehumanized the enemy and kept the 'home fires burning'.[31] Another feature of People's War/Total War is that people fight for ideological rather than mercenary considerations.[32]

To an extent, the 1857 Uprising conformed to certain characteristics of the People's War.[33] According to one estimate, about 75 per cent of the adult male population of Awadh took part in the 1857 revolt.[34] In 1857 India, the rural populace of north and central India at times rose both spontaneously and occasionally under the leadership of the landed magnates. In other words, the rural areas experienced both vertical mobilization (zamindars mobilizing their dependants and retainers) as well as horizontal mobilization (caste and clan solidarity resulted in mobilization across several villages).[35] Cooperation between civilians and military personnel was a characteristics of the 1857 uprising: for example, in May 1857 the civilians of Bulandshahr in collaboration with rebel soldiers burnt the military station and looted the treasury.[36]

The role of ideology in warfare which is a crucial constituent of the People's War model remains problematic. Large scale desertion was common both in the armies of the American Civil War and in the rebel armies of India. Brian Holden Reid and John White assert that men enlisted for cash bounties and then deserted. They argue that desertion was due to absence of regimental loyalty because of the impermanence of the fighting units and a lack of welfare measures such as adequate apparel and food.[37] And the rebel soldiery in Delhi during August–September 1857 demanded cash from Badshah Bahadur Shah II and the indigenous commercial elements for fighting the *ferangis*.[38]

It seems that Wesseling is aware of the problematic that elements of Total War are embedded in his model of Colonial War. Thus, he brings in modernizing/humanistic elements in his framework of Colonial Warfare. Wesseling asserts that whether it was the French Army in North Africa or the American Army in the Philippines at the end of the nineteenth century, the imperial war machines after their colonial conquest functioned as agents of Western civilization.[39] This sort of argument gels with those historians who believe that British rule in India was a blessing in disguise. This school claims that the overseas empires were indeed a positive thing in the course of historical development.

An example of this line of thinking is Rod Thornton. He argues that the central concept of British counter-insurgency task even today remains the 'minimum force philosophy' which in turn is a legacy of colonial policing by the British and the presence of Victorian values. The Victorian values could be traced back to Protestant ethics. The moral principles of the evangelical Protestant movement that developed during the later seventeenth and eighteenth centuries formed the basis of Victorian liberalism. Evangelical Protestantism created the chivalrous Victorian gentleman. The public school system and juvenile literature, inculcated the altruistic ideal of chivalry among the younger generation of British males. The public schools were designed to produce Christian gentlemen with 'character' and a sense of honour. And their duty was to provide the benefits of Christian civilization to the 'coloured heathen' of the empire without showing undue cruelty. It is to be noted that most of the British military officers were drawn from the public schools. In addition, fiction, poetry, theatre, and painting emphasized the values of manliness, patriotism, service, sacrifice, comradeship, and courage. The media pushed the idea of the civilizing mission conducted by the 'noble warriors'. Besides ideology, minimal amount of force was used while conducting pacification campaigns in the colonies due to the pragmatic demand of controlling enormous populations.[40]

Most nineteenth-century European officials held the view of empire as a civilizing force. And this brings us to the question of military orientalism. In his study of nineteenth-century Dutch expeditions to the Indonesian Archipelago, J.A. de Moor writes that the Dutch believed that the common Indonesians wanted to be liberated from the fanatical (pagan) priests and tyrannical 'native' rulers.[41] The British rulers of India too operated with a similar set of assumptions.

At the other extreme, historians like Rudrangshu Mukherjee assert that the basic component of British rule in India was violence and the colonizers denied the colonized any humanness by treating the latter as animals.[42] Rajat Kanta Ray finds that the

British viewed the Indians as *untermenschen* (sub-humans). Since white soldiery regarded its opponents as savages, they had no compunction in outdoing the latter in savagery.[43] And as regards the issue of collaboration of the colonized with the colonizers, Ray says that the necessity to earn a livelihood was sufficient to ensure collaboration.[44] It was a collaboration based on fear and the forces of deterrence.

However, Wesseling is right in pointing out that though the aims of colonial wars were total, the tools employed were limited. In other words, the colonial armies were relatively small. In addition, a significant proportion of these were staffed by the local subjects. Though European colonialism exhibited continuous violence, European imperialism remained based on 'native' collaboration.[45]

Figures seem to speak for themselves. In 1815, there were only 5,000 European soldiers and 5,500 Indonesian soldiers in the Dutch East Indies. By the end of the nineteenth century, there were 14,000 European soldiers and 22,000 Indonesian troops. European and Indonesian non-commissioned officers and privates served in joint corps.[46] In the context of 1857 Uprising, Major H. Daly noted the vital role played by the Punjabi troops in crushing the mutineers in the following words: 'Had the Mutiny overtaken us at such a time, and after the Sikh had forgotten his war calling and his contempt for Pandy, it is hard to say what amount of British troops could have reconquered India for us.'[47] The British raised ex-*Khalsa* soldiers for fighting against the rebels.[48] In addition, the 41,705 Indian personnel of the Madras Army remained loyal to the EIC.[49]

The small size of the armies deployed becomes clear when one analyses particular battles and sieges that occurred between 1857 and 1859 in India and elsewhere in the colonial world. In the First Opium War (1839–42), with 10,000 soldiers and 16 ships, Britain defeated the Chinese Empire.[50] Just before the 1857 revolt, about 20,000 British troops (one-third of the standing British Army) were deployed in India.[51] When the rebellion began, the British government in Punjab had at its disposal 40,000 men including 12,000 European soldiers. And these soldiers were mostly sent against the 'mutineers' of Delhi.[52] For instance on 8 July 1857, the Delhi Field Force which laid siege to Delhi numbered 6,600 effective soldiers. At that time, the rebel soldiers in Delhi numbered 40,000 men. Due to desertions and casualties, by 12 August, the rebel strength in Delhi was less than 15,000 men.[53] In 1857, the number of regular rebel soldiers in Awadh numbered 20,000 men.[54] In July 1857, Henry Havelock marched from Allahabad towards Kanpur with an army numbering 1,400 European infantry. And in 1857, the rebel force in Kanpur numbered only 3,000 infantry and 1,000 cavalry.[55] On 12 July 1857, at Fatehpur, the rebels brought forward 3,500 troops supported by 12 brass and iron guns (one was a 24-pounder) against Havelock who had eight guns and five infantry regiments.[56] On 16 July 1857, at Kanpur, Nana Sahib concentrated 5,000 (regular and irregular) soldiers and eight guns (of them four were 24-pounders, another a 6-pounder).[57] Casualties in the European armies remained very low. After fighting the twin battles of Aong and Pandu Nadi on 15 July 1857, Havelock recorded his loss as merely 25 killed and wounded.[58] In contrast, Napoleon's wars killed one in five Frenchmen born between 1790 and 1795.[59]

In fact, the battles of 1857 were smaller affairs than some of the battles fought by the British against Indians in the preceding era. In 1803, at Assaye, the Marathas had 120 cannons (of them 80 to 90 were operational).[60] In the First Anglo–Sikh War (1845–6), at Mudki (18 December 1845) the Sikhs brought forward 2,000 infantry, 22 guns and between 8,000 and 10,000 irregular cavalry. The British loss was 872 killed and wounded. During the Battle of Ferozeshah (21–2 December 1845), the Sikhs concentrated about 30,000 infantry, 80–90 guns and 12,000 horsemen. On 10 February 1846, the Sikhs at Sobraon had 30,000 soldiers, 67 cannons and 200 *zamburaks*. Against them the EIC deployed 16,000 troops. In the battle the EIC's loss was 320 killed and 3,063 wounded and Sikh casualties were between 8,000 to 15,000 men.[61]

The real threat to the metropolitan armies proved to be not the arrows, bullets, and cannons of the colonized people but disease. Callwell tells us that the real problem which a European army faces in colonial campaigning is the physical geography of the region: 'For it is perhaps the most distinguishing characteristic of small wars as compared with regular hostilities conducted between modern armies, that they are in the main campaigns against nature.'[62] Following Callwell, David Killingray in the context of European imperialism in Africa implies that rather than the 'natives', it was tropical diseases that were more dangerous to the Western soliders.[63] In Dutch Indonesia, the death rates of European troops between 1827 and 1828 rose to 45 per cent.[64]

In 2000, Douglas Porch modified the Colonial War model by dividing colonial warfare into two phases: pre-industrial colonial warfare, and imperialism of the industrial age. In Porch's model, pre-industrial colonial warfare occurred till the 1850s and the high renaissance of imperialism occurred from the 1860s. Due to technological progress, it was only during the second phase of colonial warfare that Europeans enjoyed substantial (but not absolute) firepower superiority. In the pre-industrial phase Europeans won due to a superior ideology and organizational expertise. Porch concludes that till the advent of magazine fed rifles and machine guns, European superiority in Asia did not result from technological supremacy.[65]

The role of technology seems to be at a discount among modern historians. However, the British military commanders realized the importance of hardware. After winning the Battle of Fatehpur, Havelock mentioned in his dispatch: 'But our fight was fought, neither with musket nor bayonet, nor saber, but with Enfield rifles, and cannon, so we lost no men. The enemy's fire scarcely touched us; ours, for four hours, allowed him no response.'[66] Most nineteenth-century British writers of fiction and history read the technological supremacy of the British as evidence of the superiority of the Caucasoid West Europeans over the 'orientals' (Asians).[67] Some modern scholars packaged racial superiority as cultural superiority (or uniqueness).

James Belich writes that wars outside Europe in the early modern era are often dismissed as Colonial Wars or Small Wars and remain at the fringes of military historiography. The nomenclature, claims Belich, is in itself ethnocentric. Not all battles which were fought outside Europe were small, whereas many European battles were indeed small. Further, whatever may be the size of these extra-European conflicts, these wars were of vital importance for the local people of the area concerned.[68]

There existed similarity between the tactics followed by the regular armies in the European battlefields and their non-European opponents in the theatres of war beyond Europe. The

Maratha artillery tactics at Assaye was to open grape shot fire at the linear formation of advancing British infantry at ranges between 600 to 200 metres.[69] Maratha artillery doctrine was influenced by ex-Napoleonic officers who served as instructors in the Maratha forces. And the Duke of Wellington honed his skill especially as regards logistical affairs in the course of fighting the Marathas. Wellington's skill in feeding an army on the march aided him when he fought Napoleon's marshals in Spain. The British tactic during the First Anglo–Sikh War was to get within 150 yards of the enemy's batteries and then launch an infantry charge. The Sikh tactical doctrine involved building a camp fortified with trenches which bristled with artillery pieces. British horse batteries galloped within 300 yards of the Sikh trenches and opened fire. Under their support, the EIC infantry battalions stormed the Sikh entrenchment.[70] Hence, while studying military history, establishing parallels and interconnections between warfare in the non-European world and Europe is a necessity.

THE TRIUMPH OF THE WESTERN WAY OF WARFARE

A variation and inverted image of the Colonial War model is the Western Way of Warfare paradigm. This paradigm aims to explain continuous military successes of the colonizers against the colonized in the last 500 years. The Western Way of Warfare paradigm argues that as regards military affairs what the West did from the dawn of civilization has been most effective. Geoffrey Parker claims that the Western military tradition was characterized by the emphasis on technology and discipline. From the seventeenth century the tradition of writing military theory further enhanced the superiority of the Western Way of Warfare. What kept West on its toes was a challenge–response dynamic that resulted in continuous advancement.[71] The Western Way of Warfare degenerates into a linear story of triumph of the West. While some of the followers of the Western Way of Warfare focuses on managerial and technological factors, others within this paradigm emphasize the cultural uniqueness of the West.

In William H. McNeill's view, the West's military superiority over the non-West after 1500 was due to technological, institutional, and cultural factors. Among these three factors, McNeill and

Michael Howard consider the cultural uniqueness of the Europeans as the most crucial component in combat superiority.[72] McNeill writes:

> Europeans were very prone to shed blood. The cult of prowess among them sustained a ready resort to violence in defence of personal and collective honour. As a result, in confrontations with people less well armed than themselves, Europeans seldom hesitated to inflict death and destruction on their foes, sometimes with only trivial provocation.[73]

Ironically, McNeill subverts Callwell's paradigm of 'savage natives' and indirectly concludes that it was the Europeans who won due to the savage and brutal ways. The cultural superiority thesis got a new lease of life with the publication of Victor Davis Hanson's *Carnage and Culture* in 2001. An expert in Greek warfare, Hanson claims that the core of Western warfare, i.e. infantry warfare, first emerged in classical Greece. The characteristics of Western cultural ethos are egalitarianism, strict discipline, matchless weapons, and individual initiative. The net result was that Westerners sought decisive face to face encounters in which their victory was inevitable. Hanson arrogantly claims that in the last 2,500 years 'real' warfare only occurred when a Western army had met another Western army.[74]

A variant of the Western Way of Warfare is the model of Military Revolution(s). Now, historians and political scientists are speaking of a Military Technical Revolution (hereafter MTR) or Revolution in Military Affairs (RMA). Both are considered to be much narrower in implication than the Military Revolution concept and concentrate mostly on the technological and tactical aspects of warfare.[75] For Emily O. Goldman 'RMAs are combinations of technological, doctrinal and organizational innovations that produce a dramatic increase in the combat potential of armed forces.... These fundamental discontinuities with the existing status quo signal a shift in the dominant modes of war-fighting.'[76] A Military Revolution occurs at three levels: conceptual, organization and technological. It seems that western Europe experienced a series of Military Revolutions. Laurent Henninger writes that early modern Europe experienced one that resulted in the genesis of modern warfare.[77] Geoffrey L. Herrera asserts that nineteenth-century western Europe experienced another Military Revolution. While the rifle transformed tactics, the railroad transformed operations and strategy. The increasing range, accuracy and speed of firing of the breech loading rifles resulted in the linear formation of infantry being replaced by infantry organized in a loose skirmishing order and focusing on marksmanship.[78] Against these techniques and technologies, low skilled indisciplined and technologically backward non-Westerners were blown away quickly and easily.

The Herodotean tradition of dividing the world into Orient and the Occident, a principle followed by the spokesmen of Western Way of Warfare, is erroneous. It is time now to get out of such a bipolar division in world history. To argue that discipline was an instance of Western exclusivity is nonsense. It is impossible to prove that the West was technologically superior to the rest of the world from the dawn of civilization. After all, both the stirrup and gunpowder came to Europe from China. Again, why did the challenge–response dynamic operate only in the West? One is also curious why a comparatively small region of the world repeatedly and continuously experienced a series of Military Revolutions (or RMAs). The onus is on those who talk about Military Revolutions to explain the peculiar Western exclusivity of such revolutions. Even if we accept Herodotus' bipolar model, the military superiority of the West over the non-West throughout history is erroneous. Except Alexander and some Roman emperors (like Trajan and Julian), it was the so-called non-West which spilled into new territories. For instance the Arab conquest of Spain and the Ottoman control of the Balkans had more lasting influence than the ephemeral advances of Alexander and Trajan into Asia. And in North Africa, after Roman and Vandal occupation, the Caliphate and the Ottomans were calling the shots. European control over North Africa was re-established only in the nineteenth century. Finally, from the time of Attila till Chingiz Khan, the Eurasian steppe nomads were spilling into European part of Russia rather than vice versa.[79] Only in the nineteenth century was European Russia able to overcome the steppe nomads of Central Asia. Hanson has no knowledge of warfare in China, and the aggressive Eurasian steppe nomadic warfare that occurred till the eighteenth century. For example, Chingiz Khan's war in China was greater in scope and lethality than anything occurring in Europe at that time.[80]

THE 1857 UPRISING AS A GLOBAL CIVIL WAR

In recent times, a group of historians taking a transcontinental approach has attempted to explain the parallel rise of Germany and USA from mid-nineteenth century to Second World War. Michael Geyer and Charles Bright assert that local wars are shaped by region-specific factors and comparison does not require linkages. Prussia and the USA were located at the epicentre of an arc of violence which extended from Europe to America. One could extend the arc of violence further eastward to include China. After all, the Taiping Rebellion (1851–64) was a major conflict in terms of duration and deadliness. More than 30 million Chinese perished before it was crushed. Geyer and Bright continue that nineteenth-century statistical data on civil wars show that low-intensity warfare characterized by weak states was probably more deadly than inter-state warfare in the heartland of Europe. In other words, scattered violence as part of millenarian agrarian rebellions outside Europe were more deadly than decisive battles fought by the great European powers.[81] One might add that even today the Hutu-Tutsi struggle has caused more casualties than USA's two high technology conventional wars against Iraq.

Geyer and Bright write that advances in communication and transportation increased the mobility of forces and facilitated the simultaneous and coordinated deployment of force in various regions without loss of central control. The deployment of force was based on the metropolitan ability to concentrate resources and move them at will. Power projection depended on sub-imperial posts like coaling stations, naval bases, communication nodes, etc. The capacity to be present globally became the mark of a world superpower. The vital issue became not the force at hand at a particular spot in an empire but the force that could be generated and put into place. Thus, the sea lanes and communication lines across the world became critical to the conduct of war at a global level.[82]

1857 was in many ways a civil war. The mutiny of the Bengal Army (which itself was a crucial component of the colonial regime) opened the way for the disaffected subjects to rebel. Moreover, Indians in the Bombay and Madras armies and in the Punjab Frontier Force (also known as Punjab Irregular Force) fought on the side of the British against the rebels. The Uprising had inter-linkages with the other great conflicts that occurred across Eurasia in the nineteenth century. Haraprasad Chattopadhyay rightly asserts that 1857 was not inevitable. Had there been a large number of European soldiers stationed in India, the *Pandies* would never have rebelled.[83] Due to the Crimean War, British units were withdrawn from India. As a result, only 40,000 British troops remained in the subcontinent along with 226,000 Indian soldiers.[84] And this enabled the civil war to actually occur in India. This civil uprising was part of a series of large-scale violent uprisings which occurred across the rim of Eurasia in the middle of the nineteenth century.

British grand strategy in the mid-nineteenth century represented a fusion of continental and maritime strategies. Continental strategy was geared to maintain a balance of power in Europe while maritime strategy aimed at command of the seas, essential for maintaining an overseas empire.[85] In fact, the global maritime linkages also played a part in allowing the British to survive the 1857 Uprising. As early as 18 May 1857, John Lawrence, the Chief Commissioner of Punjab informed G.F. Edmonstone, Secretary in the Foreign Department of the Government of India: 'The whole Native Regular Army are ready to break out, and unless a blow be soon struck the Irregulars as a body will follow their example. Send for our troops from Persia. Intercept the force now on its way to China and bring it to Calcutta.'[86] Along with naval superiority in the oceans, British naval supremacy along the rivers also allowed the EIC to deploy troops rapidly deep in the heartland of India. To give an example, on 19 May 1857, the British made use of the steamers along the Ganga to send troops from Calcutta to Allahabad.[87] Despite the importance of riverine warfare, naval historians choose only to concentrate on the cataclysmic conflicts involving battle fleets of the great powers which had raged across the oceans.

Warfare in the nineteenth century was transformed due to the increasing use of telegraphs, railroads, rifles and mass armies. The nineteenth century witnessed the emergence of modern warfare. Modern warfare is industrialized, bureaucratized, and nationalized. The command appointments now depended on merit and examination rather than on money and birth. The mechanics of command depended on the telegraph rather than the voice and bugle. The breech loading conical cylindrical bullets and mass manufacturing techniques are the hallmarks of such warfare. Due to the rise of firepower, densely packed linear formations of infantry soldiers on the battlefield were replaced by dispersed soldiers digging into the earth for protection against a storm of steel.[88] Populations rose in Europe from 187,000,000 in 1800 to 401,000,000 in 1900.[89] This meant that many more Europeans were dispensable. The British troops in both the Crimean War (1854–6) and during the 1857 Uprising (1857–9) fought with Minie rifles.[90] The American military units during the American Civil War and the European armies during First World War took losses of over 50 per cent in single battles.[91] War correspondents appeared in the Crimean War, 1857 Uprising and in the American Civil War. For instance, William Howard Russell covered both the Crimean War and the 1857 Uprising from the British side. During the American Civil War, 22,000 miles of railway lines gave the North an advantage over the South which had only 9,000 miles of tracks. Between 1840 and 1860, the railroad in Prussia rose from 291 miles to 3,500 miles. By 1900, Britain had 20,000 miles of railway tracks in India which aided the British–Indian Army not only to launch repeated border campaigns but also in the internal pacification campaigns.[92] The rebels of 1857 were aware of the importance of railway in British power projection. Near Allahabad, for instance, the rebels uprooted tracks and put railway engines and stations to flames.[93] In 1857 India, while the rebel soldiers of the Bengal Army conducted conventional operations against the EIC, armed militias carried out guerrilla attacks against the British and their collaborators.

One of the principal components of Colonial War, Small War and Civil Uprisings is guerrilla warfare. Ivan Arreguin-Toft writes that in asymmetric wars the weaker adversary can avoid the firepower superiority of the stronger adversary.[94] Hence, guerrilla warfare is a weapon of the weak. It involves small bands of irregulars fighting an invading army or attempting to weaken the latter's hold over a conquered territory. For both Carl von Clausewitz and Baron Jomini, guerrilla war was subsidiary and supplementary to conventional operations against the enemy. In Jomini's framework, guerrilla warfare is a sort of national uprising against the enemy and this ought to be supported by a nucleus of disciplined troops. Guerrilla warfare comprises hit-and-run operations and ambushes and hence guerrillas carry light weapons.[95] For Arreguin-Toft, guerrilla warfare strategy requires physical sanctuary (swamps, mountains, thick forests or border areas controlled by friendly states) and a supportive population who supplies intelligence, recruits, and logistical facilities.[96] In guerrilla war, writes Thomas A. Marks, terror is always an important constituent.[97] Guerrilla war and insurgency are interrelated. James D. Fearon and David D. Latin come up with a definition of insurgency: 'Insurgency is a technology of military conflict characterized by small, lightly armed bands practising guerrilla warfare from rural base areas.'[98]

Most of the literature on civil wars concentrates on the conflicts which began in the late twentieth century. This is because most studies of civil war have been made by political scientists. Nevertheless, some of the studies done by the political scientists could be used for gaining insights on the nature of 1857. Any sort of violence which involves at least 1,000 deaths could be categorized as a civil conflict.[99] Civil War could be of various types: for gaining control over the state apparatus as well as for seceding from a particular state. Rebel groups who aim to seize power from the state will tend to fight their wars closer to the capital city compared to the secessionist groups. It is to be noted that the primary aim of the rebels in 1857 was to retain Delhi, the historic capital of pre-British India. The nature of a civil war is shaped by size of a country, its location, the nature of its borders and the presence of natural resources which are required in financing the purchase of arms.[100] Some other scholars agree that in case of the poorest countries, development may actually stimulate violence. Civil War occurs more frequently in countries with a substantial population of many ethnic, linguistic and religious groups.[101]

Credit is due to C.A. Bayly for making the first attempt to compare and contrast the 1857 Uprising with other anti-colonial movements. Bayly writes that both the Java War of 1825–30 and the Indian 'Mutiny' of 1857–9 were anti-colonial movements directed against a maritime European power. Each was an amalgam of three trends: reaction against colonial interference led by the 'native' courts, agrarian revolts and the emergence of Islamic and millenarian ideologies which drove popular resistance. Nevertheless, there were dissimilarities in these two movements.

While in India, the colonial army took the initiative to challenge British rule, the colonial army in Java remained more or less loyal to the Dutch. The timing and duration of the Indian 'Mutiny', claims Bayly, was determined by the military mutiny and not by economic depression as was the case in Java. In fact, says Bayly, the north Indian economy was on an upturn when the military mutiny erupted. During the Java War, the villagers were swayed by the strong magical element in the Hindu–Buddhist tradition. In accordance with this tradition, King Dipanagara was supposed to be able to mobilize cosmic forces to defeat his enemy. There was also mixture of elements from Muslim messianic tradition. The king saw himself as protector of the Javanese culture from the encroachments of the Christian colonizers. In Bayly's eyes, social unease bred millenarian expectations. Bayly finds similarities in the legacies of both the Java War and the Indian 'Mutiny'. After suppressing the movements, both imperial powers discovered 'martial races': Punjabis and Gurkhas in the case of India and Amboinese and Moluccans in the case of Java.[102]

There are two lacunae in Bayly's paradigm. Bayly accepts the importance of the military dimension of the 1857–9 rebellion but refuses to deal with it adequately. Second, Bayly does not focus on the course of the Java War and the Indian 'Mutiny'. Turning the limelight on the course of the 1857 Uprising does not mean a reversion to narrative history or recounting a tale of great battles where the combatants (especially the British) displayed heroic bravery. Rather, the course of the Indian 'Mutiny' was inextricably intermeshed with the causes and legacies of 1857–9. Bayly's excellent model could be expanded to include not only other anti-colonial struggles which were going on in various parts of the world during the nineteenth century but also civil wars which erupted more or less in the same time along the vast rim which stretched from China Sea in the east up to the Pacific coast of USA in the west.

The 1857–9 Uprising can be compared and contrasted with both the Taiping Rebellion and the American Civil War. The Taiping Rebellion described in this volume occurred between 1850 and 1864 in south China and Yangtze provinces. The rebellion was led by one who claimed to be the second son of God. The rebellion cost between 30-40 million lives. The Taiping capital was Nanjing, a principal city on the Yangtze River not far from Shanghai. The Qing regime mobilized regional armies from the settled peasant population, under elite supervision.[103] The Manchu dynasty saved itself by enrolling literate Han degree holders, who organized the local militia for fighting the mass Taiping armies. The Han elite's background in the classical Chinese tradition, their school and family ties, and their mastery of the classical script held them together.[104] These armies got rifles from the Western powers and the support of British naval guns to dislodge the Taiping from the walled cities.[105]

One is reminded of a stark parallel with the British naval brigades discharging their super heavy guns in order to dislodge the rebels from the fortifications within Lucknow in March 1858. The 1857 Uprising, like the Taiping Rebellion, was an agrarian millenarian revolt. In Mukherjee's argument, the sepoys were peasants in uniform and they became the peasant in arms during the 1857 Uprising.[106] Just after the rebellion, argues Mukherjee, the sepoys tore off their uniforms which were those of an alien regime and identified themselves with the peasants.[107] After the sepoy mutinies, it was the talukdars' actions which transformed the military mutiny into a popular struggle. In Awadh, about 60 per cent of the fighting force was drawn from the peasants and retainers of the talukdars.[108]

Both the 1857 Uprising and the American Civil War experienced guerrilla operations along with conventional operations. Against the Union armies and their long lines of supply, small bands of Confederate cavalry proved effective. Many Confederate commanders found that the irregular units were inexpensive to organize and effective against the Union's regulars in hit-and-run expeditions. In western Virginia and western Missouri, guerrilla warfare persisted because of the pro-Southern sympathy of 40 per cent of the population and the difficult terrain.[109] After losing Lucknow in March 1858, the rebels took to guerrilla warfare. Had they utilized the option of guerrilla warfare in mid-1857, history might have taken a different turn in South Asia in particular and in the world in general.[110]

Monica Duffy Toft writes that religious civil wars are more destructive than civil wars fought over other issues, and they last longer. Christianity and Islam, she says, encourage followers to discount their physical survival. The Abrahamic religions tend to be uncompromising because the texts like Old Testament, New

Testament and Koran place strong limits on the conduct of the followers. The more central a religion is to a violent conflict, the less likely that conflict will be resolved through negotiations. This is because the more central religion is to an insurgency, the less likely the combatants are to restrain themselves from using force against even enemy non-combatants who are portrayed as unbelievers.[111] Hans Kung writes that in Islamic doctrine one could become a *shahid* not only by passively suffering for faith but also by actively fighting for his faith.[112]

The 1857 Uprising had a religious dimension. The rebels conceptualized the church as symbol of alien religion and *ferangi* domination. When the Indian infantry at Ferozepur revolted in May 1857, they burnt down the church and the British bungalows.[113] For the rebels, religion served as the source of solidarity and fraternity.[114] Rajat Kanta Ray writes that race and religion were fused into an explosive psychological compound. Religion constituted the very basis of the community in 1857.[115] In north India, religious men played a very important role in spreading rumour, prophecies, and anti-British sentiment among the populace.[116] Ray continues that nationalism is a recent phenomenon but patriotism is far older than that. The 'rebels' patriotism expressed itself in the specific form of combined (joint Hindu–Muslim) religious crusade to protect *dharma* and *deen*. The rebels of 1857 belonged to a world which had no notion of political sovereignty.[117] One wonders why—after all, pre-British India had experienced the existence of large agrarian bureaucratic empires for centuries. And, pre-British India was not a stateless society as Aidan Southall and Burton Stein would argue.[118] Ray points out that the 1857 Uprising on part of the Indians was a multi-layered rebellion, partly a racial war of black subject people against their white oppressors, and the race war was ideologically packaged as a religious war between true and false religions.[119] Mukherjee accepts that the religious men predominated among the Awadh 'mutineers'. The religious leaders were bitter in their hostility to the government and stirred up anti-British feelings in the populace, which strengthened the morale of the rebel soldiery. These religious leaders deliberately portrayed the revolt as a religious war in order to mobilize the masses against imperialism.[120]

A holistic model within the emergent field of global history approach which accounts for the varied characteristics of the 1857 Uprising and establishes parallels with other armed uprisings in different parts of the world, ought to take into account both the social and cultural factors, collectively held semi-conscious or unconscious images, assumptions, codes, and scripts that define the external environment. Cultural assumptions also constitute a system of inherited conceptions expressed in symbolic forms by means of which men communicate, perpetuate and develop their knowledge about attitudes towards life. To an extent, the military culture of mid-nineteenth-century South Asia was also a product of the macro-environmental level which comprised of geography, ethno-cultural characteristics and historical traditions. It is to be noted that military culture of a particular group is deeply rooted not only in historical practice but also in a particular generation's recent experience.[121] Along with culture, there is the role of social structure. Stephen Peter Rosen asserts that social divisions created by dominant social structures are carried over into the military organizations which in turn affect the combat effectiveness of those organizations. Again, states aware of the nature of internal social structures of their enemies are able to exploit the weaknesses that they create.[122]

CONCLUSION

Categorizing the 1857 Uprising as a civil war might raise hiccups among Indian historians who are prone to look at the EIC regime as an alien intrusion in Indian society. However, there can be no denying that the colonial regime was based on the collaboration of the colonized, whatever may be the latter's motivation. There can be no doubt that Indian soldiers were crucial agents of colonialism, providing not only auxiliary support but also constituting a determining factor during the imperial military crisis. Small is not always beautiful. It is time to move away from micro analysis to macro synthesis. Instead of pouring over the agrarian records of a particular *taluka*, it is necessary to put 1857 in global perspective in order to assess the true nature of the Uprising. All the theories discussed above, except the last, are Eurocentric in perspective and the present attempt is to integrate a local phenomenon as part of a macro-historical phenomenon.

It is time to throw away the binary model of civilization–savagery, and of West *versus* East, and to merge Eurasian history into one single stream.

There was no direct correlation between economic decline and the incidence of armed violence in 1857. Any sort of Whiggish teleology is erroneous. The primitivization of the warfare conducted by the rebels would not be of much help. Rather than looking for inherent efficiency of a military organization, says Jeremy Black, it is better to understand that all military organizations in history were products of specific circumstances (especially the political context) rather than a stage in military progress. In other words, no uniform global model based on technology or operational effectiveness is possible.[123] Any model, despite its overarching interpretations and synthesis, should take care of the local contingent factors. Counter-factual history could prove nothing but at least could point out the vulnerabilities of teleological determinism. For instance had there been no Crimean War, there would have been no 1857 at least not the type which India witnessed in the mid-nineteenth century.

NOTES

1. Christopher Hibbert, *The Great Mutiny India 1857* (1978, rpt., Harmondsworth: Penguin, 1980); Saul David, *The Indian Mutiny* (London: Viking, 2002).
2. Alan Beyerchen, 'Clausewitz, Nonlinearity, and the Unpredictability of War', *International Security*, vol. 17, no. 3 (1992–3), pp. 62–3, 65.
3. Literally it means that a butterfly flapping its wing in California might cause a weather storm in China. A Beyerchen, 'Clausewitz, Nonlinearity, and the Unpredictability of War', p. 66.
4. Beyerchen, 'Clausewitz, Nonlinearity, and the Unpredictability of War', p. 77.
5. Stuart Kinross, 'Clausewitz and Low-Intensity Conflict', *JSS*, vol. 27, no. 1 (2004), pp. 35–8.
6. John P. Cann, 'Low-Intensity Conflict, Insurgency, Terrorism and Revolutionary War', in Matthew Hughes and William J. Philpott (eds.), *Modern Military History* (Houndmills, Basingstoke: Palgrave Macmillan, 2006), pp. 108–9.
7. Peter Robb, 'Introduction: South Asia and the Concept of Race', in Peter

Robb (ed.), *The Concept of Race in South Asia* (New Delhi: Oxford University Press, 1995), pp. 1–76.

8. Colonel C.E. Callwell, *Small Wars: A Tactical Textbook for Imperial Soldiers* (1896, rpt., London: Greenhill, 1990), p. 21.
9. Ibid., p. 22.
10. Ibid., p. 24.
11. Ibid., p. 26.
12. Ibid., p. 27.
13. Ibid., p. 40.
14. Ibid., p. 42.
15. Cann, 'Low-Intensity Conflict, Insurgency, Terrorism and Revolutionary War', in Hughes and Philpott (eds.), *Modern Military History*, p. 109.
16. Callwell, *Small Wars*, p. 33.
17. 'The Mutiny Day by Day, being Extracts from the Letters of General Archdale Wilson, to his wife', *JUSII*, vol. XLIX, no. 221 (1920), pp. 290–1.
18. Ibid., p. 290.
19. *Memoirs of Major-General Henry Havelock*, by John Clark Marshman (London: Longman, 1861), p. 277.
20. Ibid., p. 282.
21. H.L. Wesseling, 'Colonial Wars: An Introduction', in J.A. de Moor and Wesseling (eds.), *Imperialism and War: Essays on Colonial Wars in Asia and Africa* (Leiden: E.J. Brill, 1989), pp. 3–4.
22. Douglas Porch, *Wars of Empire* (2000, rpt., London: Cassell, 2001), p. 46.
23. Ibid., p. 63.
24. Ibid., p. 64.
25. William J. Philpott, 'Total War', in Hughes & Philpott (eds.), *Modern Military History*, p. 131.
26. Ibid., p. 132.
27. Jeremy Black, 'Revolutionary and Napoleonic Warfare', in J. Black (ed.), *European Warfare: 1453–1815* (Houndmills, Basingstoke: Macmillan, 1999), pp. 228, 234.
28. Stig Forster and Jorg Nagler, 'Introduction', in S. Forster and J. Nagler (eds.), *On the Road to Total War: The American Civil War and the German .Wars of Unification, 1861–1871* (Cambridge: Cambridge University Press, 1997), pp. 2–3.
29. Forster and Nagler, 'Introduction', in Forster and Nagler (eds.), *On the Road to Total War*, p. 7.
30. Ibid., p. 8.
31. Ibid., p. 21.
32. Mark E. Neely Jr., 'Was the Civil War a Total War?', in Forster and Nagler (eds.), *On the Road to Total War*, p. 36.

33. Kaushik Roy in 'The Beginning of "People's War" in India', *Economic and Political Weekly*, vol. XLII, no. 19 (2007), pp. 1720–8 argues that 1857 was indeed a People's War.
34. Douglas Peers, 'South Asia', in Jeremy Black (ed.), *War in the Modern World Since 1815* (London/New York: Routledge, 2003), p. 48.
35. The so-called Subaltern School argument is that the common people took the initiative and mobilized themselves and at times forced the elite to cooperate with the faceless and nameless mass to lead the anti-colonial struggle. Gautam Bhadra, 'Four Rebels of Eighteen-Fifty-Seven', in Ranajit Guha (ed.), *Subaltern Studies: Writings on South Asian History and Society*, vol. 4 (New Delhi: Oxford University Press, 1985), pp. 229–75; Tapti Roy, *The Politics of a Popular Uprising: Bundelkhand in 1857* (New Delhi: Oxford University Press, 1994).
36. 'The Mutiny Day by Day being Extracts from the Letters of General Archdale Wilson', p. 276.
37. Brian Holden Reid and John White, '"A Mob of Stragglers and Cowards": Desertion from the Union and Confederate Armies, 1861-65', *JSS*, vol. 8, no. 1 (1985), pp. 68, 70, 72–4.
38. Kaushik Roy, 'Structural Anatomy of the Rebel Forces during the Great Mutiny of 1857–58: Equipment, Logistics and Recruitment Reconsidered', in Sabyasachi Bhattacharya (ed.), *Rethinking 1857* (New Delhi: Orient Longman, 2007), pp. 296–9.
39. Wesseling, 'Colonial Wars', in Moor and Wesseling (eds.), *Imperialism and War*, p. 5.
40. Rod Thornton, 'The British Army and the Origins of its Minimum Force Philosophy', *Small Wars and Insurgencies*, vol. 15, no. 1 (2004), pp. 83–106.
41. J.A. de Moor, 'Warmakers in the Archipelago: Dutch Expeditions in Nineteenth Century Indonesia', in Moor and Wesseling (eds.), *Imperialism and War*, p. 67.
42. Rudrangshu Mukherjee, '"Satan Let Loose Upon Earth": The Kanpur Massacres in India in the Revolt of 1857', *Past and Present*, no. 128 (August 1990), p. 93.
43. Rajat Kanta Ray, *The Felt Community: Commonalty and Mentality Before the Emergence of Indian Nationalism* (New Delhi: Oxford University Press, 2003), p. 365.
44. Ibid., p. 471.
45. Wesseling, 'Colonial Wars', in Moor and Wesseling (eds.), *Imperialism and War*, pp. 5–11.
46. Martin Bossenbroek, 'The Living Tools of Empire: The Recruitment of European Soldiers for the Dutch Colonial Army, 1814–1909', *JICH*, vol. 23, no. 1 (1995), p. 29.
47. Major H. Daly, *Memoirs of General Henry Dermot Daly* (London: John Murray, 1905), p. 222.

48. *Mutiny Records: Correspondence, Part I* (Lahore: Punjab Govt. Press, 1911), p. 43.
49. Haraprasad Chattopadhyay, 'Sepoy Army: Its Strength and Composition', *Calcutta Review,* vol. 30 (August 1856), p. 104.
50. Michael S. Neiberg, *Warfare in World History* (London and New York: Routledge, 2001), p. 56.
51. Peter Burroughs, 'Imperial Defence and the Victorian Army', *JICH,* vol. 15, no. 1 (1986), p. 59.
52. *Mutiny Records,* Part I, p. 30.
53. Daly, *Memoirs of Henry Dermot Daly,* pp. 143, 170.
54. *Memoirs of Major-General Henry Havelock,* p. 275.
55. Ibid. pp. 278, 282–3.
56. Ibid. pp. 292–3.
57. Ibid., p. 305.
58. Ibid., p. 302.
59. Neiberg, *Warfare in World History,* p. 54.
60. Randolf G.S. Cooper, 'Wellington and the Marathas', *International History Review,* vol. 11, no. 1 (1989), p. 35.
61. Lieutenant-Colonel H.M. Sinclair, 'The First Sikh War, 1845–6', *JUSII,* vol. 28, no. 134 (1899), pp. 7–9, 17–18.
62. Callwell, *Small Wars,* p. 44.
63. David Killingray, 'Colonial Warfare in West Africa: 1870–1914', in Moor and Wesseling (eds.), *Imperialism and War,* p. 150.
64. Bossenbroek, 'The Living Tools of Empire', p. 30.
65. Porch, *Wars of Empire,* p. 28.
66. *Memoirs of Major-General Henry Havelock,* p. 295.
67. Gautam Chakravarty, *The Indian Mutiny and the British Imagination* (Cambridge: Cambridge University Press, 2006), p. 4.
68. James Belich, 'The Victorian Interpretation of Racial Conflict and the New Zealand Wars: An Approach to the Problem of One-Sided Evidence', *JICH,* vol. 5 (1986–7), p. 123.
69. Cooper, 'Wellington and the Marathas', p. 35.
70. Sinclair, 'The First Sikh War, 1845–6', pp. 10, 16.
71. Geoffrey Parker (ed.), *The Cambridge Illustrated History of Warfare: The Triumph of the West* (Cambridge: Cambridge University Press, 1995).
72. W.H. McNeill, 'European Expansion, Power and Warfare since 1500', and Michael Howard, 'Colonial Wars and European Wars', in Moor and Wesseling (eds.), *Imperialism and War,* pp. 17, 221.
73. Ibid., pp. 19–20.
74. Victor Davis Hanson, *Carnage and Culture: Landmark Battles in the Rise of Western Power* (New York: Doubleday, 2001).
75. Laurent Henninger, 'Military Revolutions and Military History', in Hughes and Philpott (eds.), *Modern Military History,* p. 16.

76. Emily O. Goldman, 'Introduction: Information Resources and Military Performance', *JSS*, vol. 27, no. 2 (2004), pp. 212–13.
77. Henninger, 'Military Revolutions and Military History', in Hughes and Philpott (eds.), *Modern Military History*, p. 17.
78. Geoffrey L. Herrera, 'Inventing the Railroad and Rifle Revolution: Information, Military Innovation and the Rise of Germany', *JSS*, vol. 27, no. 2 (2004), pp. 247–8, 266.
79. See Peter Heather, 'The Huns and the End of the Roman Empire in Western Europe', *English Historical Review*, vol. CX, no. 435 (1995), pp. 4–41.
80. At least one Western scholar, Jeremy Black, is aware of the rabid Eurocentric perspective prevalent in the work of most of the Western writers of military history. See Black, *Rethinking Military History* (London and New York: Routledge, 2004).
81. Michael Geyer and Charles Bright, 'Global Violence and Nationalizing Wars in Eurasia and America: The Geopolitics of War in the Mid-Nineteenth Century', *CSSH*, vol. 38, no. 4 (October 1996), pp. 619–29; Carl N. Degler, 'The American Civil War and the German Wars of Unification: The Problems of Comparison', in Forster and Nagler (eds.), *On the Road to Total War*, p. 53.
82. Geyer and Bright, 'The Geopolitics of War', pp. 651–2.
83. Haraprasad Chattopadhyay, 'Sepoy Army: Its Strength and Composition', *Calcutta Review*, vol. 30 (September 1956), p. 201.
84. Bruce Watson, *The Great Indian Mutiny: Colin Campbell and the Campaign at Lucknow* (New York, Westport, Connecticut, London: Praeger, 1991), p. 23.
85. Hew Strachan, 'The British Way in Warfare Revisited', *Historical Journal*, vol. 26, no. 2 (1983), pp. 447–61.
86. *Mutiny Records*, Part I, p. 39.
87. *Memoirs of Major-General Henry Havelock*, p. 269.
88. Hans J. van de Ven, 'War in the Making of Modern China', *MAS*, vol. 30, no. 4 (1996), pp. 745–6.
89. Neiberg, *Warfare in World History*, p. 49.
90. Ibid., p. 51.
91. Stephen Peter Rosen, 'Military Effectiveness: Why Society Matters', *International Security*, vol. 19, no. 4 (1995), p. 11.
92. Neiberg, *Warfare in World History*, p. 53.
93. *Memoirs of Major-General Henry Havelock*, p. 279.
94. Ivan Arreguin-Toft, 'How the Weak Win Wars: A Theory of Asymmetric Conflict', *International Security*, vol. 26, no. 1 (2001), p. 123.
95. Azeem Ibrahim, 'Conceptualisation of Guerrilla Warfare', *Small Wars & Insurgencies*, vol. 15, no. 3 (2004), pp. 112–13.
96. Arreguin-Toft, 'How the Weak Win Wars', p. 104.
97. Thomas A. Marks, 'Ideology of Insurgency: New Ethnic Focus or Cold

War Distortions?', *Small Wars and Insurgencies*, vol. 15, no. 1 (2004), p. 107.

98. James D. Fearon and David D. Latin, 'Ethnicity, Insurgency and Civil War', *American Political Science Review*, vol. 97, no. 1 (February 2003), p. 75.
99. Arreguin-Toft, 'How the Weak Win Wars', p. 94.
100. Halvard Buhag and Scott Gates, 'The Geography of Civil War', *Journal of Peace Research*, vol. 39, no. 4 (2002), pp. 418–19, 421.
101. Havard Hegre, Tanja Ellingsen, Scott Gates and Nils Petter Gleditsch, 'Towards a Democratic Civil Peace? Democracy, Political Change, and Civil War, 1816-1992', *American Political Science Review*, vol. 95, no. 1 (2001), p. 37.
102. C.A. Bayly, 'Two Colonial Revolts: The Java War, 1825–30, and the Indian "Mutiny" of 1857–59', in C.A. Bayly and D.H.A. Kolff (eds.), *Two Colonial Empires: Comparative Essays on the History of India and Indonesia in the Nineteenth Century* (Dordrecht: Martinus Nijhoff, 1986), pp. 111–35.
103. Hans van de Ven, 'Military Mobilization in China: 1840–1949', in Black (ed.), *War in the Modern World*, pp. 25–6.
104. Peter C. Perdue, 'Military Mobilization in Seventeenth and Eighteenth-Century China, Russia, and Mongolia', *MAS*, vol. 30, no. 4 (1996), p. 785.
105. Hans van de Ven, 'Military Mobilization in China: 1840–1949', in Black (ed.), *War in the Modern World since 1815*, p. 27.
106. Rudrangshu Mukherjee, 'The Sepoy Mutinies Revisited', in Mushirul Hasan and Narayani Gupta (eds.), *India's Colonial Encounter: Essays in Memory of Eric Stokes* (New Delhi: Manohar, 1993), p. 130.
107. Mukherjee, '"Satan Let Loose Upon Earth"', p. 99.
108. Rudgrangshu Mukherjee, *Awadh in Revolt: 1857–58: A Study of Popular Resistance* (New Delhi: Oxford University Press, 1984), pp. x, 95.
109. John D. Waghelstein and Donald Chisholm, 'The Road Not Taken: Conflict Termination and Guerrillaism in the American Civil War', *JSS*, vol. 29, no. 5 (2006), pp. 874, 877.
110. Kaushik Roy, 'Company *Bahadur* Against the *Pandies*: The Military Dimension of 1857 Mutiny Revisited', *Jadavpur University Journal of History*, vol. 19 (2001–2), pp. 40–3.
111. Monica Duffy Toft, 'Getting Religion? The Puzzling Case of Islam and Civil War', *International Security*, vol. 31, no. 4 (2007), pp. 98, 100, 106.
112. Hans Kung, 'Religion, Violence and "Holy Wars"', *International Review of the Red Cross*, vol. 87, no. 858 (June 2005), p. 262.
113. *Mutiny Records*, Part I, p. 31.

114. Mukherjee, 'Sepoy Mutinies Revisited', in M. Hasan and N. Gupta (eds.), *India's Colonial Encounter*, p. 128.
115. Rajat Kanta Ray, 'Race, Religion and Realm: The Political Theory of "The Reigning Indian Crusade", 1857', in M. Hasan and N. Gupta (eds.), *India's Colonial Encounters*, pp. 137–8.
116. Mukherjee, *Awadh in Revolt*, p. 105.
117. Ray, *Felt Community*, pp. 355, 358.
118. Aidan Southall, 'The Segmentary State in Africa and Asia', *CSSH*, vol. 30, no. 1 (1988), pp. 52–82.
119. Ray, *Felt Community*, p. 357.
120. Mukherjee, *Awadh in Revolt*, pp. 143, 150–1.
121. Alastair Iain Johnston, 'Thinking about Strategic Culture', *International Security*, vol. 19, no. 4 (1995), pp. 37, 41, 44.
122. Rosen, 'Military Effectiveness', pp. 19, 28.
123. Jeremy Black, 'Military Organizations and Military Change in Historical Perspective', *JMH*, vol. 62 (October 1998), pp. 871–92.

Bibliography

BOOKS AND ARTICLES

ARMED FORCES AND WARFARE

Allen, Charles (ed.), *A Soldier of the Company: Life of an Indian Ensign 1833-1843* (London: Michael Joseph in association with the National Army Museum, 1988).

Allen, Charles, *Soldier Sahibs: The Men Who Made the North-West Frontier* (London: Viking, 2000).

Arreguin-Toft, Ivan, 'How the Weak Win Wars: A Theory of Asymmetric Conflict', *International Security*, vol. 26, no. 1 (2001).

Balasubramaniam, R., *The Saga of Indian Cannons* (New Delhi: Aryan Books International, 2002).

Barua, Pradeep, 'Military Developments in India: 1750-1850', *JMH*, vol. 58, no. 4 (1994).

Black, Jeremy, 'Military Organizations and Military Change in Historical Perspective', *JMH*, vol. 62 (October 1998).

———, 'Revolutionary and Napoleonic Warfare', in J. Black (ed.), *European Warfare: 1453-1815* (Houndmills, Basingstoke: Macmillan, 1999).

Blacker, Valentine, *Memoir of Operations of the British Army in India during the Maratha War of 1817, 1818 & 1819* (London: Black, Kingsbury, Parbury and Allen, 1821).

Bossenbroek, Martin, 'The Living Tools of Empire: The Recruitment of European Soldiers for the Dutch Colonial Army, 1814–1909', *JICH*, vol. 23, no. 1 (1995).

Broome, Arthur, *History of the Rise and Progress of the Bengal Army* (London, 1850).

Brown, R.R., 'Taming the Tigers: An East India Company Gun from Museum Bronbeek, Arnhem', *JOS*, vol. 16 (2004).

Buhag, Halvard and Scott Gates, 'The Geography of Civil War', *Journal of Peace Research*, vol. 39, no. 4 (2002).

Burroughs, Peter, 'Imperial Defence and the Victorian Army', *JICH*, vol. 15, no. 1 (1986).

Burton, R.G., 'Battles of the Deccan: Assaye', *JUSII*, vol. 20 (1891).

Cadell, Patrick, *History of the Bombay Army* (London, 1938).

Callahan, Raymond, *The East India Company and Army Reform: 1783–1798* (Cambridge, MA: Harvard University Press, 1972).

———, 'Servants of the Raj: The Jacob Family in India: 1817–1926', *JSAHR* (Spring 1978).

———, 'The Great Sepoy Mutiny', in Daniel Marston and Chandar Sundaram (eds.), *A Military History of India and South Asia: From the East India Company to the Nuclear Era* (Westport, CT: Praeger, 2007).

Callwell, Colonel C.E., *Small Wars: A Tactical Textbook for Imperial Soldiers* (1896, rpt., London: Greenhill, 1990).

Cann, John P., 'Low-Intensity Conflict, Insurgency, Terrorism and Revolutionary War', in Matthew Hughes and William J. Philpott (eds.), *Modern Military History* (Houndmills, Basingstoke: Palgrave Macmillan, 2006).

Carleton, N. and M. Buck, 'Guns of the Rajahs: Indian Artillery from the Mughals to the Sikhs', *JOS*, vol. 16 (2004).

Chatterjee, S.K., *Vintage Guns of India* (New Delhi: Macmillan, 2001).

Chattopadhyay, Haraprasad, 'Sepoy Army—Its Strength and Composition', *Calcutta Review*, vol. 30 (July 1956).

———, 'Sepoy Army—Its Strength and Composition', *Calcutta Review*, vol. 30 (August 1956).

———, 'Sepoy Army—Its Strength and Composition', *Calcutta Review*, vol. 30 (September 1956).

———, *The Sepoy Mutiny, 1857: A Social Study and Analysis* (Calcutta: Bookland Pvt. Ltd., 1957).

Cooper, Randolf G.S., 'Wellington and the Marathas', *International History Review*, vol. 11, no. 1 (1989).

Cooper, R.G.S. and N.K. Wagle, 'Maratha Artillery: From Dabhoi to Assaye', *JOS*, vol. 7 (1995).

Daly, Lieutenant-General Sir H., 'The Punjab Frontier Force', *Journal of the Royal United Service Institution*, vol. 28 (June, 1884).

Daly, Major H., *Memoirs of General Henry Dermot Daly* (London: John Murray, 1905).

David, Saul, *The Indian Mutiny* (London: Viking, 2002).

———, *Victoria's Wars: The Rise of Empire* (London: Viking, 2006)

de Moor, J.A., 'Warmakers in the Archipelago: Dutch Expeditions in Nineteenth Century Indonesia', in J.A. de Moor and H.L. Wesseling (eds.), *Imperialism and War: Essays on Colonial Wars in Asia and Africa* (Leiden: E.J. Brill, 1989).

Degler, Carl N., 'The American Civil War and the German Wars of Unification: The Problems of Comparison', in Stig Forster and Jorg Nagler (eds.), *On the Road to Total War: The American Civil War and the German Wars of Unification, 1861-1871* (Cambridge: Cambridge University Press, 1997).

Deloche, J., *Senji (Gingi), ville fortifiée du pays tamoul* (Paris/Pondichery: Institut Francais De Pondichery, 2000).

———, 'Études sur les fortifications de l'Inde: III. La fortification hindoue dans le Sud de l'Inde (VIc-XVIIIc siècle)', *Bulletin de L'École Française D'Extrême-Orient*, vol. 88 (2001).

———, 'Études sur les fortifications de l'Inde: IV. La fortification musulmane dans le Dekkan méridional (XVc-XVIIIc siècle)', *Bulletin de L'École Française D'Extrême-Orient*, vol. 89 (2002).

———, 'Gunpowder Artillery and Military Architecture in South India (15th–18th Century)', *IJHS*, vol. 40 (2005).

———, *Studies on Fortification in India* (Pondichery: Institut Francais De Pondichery, 2007).

Dey, R.S., *A Brief Account of the Punjab Frontier Force from 1849 to 31 March 1903* (Calcutta: W. Newman, 1905).

Egerton, W., *Illustrated Handbook of Indian Arms* (1880, rpt., Bangkok: White Orchid Press, 1986).

Fearon, James D. and David D. Latin, 'Ethnicity, Insurgency and Civil War', *American Political Science Review*, vol. 97, no. 1 (February 2003).

Forster, Stig and Jorg Nagler, 'Introduction', in Forster and Nagler (eds.), *On the Road to Total War: The American Civil War and the German Wars of Unification, 1861-1871* (Cambridge: Cambridge University Press, 1997).

Fraser, John, 'The Letters of Brevet Lieutenant-Colonel Robert Abercomby Yule: Part One', *JSAHR*, vol. 61 (1983).

Geyer, Michael and Charles Bright, 'Global Violence and Nationalizing Wars in Eurasia and America: The Geopolitics of War in the Mid-Nineteenth Century', *CSSH*, vol. 38, no. 4 (1996).

Goldman, Emily O., 'Introduction: Information Resources and Military Performance', *JSS*, vol. 27, no. 2 (2004).

Gommans, Jos and D.H.A. Kolff, 'Introduction', in Gommans and Kolff (eds.), *Warfare and Weaponry in South Asia: 1000-1800 AD* (New Delhi: Oxford University Press, 2001).

Graham, Brigadier-General C.A., *A History of the Indian Mountain Artillery* (Aldershot: Gale and Polden, 1957).

Greenhut, Jeffrey, 'Sahib and Sepoy: An Inquiry into the Relationship between the British Officers and Native Soldiers of the British Indian Army', *Military Affairs*, vol. XLVIII, no. 1 (January 1984).

Gregorian, Raffi, 'Unfit for Service: British Law and Looting in India in the mid-Nineteenth Century', *South Asia*, vol. 13, no. 1 (1990).

Hanson, Victor Davis, *Carnage and Culture: Landmark Battles in the Rise of Western Power* (New York: Doubleday, 2001).

Heathcote, T.A., *The Indian Army: The Garrison of British Imperial India, 1822–1922* (New York/Manchester: Manchester University Press, 1974).

Hegre, Havard, Tanja Ellingsen, Scott Gates and Nils Petter Gleditsch,

'Towards a Democratic Civil Peace? Democracy, Political Change, and Civil War, 1816–1992', *American Political Science Review*, vol. 95, no. 1 (2001).

Henninger, Laurent, 'Military Revolutions and Military History', in Matthew Hughes and William J. Philpott (eds.), *Modern Military History* (Houndmills, Basingstoke: Palgrave Macmillan, 2006).

Herrera, Geoffrey L., 'Inventing the Railroad and Rifle Revolution: Information, Military Innovation and the Rise of Germany', *JSS*, vol. 27, no. 2 (2004).

Hervey, Albert, *Ten Years in India, or, The Life of a Young Officer*, 3 vols. (London, 1850).

History of the 1st Punjab Cavalry (Lahore: Govt. Central Gazette Press, 1887).

History of the Second Punjab Cavalry (London: Kegan Paul Trench, 1888).

History of the 23rd Cavalry (Frontier Force), late 3rd Regiment, Punjab Cavalry (no imprint, *c.* 1910).

Hoover, James W., 'The Recruitment of the Bengal Army: Beyond the Myth of the Zemindar's Son', *Indo-British Review*, vol. 21, no. 2 (1996).

———, *Men Without Hats: Dialogue, Discipline and Discontent in the Madras Army, 1806-1807* (New Delhi: Manohar, 2007).

Howard, Michael, 'Colonial Wars and European Wars', in J.A. de Moor and H.L. Wesseling (eds.), *Imperialism and War: Essays on Colonial Wars in Asia and Africa* (Leiden: E.J. Brill, 1989).

Ibrahim, Azeem, 'Conceptualisation of Guerrilla Warfare', *Small Wars and Insurgencies*, vol. 15, no. 3 (2004).

Johnston, Alastair Iain, 'Thinking about Strategic Culture', *International Security*, vol. 19, no. 4 (1995).

Khan, I.A., *Gunpowder and Firearms: Warfare in Medieval India* (New Delhi: Oxford University Press, 2004).

Killingray, David, 'Colonial Warfare in West Africa: 1870-1914', in J.A. de Moor and H.L. Wesseling (eds.), *Imperialism and War: Essays on Colonial Wars in Asia and Africa* (Leiden: E.J. Brill, 1989).

Kinross, Stuart, 'Clausewitz and Low-Intensity Conflict', *JSS*, vol. 27, no. 1 (2004).

Lambrick, H.T., *Sir Charles Napier and Sind* (Oxford, 1952).

———, *John Jacob of Jacobabad* (London, 1960).

Leasor, James, *The Red Fort: An Account of the Siege of Delhi in 1857* (1956).

MacCrory, Patrick, *Signal Catastrophe: The Retreat from Kabul 1842* (London: Hodder and Stuughton, 1966).

MacKinnon, Major W., 'Jezail Experiments', *Proceedings of the United Service Institution of India*, vol. 20, no. 4 (1875).

Macpherson, W.C. (ed.), *Soldering in India 1764-1787: Extracts from*

Journals and Letters Left by Lieutenant-Colonel Allan Macpherson and Lieutenant-Colonel John Macpherson of the East India Company's Service (Edinburgh/London: William Blackwood & Sons, 1928).

Marks, Thomas A., 'Ideology of Insurgency: New Ethnic Focus or Cold War Distortions?', *Small Wars & Insurgencies*, vol. 15, no. 1 (2004).

Mason, Philip, *A Matter of Honour: An Account of the Indian Army, Its Officers and Men* (London, 1974).

McNeill, W.H. 'European Expansion, Power and Warfare since 1500', in J.A. de Moor and H.L. Wesseling (eds.), *Imperialism and War: Essays on Colonial Wars in Asia and Africa* (Leiden: E.J. Brill, 1989).

Memoirs of Major-General Henry Havelock, by John Clark Marshman (London: Longman, 1861).

Menezes, S.L., *Fidelity and Honour: The Indian Army from the Seventeenth to the Twenty-first Century* (Delhi: Viking, 1999).

Mitchell, William Forbes, *Reminiscences of the Great Mutiny 1857–59* (London: Macmillan and Co., 1893).

Moore, Edward, *A Narrative of the Operations of Captain Little's Detachment of the Maratha Army* (London, 1794).

Moreman, T.R., *The Army in India and the Development of Frontier Warfare 1849-1947* (Houndmills, Basingstoke, London: Macmillan, 1998).

Neely Jr., Mark E., 'Was the Civil War a Total War?', in Stig Forster and Jorg Nagler (eds.), *On the Road to Total War: The American Civil War and the German Wars of Unification, 1861-1871* (Cambridge: Cambridge University Press, 1997).

Neiberg, Michael S., *Warfare in World History* (London and New York: Routledge, 2001).

Nevill, Captain H.L., *Campaigns on the North-West Frontier* (London: John Murray, 1912).

North, R., *The Punjab Frontier Force. A Brief Record of their Services* (Dera Ismail Khan: Commercial Steam Press, 1934).

Pant, G.N., *Studies in Indian Weapons and Warfare* (New Delhi: Army Educational Stores, 1970).

Parker, Geoffrey (ed.), *The Cambridge Illustrated History of Warfare: The Triumph of the West* (Cambridge: Cambridge University Press, 1995).

Peers, Douglas M., 'War and Public Finance in Early Nineteenth-Century British India: The First Burma War', *International History Review*, vol. 11, no. 4 (1989).

———, *Between Mars and Mammon: Colonial Armies and the Garrison State in India 1819–1835* (London: I.B. Tauris, 1995)

———, 'South Asia', in Jeremy Black (ed.), *War in the Modern World since 1815* (London/New York: Routledge, 2003).

———, 'Colonial Knowledge and the Military in India, 1780–1860', *JICH*, vol. 33, no. 2 (May 2005).

Pemble, John, *The Invasion of Nepal: John Company at War* (Oxford: Clarendon Press, 1971).

Perdue, Peter C., 'Military Mobilization in Seventeenth and Eighteenth-Century China, Russia, and Mongolia', *MAS*, vol. 30, no. 4 (1996).

Philpott, William J., 'Total War', in Matthew Hughes and William J. Philpott (eds.), *Modern Military History* (Houndmills, Basingstoke: Palgrave Macmillan, 2006).

Porch, Douglas, *Wars of Empire* (2000, rpt., London: Cassell, 2001).

Reid, Brian Holden and John White, '"A Mob of Stragglers and Cowards": Desertion from the Union and Confederate Armies, 1861–65', *JSS*, vol. 8, no. 1 (1985).

Roberts, Field-Marshal Lord, *Forty One Years in India: From Subaltern to the Commander-in-Chief* (London, 1897).

Rosen, Stephen Peter, 'Military Effectiveness: Why Society Matters', *International Security*, vol. 19, no. 4 (1995).

Roy, Kaushik, 'Company *Bahadur* against the *Pandies*: The Military Dimension of 1857 Mutiny Revisited', *Jadavpur University Journal of History*, vol. 19 (2001–2).

———, 'Equipping Leviathan: Ordnance Factories of British India', *War in History*, vol. 10, no. 4 (2003).

———, 'Firepower-Centric Warfare in India and the Military Modernization of the Marathas: 1740-1818', *IJHS*, vol. 40 (2005).

———, 'The Beginning of "People's War" in India', *Economic and Political Weekly*, vol. XLII, no. 19 (2007).

———, 'Structural Anatomy of the Rebel Forces during the Great Mutiny of 1857–58: Equipment, Logistics and Recruitment Reconsidered', in Sabyasachi Bhattacharya (ed.), *Rethinking 1857* (New Delhi: Orient Longman, 2007).

Sarkar, Jagadish Narayan, 'Limitations of the Art of War in Medieval India', *Journal of the Bihar Research Society*, vol. LIX (1973).

Sinclair, Lieutenant-Colonel H.M., 'The First Sikh War, 1845–6', *JUSII*, vol. 28, no. 134 (1899).

Spiers, E.M., *The Army and Society: 1815–1914* (London: Longman, 1980).

Stanley, Peter, '"Dear Comrades": Barrack Room Culture and the "White Mutiny" of 1859-60', *Indo-British Review*, vol. 21, no. 2 (1996).

Strachan, Hew, 'The British Way in Warfare Revisited', *Historical Journal*, vol. 26, no. 2 (1983).

'The Mutiny Day by Day, being Extracts from the Letters of General Archdale Wilson, to his wife', *JUSII*, vol. XLIX, no. 221 (1920).

Thornton, Rod, 'The British Army and the Origins of its Minimum Force Philosophy', *Small Wars and Insurgencies*, vol. 15, no. 1 (2004).

Toy, Sidney, *The Strongholds of India* (London, 1957).

Vaughan, J.L., *My Service in the Indian Army—and After* (London, 1904).

Ven, Hans J. van de, 'War in the Making of Modern China', *MAS*, vol. 30, no. 4 (1996).

———, 'Military Mobilization in China: 1840-1949', in Jeremy Black (ed.), *War in the Modern World since 1815* (London/New York: Routledge, 2003).

Waghelstein, John D. and Donald Chisholm, 'The Road not Taken: Conflict Termination and Guerrillaism in the American Civil War', *JSS*, vol. 29, no. 5 (2006).

Watson, Bruce, *The Great Indian Mutiny: Colin Campbell and the Campaign at Lucknow* (New York, Westport, Connecticut, London: Praeger, 1991).

Wesseling, H.L., 'Colonial Wars: An Introduction', in J.A. de Moor and H.L. Wesseling (eds.), *Imperialism and War: Essays on Colonial Wars in Asia and Africa* (Leiden: E.J. Brill, 1989).

Wilson, W.J., *History of the Madras Army*, 4 vols. (Madras: Govt. Press, 1882).

Young, H.A., *The East India Company's Arsenals & Manufactories* (Oxford, 1937).

Younghusband, George, *The Story of the Guides* (London: Macmillan, 1908).

1857 AND INDIAN SOCIETY

Ahmed, A.S., 'Pukhtun Tribes in the Great Game', *Asian Affairs*, vol. 11, (1980).

Ashraf, K.M., 'Muslim Revivalists and the Revolt of 1857', in P.C. Joshi (ed.), *Rebellion 1857: A Symposium* (1957, rpt., Kolkata: K.P. Bagchi, 1986).

Bandopadhyay, Sekhar, *From Plassey to Partition: A History of Modern India* (New Delhi: Orient Longman, 2004).

———, 'Eighteen Fifty-Seven and its Many Histories', in *1857: Essays from Economic and Political Weekly* (Hyderabad: Orient Longman in association with the Sameeksha Trust, 2008).

Barui, Balai Chandra, 'Laban Ekadhipatyar Biruddhe Pratirodh, Company Banam Sthaniya Zamindar (1772-1800)', *Sampratik Itihas Charcha*, 2005 [in Bengali].

Bashiruddin, *Waqiat-i Darul Hakumat Dilli* (Delhi, 1919).

Basu, Swapan, 'Kolkata; 1857', *Saradiya Bartaman*, 2004 (in Bengali).

Bayly, C.A., 'Two Colonial Revolts: The Java War, 1825-30, and the Indian "Mutiny" of 1857-59', in C.A. Bayly and D.H.A. Kolff (eds.), *Two Colonial Empires: Comparative Essays on the History of India and Indonesia in the Nineteenth Century* (Dordrecht: Martinus Nijhoff, 1986).

Beal, T.W., *Oriental Biographical Dictionary* (n.d., rpt., Delhi, 1971).

Bhadra, Gautam, 'Four Rebels of Eighteen-Fifty-Seven', in Ranajit Guha (ed.), *Subaltern Studies: Writings on South Asian History and Society*, vol. 4 (New Delhi: Oxford University Press, 1985).

Bhattacharya, Sabyasachi, 'Rethinking 1857', in Sabyasachi Bhattacharya (ed.), *Rethinking 1857* (New Delhi: Orient Longman, 2007).

Brodkin, E.I., 'The Struggle for Succession: Rebels and Loyalists in the Indian Mutiny of 1857', *MAS*, vol. 6, no. 3 (1972).

Brown, Reverend J. Cave, *The Punjab and Delhi in 1857*, vol. 1 (n.d., rpt., Delhi, 1970).

Burns, A., *Travels into Bokhara*, vol. 1 (London, 1831).

Carey, W.H., *The Good Old Day of Honourable John Company: 1600-1858* (compiled from newspaper and other publications), vol. 1, ed. Nisith R. Ray (Kolkata: Riddhi, 1980).

Chakravarty, Gautam, *The Indian Mutiny and the British Imagination* (Cambridge: Cambridge University Press, 2006).

Chattopadhyay, Basudeb, 'Panic Sunday in Calcutta: 14 June 1857', in Sabyasachi Bhattacharya (ed.), *Rethinking 1857* (New Delhi: Orient Longman, 2007).

Chirayata Shahitya Sangraha, vol. 1, ed. Kanchan Basu, Kolkata, July 1991 (in Bengali).

Cowasjee, Saros (ed.), *A Raj Collection* (New Delhi: Oxford University Press, 2005).

Crane, Ralph and Radhika Mohanram, 'Introduction', in Crane (ed.), *Love Besieged: A Romance of the Defence of Lucknow*, by Charles E. Pearce (New Delhi: Oxford University Press, 2003).

Dalrymple, William, *The Last Mughal: The Fall of a Dynasty, Delhi 1857* (New Delhi: Penguin Books, 2006).

———, 'Religious Rhetoric in the Delhi Uprising of 1857', in Sabyasachi Bhattacharya (ed.), *Rethinking 1857* (New Delhi: Orient Longman, 2007).

Dargah Quli Khan, Muraqqa-i Delhi, ed. Nurul Hasan Ansari (Delhi, 1982).

Datta, Kaliprasanna, *Bijoy* (Calcutta, 1883).

Davies, C.C., *The Problem of the North-West Frontier 1890-1908, with a Survey of Policy Since 1849* (London, 1932).

Elliot, Major-General J.G., *The Frontier 1839-1947* (London, 1968).

Fane, Henry, *Five Years in India*, 2 vols (London: Henry Colburn, 1842).

Fanshawe, H.C., *Shahjahan's Delhi—Past and Present* (n.d., rpt., Delhi, 1979).

Farrell, James Gordon, *The Siege of Krishnapur* (1973, rpt., Introduction by Pankaj Mishra, New York, 2004).

Fergusson, James, *History of Indian and Eastern Architecture* (n.d., rpt., Delhi, 1967).

Fichet, W.H., *Tales of the Great Mutiny* (London: Smith, Elder & Co. 1902).

Firminger, W.K., *Thackers Guide to Calcutta* (Calcutta: Thackers Spink & Co., 1906).

Fisher, Michael H., 'British Expansion in North India: The Role of the Resident in Awadh', *IESHR*, vol. 18, no. 1 (1981).

Forrest, G.W., *A History of the Indian Mutiny*, vol. 1 (Edinburgh and London: William Blackwood & Sons, 1904).

Forster, G., *A Journey from Bengal to England*, vol. 1 (London: R. Faulder, 1798).

Frank, Katherine, *Lucie Duff Gordon: A Passage to Egypt* (London: Tauris Parke Paperbacks, 2007).

Fraser, George MacDonald, *Flashman* (London, 1969).

Ghose, Benoy, 'The Bengali Intelligentsia and the Revolt', in P.C. Joshi (ed.), *Rebellion 1857: A Symposium* (1957, rpt., Kolkata: K.P. Bagchi, 1986).

——— (ed.), *Samayik Patre Banglar Samay Chitra*, vol. 3, Kolkata [in Bengali].

'Gun-Runners of Esplanade', *Statesman*, 16.10.1878.

Gupta, Narayani, 'Military Security and Urban Development: A Case Study of Delhi, 1857-1912', *MAS*, vol. 5, no. 1 (1971).

Gupta, Swarupa, 'Notions of Nationhood in Bengal: Perspectives on *Samaj*, 1867–1905', *MAS*, vol. 40, no. 2 (2006).

———, '*Samaj, Jati* and *Desh*: Reflections on Nationhood in Late Colonial Bengal', *Studies in History*, vol. 23, no. 2 (2007).

———, '1857 and Ideas about Nationhood in Bengal: Nuances and Themes', in *1857: Essays from Economic and Political Weekly* (Hyderabad: Orient Longman in association with the Sameeksha Trust, 2008).

Habib, Irfan, 'Understanding 1857', in Sabyasachi Bhattacharya (ed.), *Rethinking 1857* (New Delhi: Orient Longman, 2007).

Haldar, Gopal, 'Bengali Literature before and after 1857', in P.C. Joshi (ed.), *Rebellion 1857: A Symposium* (1957, rpt., Kolkata: K.P. Bagchi, 1986).

Harris, G., *A Lady's Diary of the Siege of Lucknow* (1858, rpt., New Delhi: Asian Educational Services, 1997).

Hibbert, Christopher, *The Great Mutiny India 1857* (1978, rpt., Harmondsworth: Penguin, 1980).

Holmes, T. Rice, *A History of the Indian Mutiny and of the Disturbances Which Accompanied it Among the Civil Population* (London: Macmillan & Co. Ltd., 1913).

Husain, S. Mahdi, *Bahadur Shah Zafar and the War of 1857 in Delhi* (1958, rpt., Delhi: Aakar Books, 2006).

Joshi, P.C., '1857 in our History', in P.C. Joshi (ed.), *Rebellion 1857: A Symposium* (1957, rpt., Kolkata: K.P. Bagchi, 1986).

Kaye's and Malleson's, *History of the Indian Mutiny of 1857–58*, ed. Col. Malleson (1897-8, rpt., Connecticut: Greenwood Press Publishers, 1971), vol. 4.

Khaldun, Talmiz, 'The Great Rebellion', in P.C. Joshi (ed.), *Rebellion 1857: A Symposium* (1957, rpt., Kolkata: K.P. Bagchi, 1986).

Khan, Syed Ahmad, *Sirat-i Faridia* (Agra, 1896).

———, *Asar-us Sanadid* (n.d., Delhi).

Koch, Ebba, 'Mughal Palace Gardens from Babur to Shah Jahan (1526–1648)', *Muqarnas*, vol. 14 (1997).

Kumar, Gyanendra Nath (ed.), *Vamsa Parichay*, vol. 1 (Kolkata, Baishakh 1328) (in Bengali).

Lakshmi, Aishwarya, 'The Mutiny Novel: Creating the Domestic Body of the Empire', in *1857: Essays from Economic and Political Weekly* (Hyderabad: Orient Longman in association with the Sameeksha Trust, 2008).

Latif, Abdul, *1857 ka Tarikh-i Roznamcha*, ed. K.A. Nizami (Delhi, 1958).

Mackenzie, John M., *The Empire of Nature: Hunting Conservation and British Imperialism* (Manchester: Manchester University Press, 1997).

Macmillan, Allister, *Seaports of India and Ceylon: Historical and Descriptive, Commercial and Industrial, Facts, Figures and Resources* (FRGS, 1928).

Marks, Thomas A., 'Ideology of Insurgency: New Ethnic Focus or Cold War Distortions?', *Small Wars & Insurgencies*, vol. 15, no. 1 (2004).

McGregor, W.L., *History of the Sikhs*, vol. 1 (London, 1846).

Metcalf, Thomas R., 'From Raja to Landlord: The Oudh Taluqdars, 1850–70', in Thomas R. Metcalf, *Forging the Raj: Essays on British India in the Heyday of Empire* (New Delhi: Oxford University Press, 2005).

———, 'The Influence of the Mutiny of 1857 on Land Policy in India', in Thomas R. Metcalf, *Forging the Raj: Essays on British India in the Heyday of Empire* (New Delhi: Oxford University Press, 2005).

Metcalfe, T., *Two Narratives of the Mutiny in India* (n.d., rpt., Delhi).

Mitra, Upendra Chandra, *Nana Saheb* (2nd edn. Calcutta, 1883).

Moitreya, Akshoykumar, *Sirajuddaula, Sekaler Sukhdukhha, Gourer Katha* (rpt., Calcutta, 1984).

Moynihan, Elizabeth B., 'The Lotus Garden Palace of Zahir al-Din Muhammad Babur', *Muqarnas*, vol. 5 (1988).

Mukherjee, Meenakshi, *Realism and Reality: The Novel and Literature in Colonial Society* (Delhi, 1985).

Mukherjee, Rudgrangshu, *Awadh in Revolt: 1857–58: A Study of Popular Resistance* (New Delhi: Oxford University Press, 1984).

———, '"Satan Let Loose Upon Earth": The Kanpur Massacres in India in the Revolt of 1857', *Past and Present*, no. 128 (1990).

———, 'The Sepoy Mutinies Revisited', in Mushirul Hasan and Narayani Gupta (eds.), *India's Colonial Encounter: Essays in Memory of Eric Stokes* (New Delhi: Manohar, 1993).

Nishbet, Hume, *The Queen's Desire: A Romance of the Indian Mutiny* (1893).

Paxton, Nancy L., *Writing Under Raj: Gender, Race and Rape in the British Colonial Imagination 1830–1947* (New Jersey: Rutgers University Press, 1999).

Pearce, Charles E., *Love Besieged: A Romance on the Defence of Lucknow*, ed. by Ralph Crane (New Delhi: Oxford University Press, 2003).

Ray, Rajat Kanta, 'Race, Religion and Realm: The Political Theory of "The Reigning Indian Crusade", 1857', in Mushirul Hasan and Narayani Gupta (eds.), *India's Colonial Encounter: Essays in Memory of Eric Stokes* (New Delhi: Manohar, 1993).

———, *The Felt Community: Commonalty and Mentality Before the Emergence of Indian Nationalism* (New Delhi: Oxford University Press, 2003).

Roy, Tapti, *The Politics of a Popular Uprising: Bundelkhand in 1857* (New Delhi: Oxford University Press, 1994).

Sarbadhikary, Jadunath, *Tirthabhraman (1853–1857)*, ed. Nagendranath Basu (Calcutta, 1915).

Sen, Indrani, 'Inscribing the Rani of Jhansi in Colonial "Mutiny" Fiction', in *1857: Essays from Economic and Political Weekly* (Hyderabad: Orient Longman in association with the Sameeksha Trust, 2008).

Sharma, Y.D., *Delhi and its Neighbourhood* (Delhi, 1982).

Sharpe, Jenny, *Allegories of Empire: The Figure of Woman in the Colonial Text* (Minneapolis: Minnesota University Press, 1993).

Shastri, Shibnath, *Ramtanu Lahiri O Tatkalin Bangasamaj* (Kolkata, 1957) [in Bengali].

Singh, Lata, '1857: Visibilising the "Other" in History: Courtesans and the Revolt', in *1857: Essays from Economic and Political Weekly* (Hyderabad: Orient Longman in association with the Sameeksha Trust, 2008).

Sinha, Pradip, *Calcutta in Urban History* (Calcutta: Firma KLM Private Ltd., 1978).

Spain, J.W., *The Pathan Borderland* (The Hague, 1963).

Spear, Percival, *Delhi: Its Monuments and History*, updated and annotated by Gupta and Sykes (Delhi, 1994).

Stokes, Eric, 'Rural Revolt in the Great Rebellion of 1857 in India: A Study of the Saharanpur and Muzaffarnagar Districts', *Historical Journal*, vol. 12, no. 4 (1969).

Symons, N.H.V., *The Story of the Government House* (Calcutta, 1935).

Tagore, Jyotirindranath, *Jhansir Rani* (Calcutta, 1903).

Taylor, P.J.O. (ed.), *A Companion to Indian Mutiny of 1857* (New Delhi: Oxford University Press, 1996).

Taylor, Philip Meadows, *Seeta* (1881, rpt., Delhi: Asian Educational Services, 1989).

The *Maharaja* of Cooch Behar, *Big Game Shooting in Eastern and North Eastern India* (New Delhi: Mittal Publishers, 1958).

Thorburn, S.S., *The Punjab in Peace and War* (Edinburgh and London, 1904).

Wilkinson, Theon, *Two Monsoons* (London, 1976).

Yadav, K.C., 'Interpreting 1857: A Case Study', in Sabyasachi Bhattacharya (ed.), *Rethinking 1857* (New Delhi: Orient Longman, 2007).

HISTORIOGRAPHY

Belich, James, 'The Victorian Interpretation of Racial Conflict and the New Zealand Wars: An Approach to the Problem of One-Sided Evidence', *JICH*, vol. 5 (1986–7).

Beyerchen, Alan, 'Clausewitz, Nonlinearity, and the Unpredictability of War', *International Security*, vol. 17, no. 3 (1992–3).

Black, Jeremy, *Rethinking Military History* (London and New York: Routledge, 2004).

Canandine, David, 'The Present and the Past in the English Industrial Revolution: 1880-1980', *Past and Present*, no. 103 (1984).

Fulbrook, Mary, *Historical Theory* (London: Routledge, 2002).

Hutcheon, Linda, *Politics of Postmodernism* (1989, rpt., London/New York: Routledge, 2003).

Kocka, Jurgen, 'Comparison and Beyond', *History and Theory*, vol. 42, no. 1 (2003).

Kung, Hans, 'Religion, Violence and "Holy Wars"', *International Review of the Red Cross*, vol. 87, no. 858 (June 2005).

Loomba, Ania, *Colonialism/Postcolonialism* (1998, rpt., New York: Routledge, 2001).

Lorenz, Chris, 'Comparative Historiography: Problems and Perspectives', *History and Theory*, vol. 38, no. 1 (1999).

Mazlish, Bruce, 'Comparing Global History to World History', *Journal of Interdisciplinary History*, vol. 28, no. 3 (1998).

McCullagh, C. Behan, 'The Truth of Historical Narratives', *History and Theory*, vol. 26 (1987).

Passmore, John, 'Narratives and Events', *History and Theory*, vol. 26 (1987).

Robb, Peter, 'Introduction: South Asia and the Concept of Race', in Peter Robb (ed.), *The Concept of Race in South Asia* (New Delhi: Oxford University Press, 1995).

Sachsenmaier, Dominic, 'World History as Ecumenical History?', *JWH*, vol. 18, no. 4 (2007).

Southall, Aidan, 'The Segmentary State in Africa and Asia', *CSSH*, vol. 30, no. 1 (1988).

Sutherland, Heather, 'The Problematic Authority of (World) History', *JWH*, vol. 18, no. 4 (2007).

Toft, Monica Duffy, 'Getting Religion? The Puzzling Case of Islam and Civil War', *International Security*, vol. 31, no. 4 (2007).

Topolski, Jerzy, 'Historical Narrative: Towards a Coherent Structure', *History and Theory*, vol. 26 (1987).

White, Hayden, 'The Historical Text as Literary Artifact', in Hayden White, *Tropics of Discourse* (1978, rpt., Baltimore, Maryland/London: John Hopkins University Press, 1985).

———, 'The Question of Narrative in Contemporary Historical Theory', in Hayden White, *The Content of the Form* (1987, rpt., Baltimore, Maryland/ London: John Hopkins University Press, 1990).

TAIPING REBELLION

Bernhardt, Kathryn, 'Elite and Peasant during the Taiping Occupation of the Jiangnan, 1860-64', *Modern China*, vol. 13, no. 4 (October 1987).

Chesneaux, Jean, *Peasant Revolts in China, 1840-1949* (London: W.W. Norton, 1973).

Deepak, B.R., 'The 1857 Rebellion and Indian Involvement in the Taiping Uprising in China', in Madhavi Thampi (ed.), *India and China in the Colonial World* (New Delhi: Social Science Press, 2005).

Kuhn, Philip A., 'The Taiping Rebellion', in John K. Fairbank (ed.), *The Cambridge History of China*, vol. 10, *Late Ch'ing, 1800-1911*, Part 1 (Cambridge: Cambridge University Press, 1978).

Lindley, A.F., *Ti-ping Tien-Kwoh* (New York: Praeger Publishers, 1970).

Meadows, Thomas Taylor, *The Chinese and their Rebellions* (London: Smith, Elder & Co., 1856).

Sheng-wu, Yu and Chang Chen-kun, 'China and India in the Mid-Nineteenth Century', in P.C. Joshi (ed.), *Rebellion 1857: A Symposium* (Calcutta: K.P. Bagchi & Co., 1986).

Shih, Vincent Y.C., *The Taiping Ideology: Its Sources, Interpretations and Influences* (Seattle and London: University of Washington Press, 1967).

Thampi, Madhavi, *Indians in China, 1800-1949* (New Delhi: Manohar, 2005).

Contributors

R. BALASUBRAMANIAM was a Professor at the Department of Materials and Metallurgical Engineering, Indian Institute of Technology, Kanpur, India. He has published on several aspects of cannon technology in early modern India. He has passed away recently.

RUTH RHYNAS BROWN is at present located at Hawthorne Cottage, Moorfield Road, Leeds. An independent scholar, Brown was formerly Senior Curator, Royal Armouries, Tower of London, England.

RAYMOND CALLAHAN is now retired from the History Department of the University of Delaware, USA and has several publications on various aspects of South Asian and South-East Asian strategic and political history. His two most noteworthy books are one on Singapore during World War II and another on the genesis of East India Company Army's officer corps in the last decade of the eighteenth century.

UTTARA CHAKRABORTY has retired from Bethune College, Kolkata. Her specialization is Kolkata in the nineteenth century.

ANASUA DUTTA teaches at the History Department of Presidency College and she is working on the gun traders of colonial Bengal.

SWARUPA GUPTA is a Fellow at the Maulana Azad Institute of Asian Studies and has published several articles in various peer reviewed journals. Her Ph.D. has been published from E.J. Brill.

IQBAL HUSAIN has retired from Aligarh Muslim University and is an expert on the Urdu sources of medieval and early modern India.

SATYAKI KANJILAL was a M.Phil student in the English Department at Kalyani University and is working on the British novels written in the colonial period.

TIM MOREMAN has done his Ph.D. from King's College, London. He has a book on India's north-west frontier warfare during the British Raj and another published by Frank Cass on the Indian and British armies in Burma during World War II. Moreman has also published many articles on British–India's frontier warfare in the *Journal of Imperial and Commonwealth History* and in the *Journal of Strategic Studies.*

KAUSHIK ROY is Senior Researcher at the Centre for the Study of Civil War (CSCW), International Peace Research Institute Oslo (PRIO) and is a Reader at the History Department of Jadavpur University, Kolkata. His most recent publication is *The Oxford Companion to Modern Warfare in India.*

MADHAVI THAMPI is a Reader in the Department of East Asian Studies, University of Delhi. She has published widely on Indian interactions with China.

Index